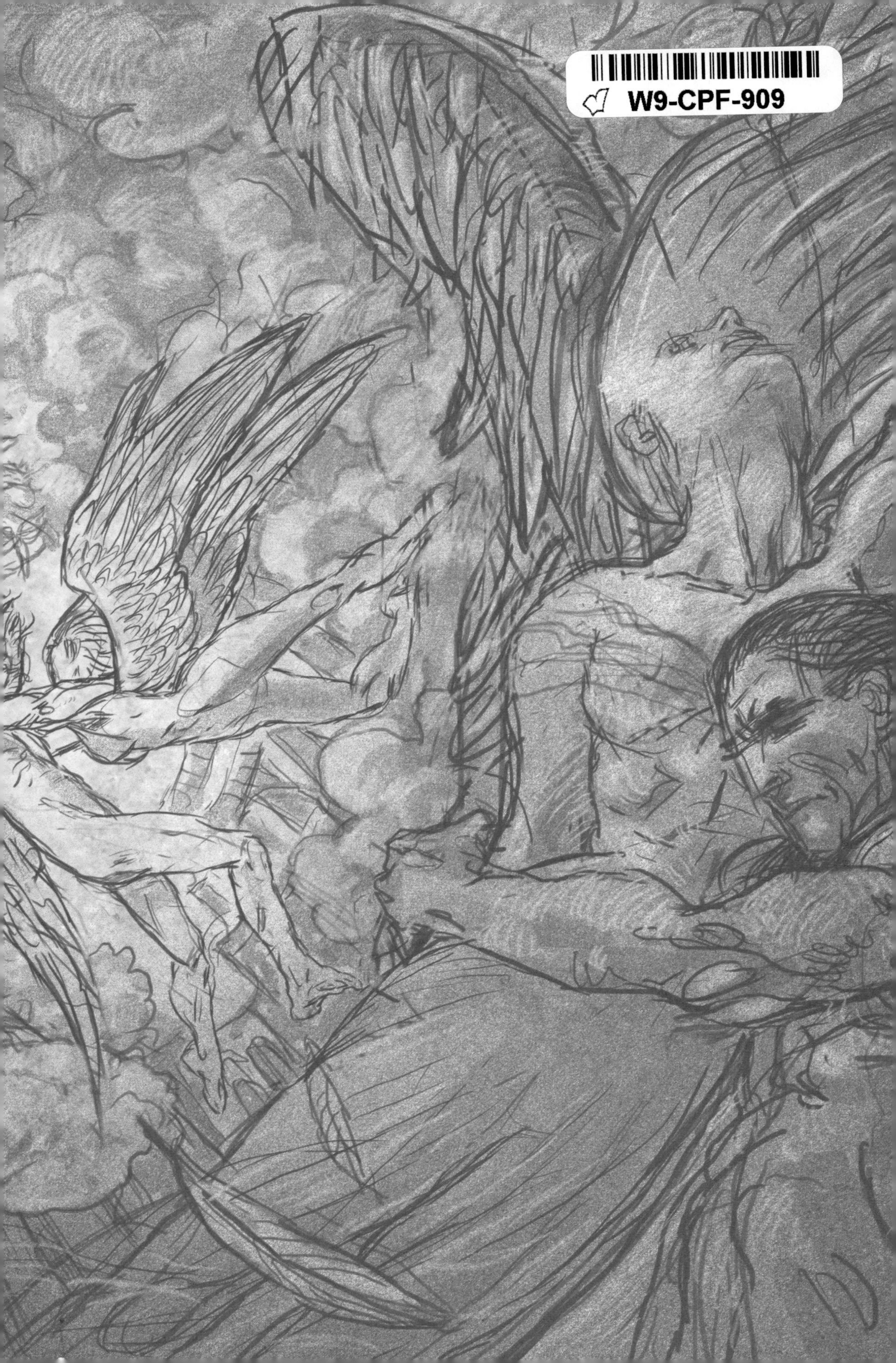

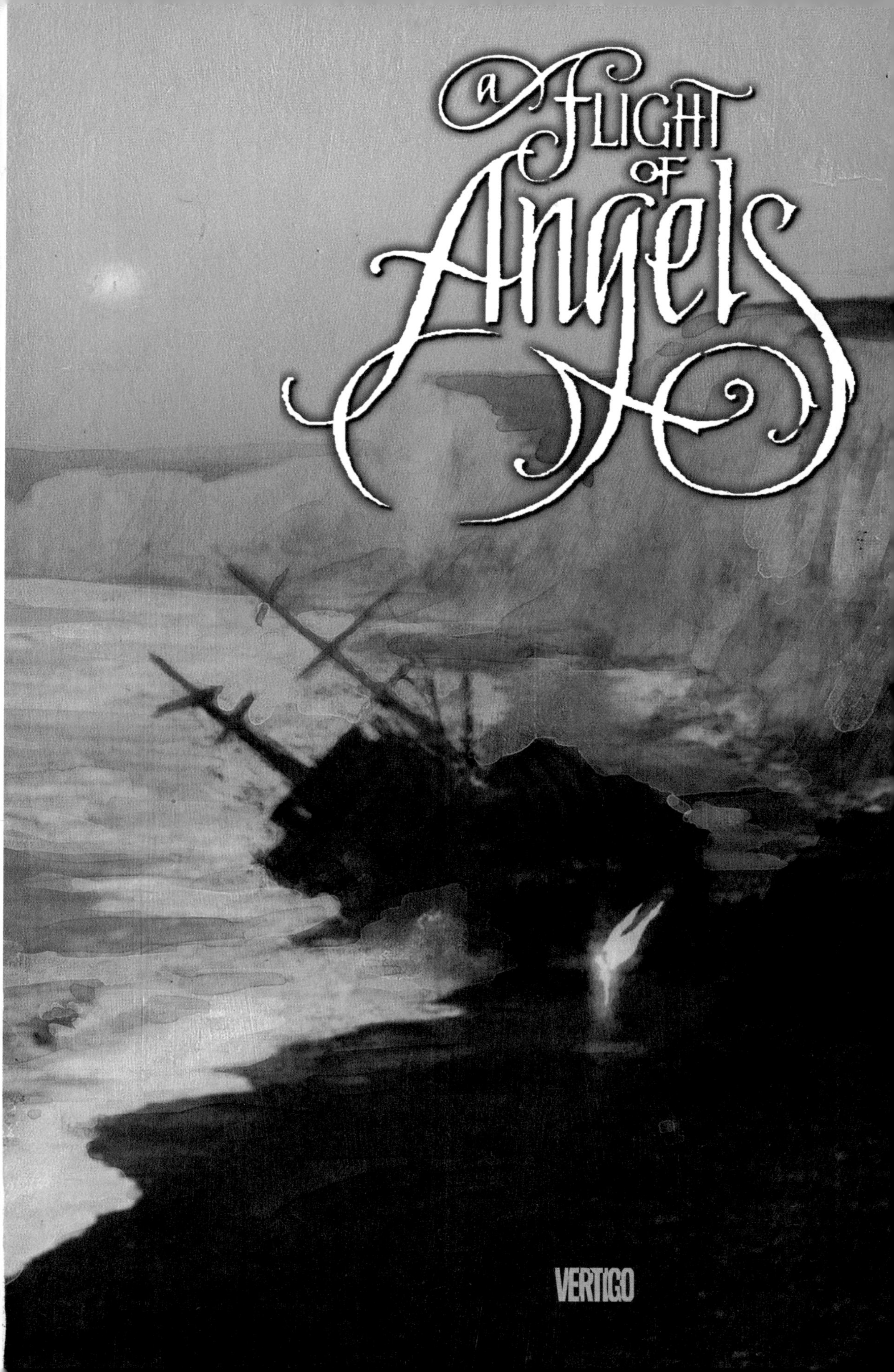
a Flight of Angels
VERTIGO

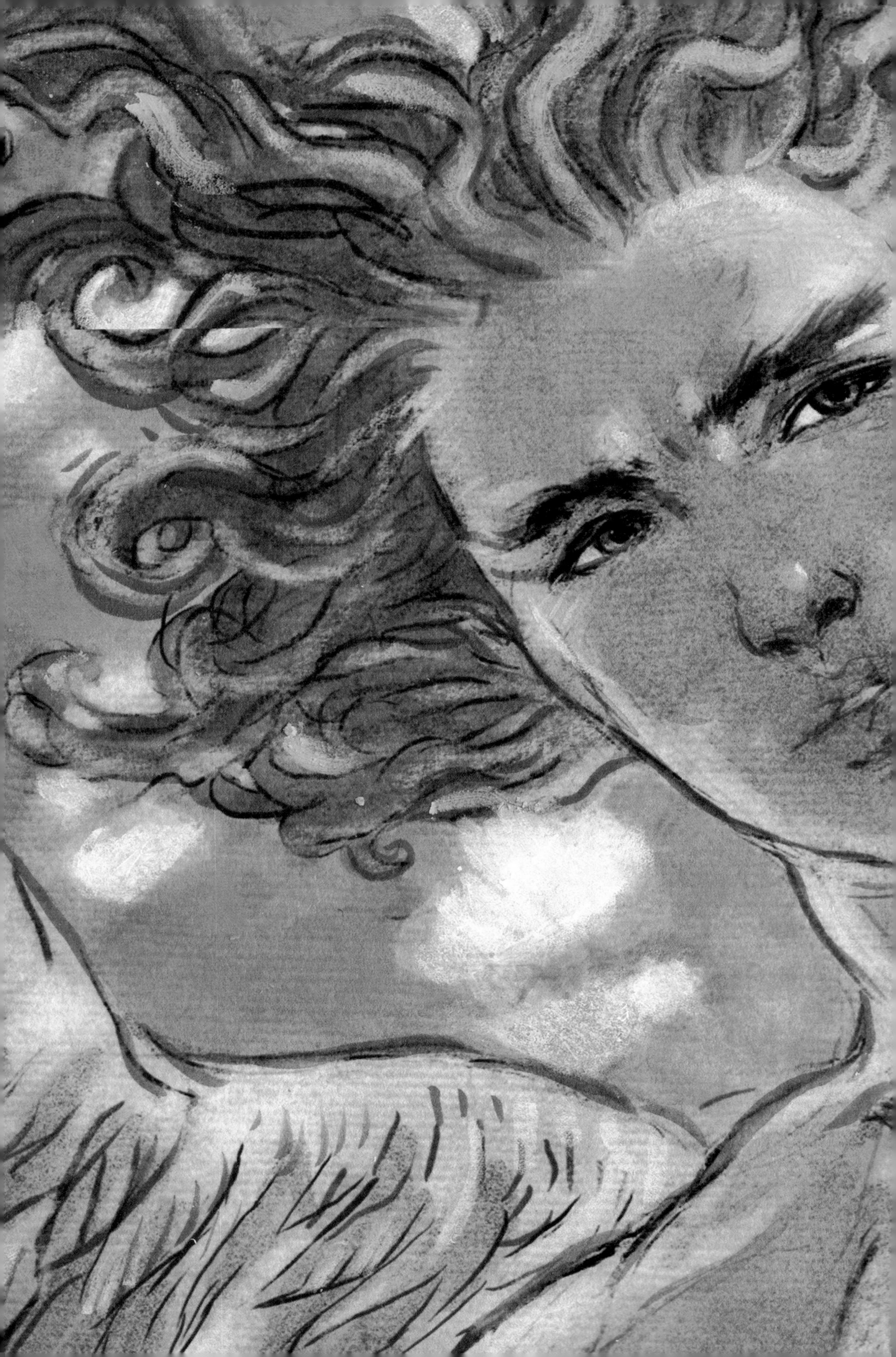

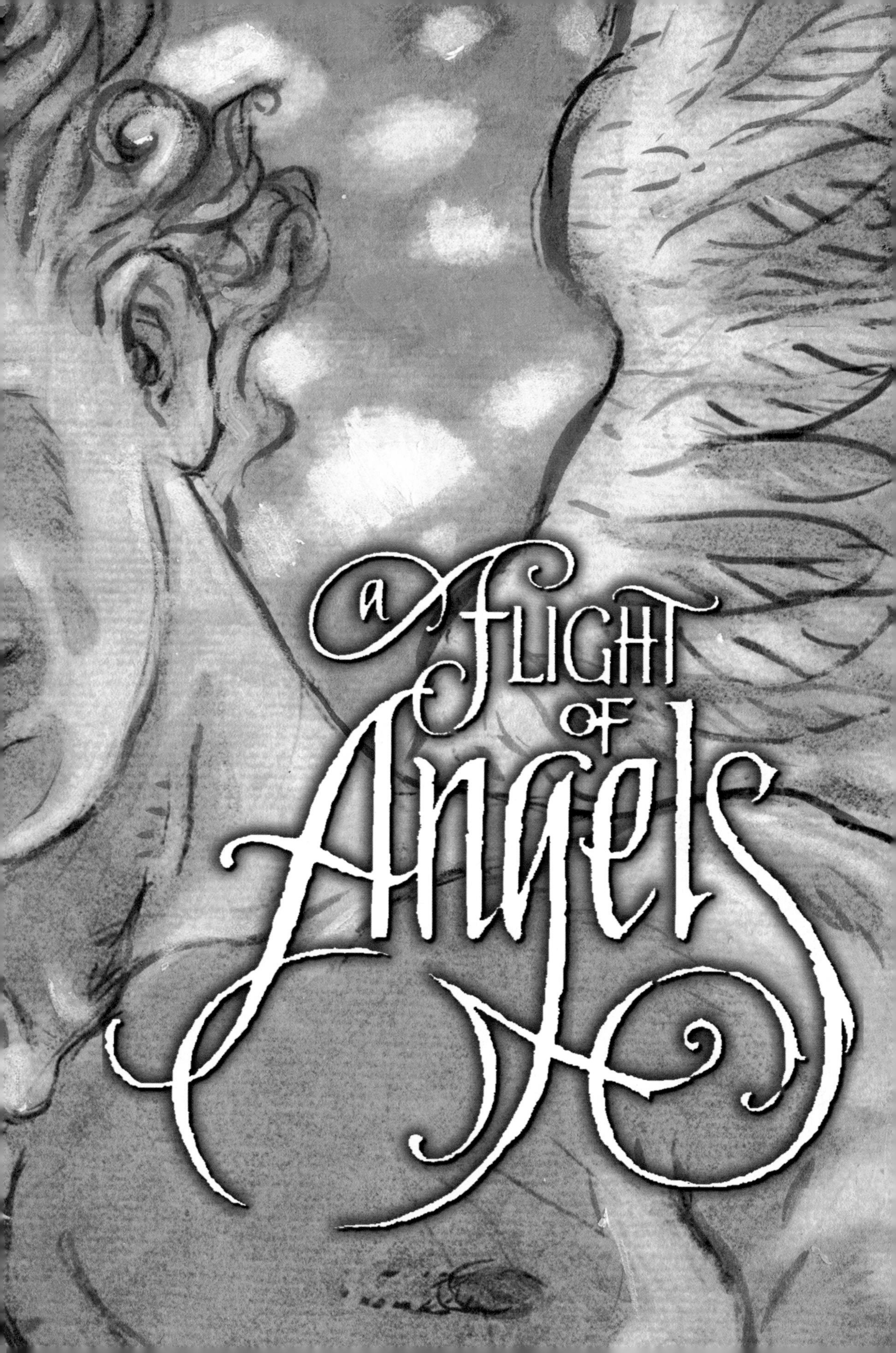
a Flight of Angels

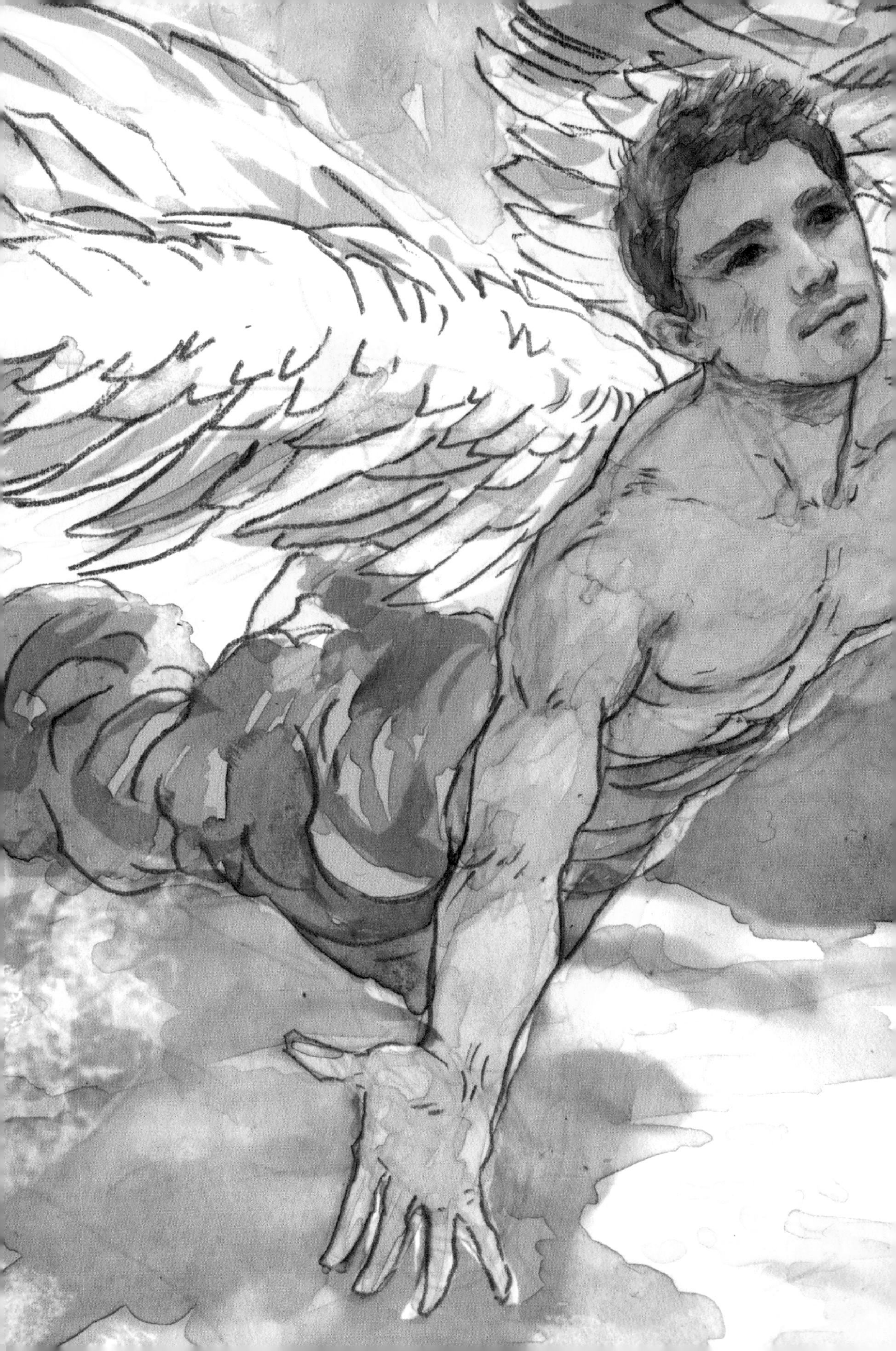

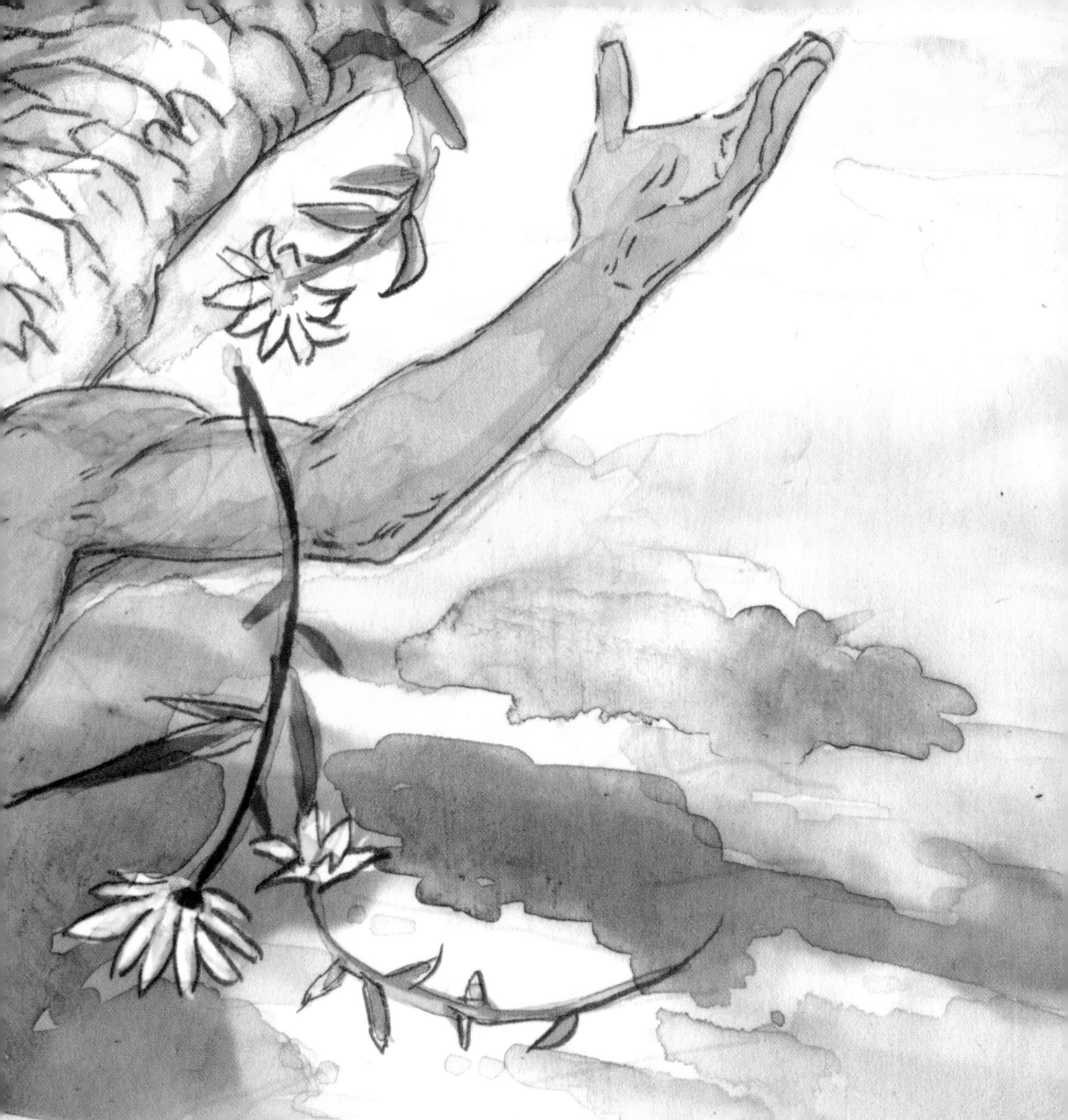

HOLLY BLACK: frame story and "Shining Host"
LOUISE HAWES: "Original Sin"
BILL WILLINGHAM: "The Story Within the Story Within"
ALISA KWITNEY: "Chaya Surah and the Angel of Death"
TODD MITCHELL: "The Guardian"

Conceived and Illustrated by **REBECCA GUAY**

Lettered by **TODD KLEIN**

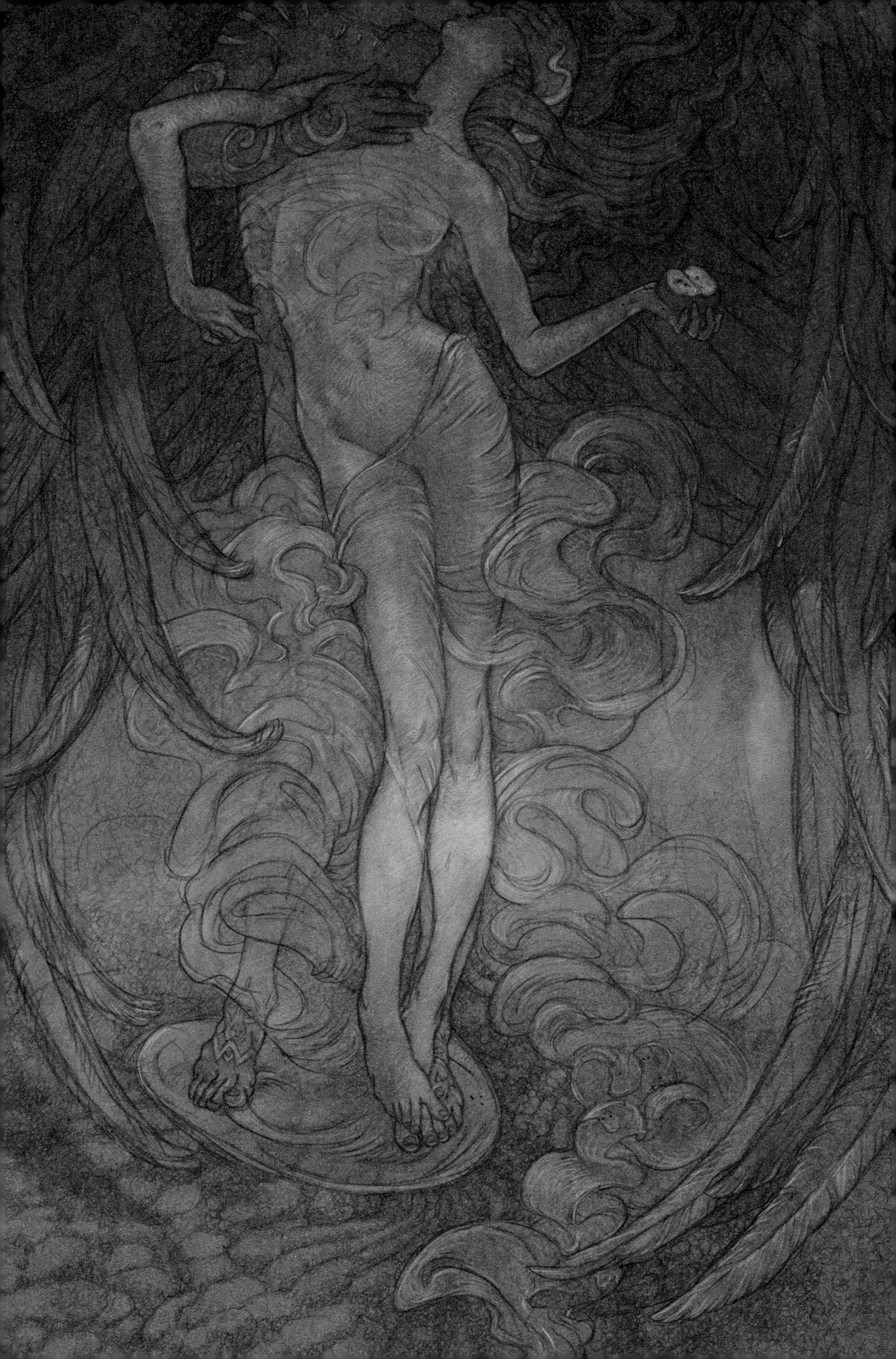

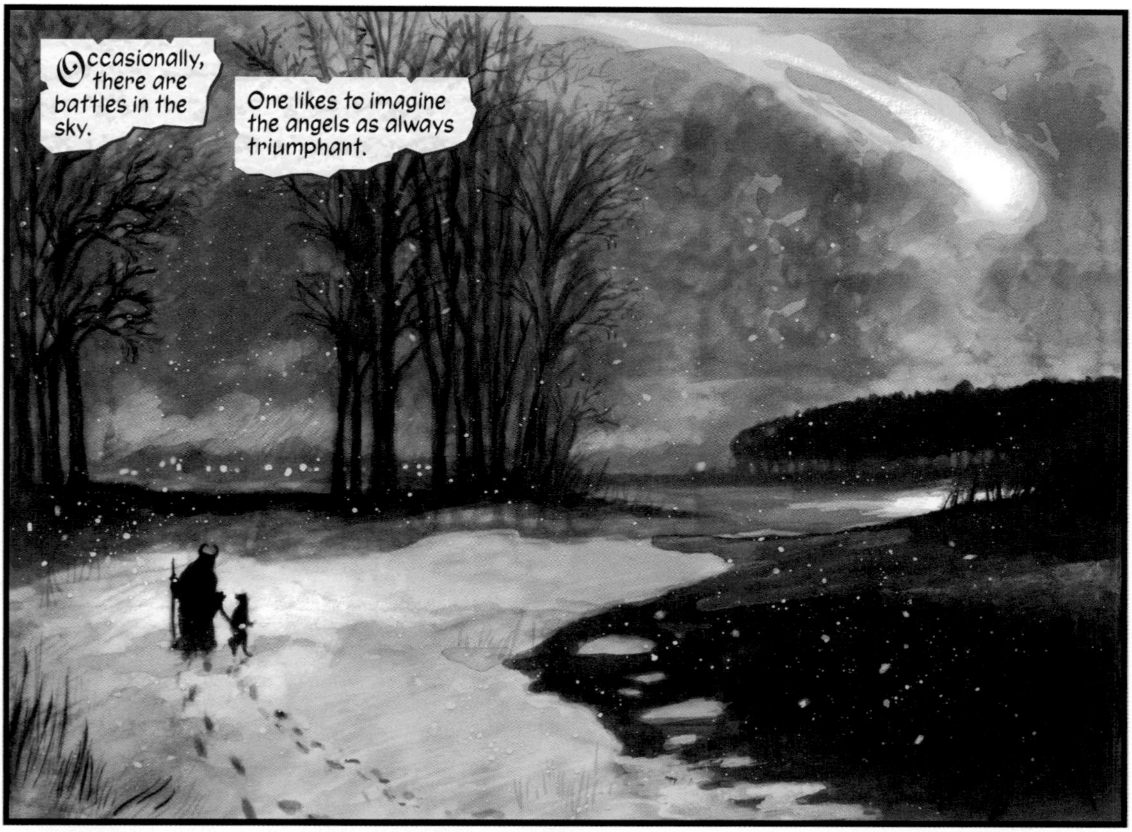
Occasionally, there are battles in the sky.
One likes to imagine the angels as always triumphant.
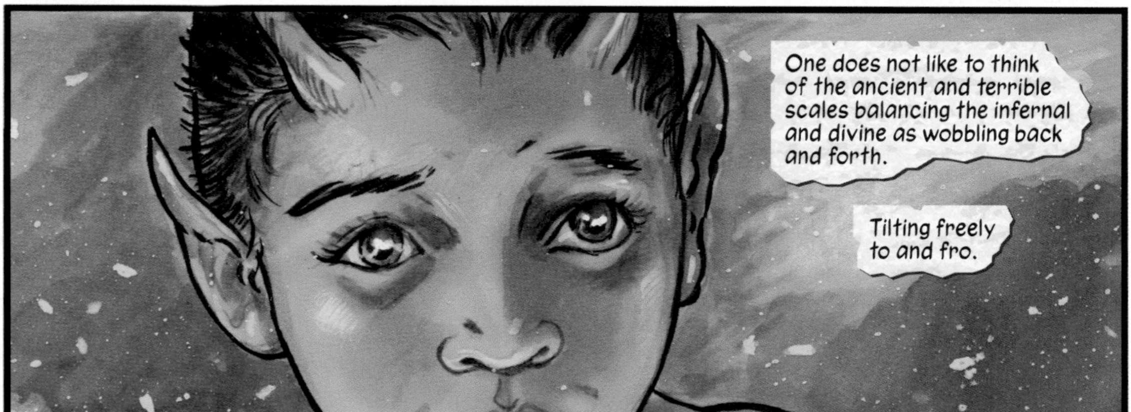
One does not like to think of the ancient and terrible scales balancing the infernal and divine as wobbling back and forth.
Tilting freely to and fro.
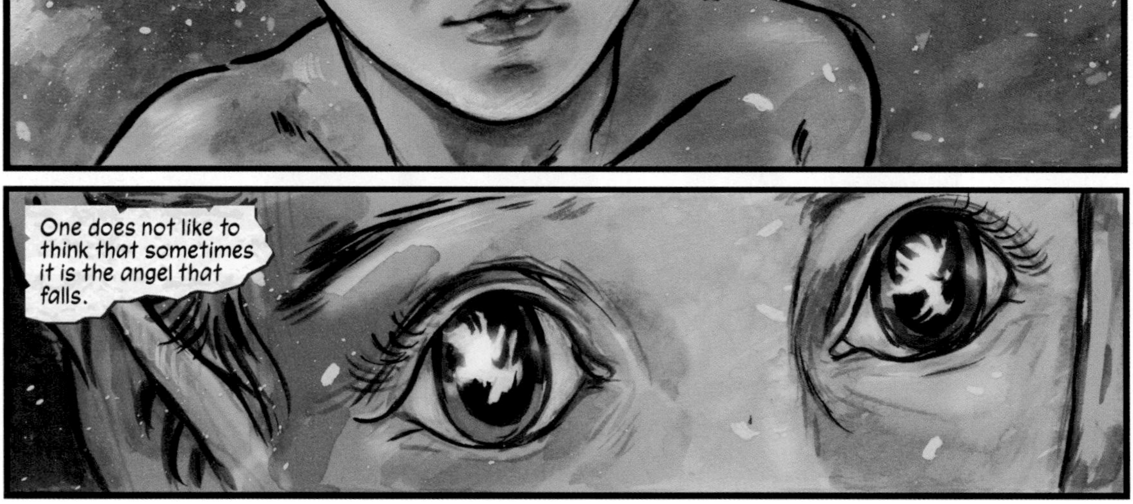
One does not like to think that sometimes it is the angel that falls.

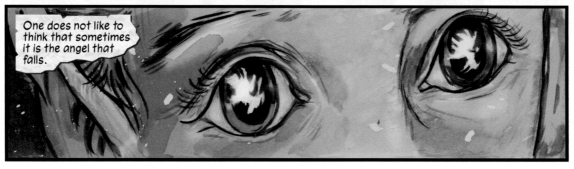

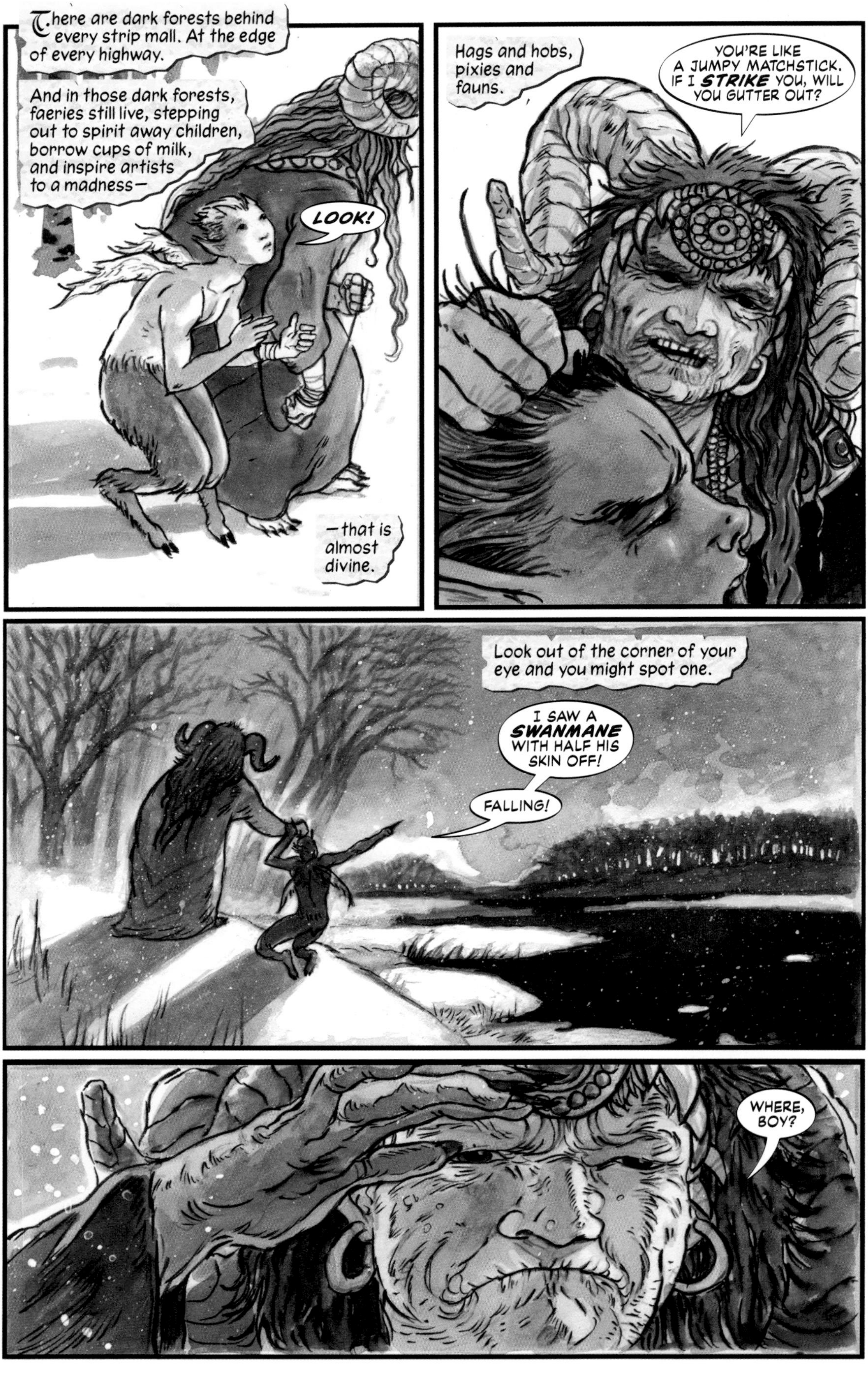
There are dark forests behind every strip mall. At the edge of every highway.
And in those dark forests, faeries still live, stepping out to spirit away children, borrow cups of milk, and inspire artists to a madness—
LOOK!
—that is almost divine.
Hags and hobs, pixies and fauns.
YOU'RE LIKE A JUMPY MATCHSTICK. IF I STRIKE YOU, WILL YOU GUTTER OUT?
Look out of the corner of your eye and you might spot one.
I SAW A SWANMANE WITH HALF HIS SKIN OFF!
FALLING!
WHERE, BOY?

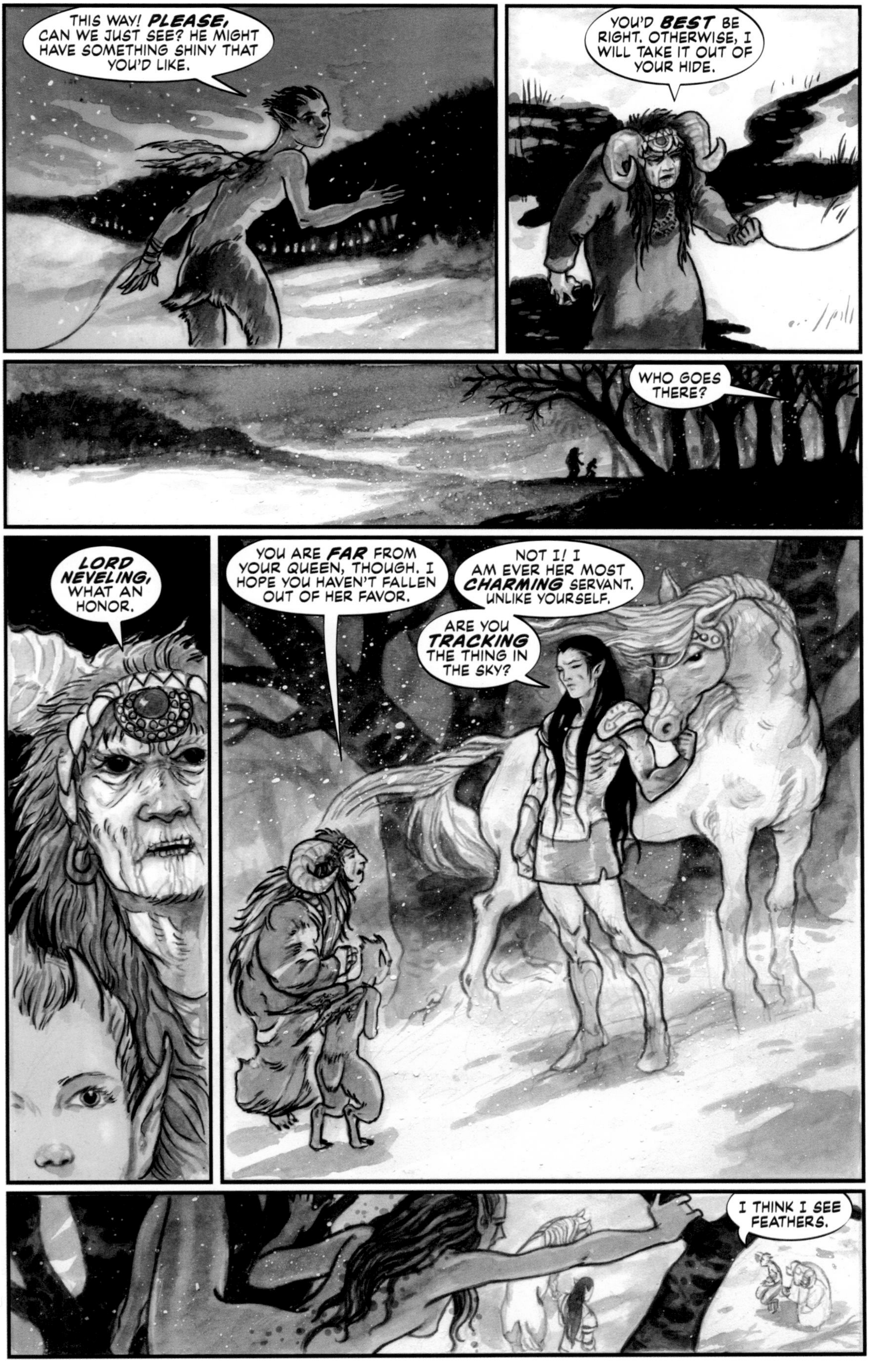
THIS WAY! PLEASE, CAN WE JUST SEE? HE MIGHT HAVE SOMETHING SHINY THAT YOU'D LIKE.
YOU'D BEST BE RIGHT. OTHERWISE, I WILL TAKE IT OUT OF YOUR HIDE.
WHO GOES THERE?
LORD NEVELING, WHAT AN HONOR.
YOU ARE FAR FROM YOUR QUEEN, THOUGH. I HOPE YOU HAVEN'T FALLEN OUT OF HER FAVOR.
NOT I! I AM EVER HER MOST CHARMING SERVANT. UNLIKE YOURSELF.
ARE YOU TRACKING THE THING IN THE SKY?
I THINK I SEE FEATHERS.

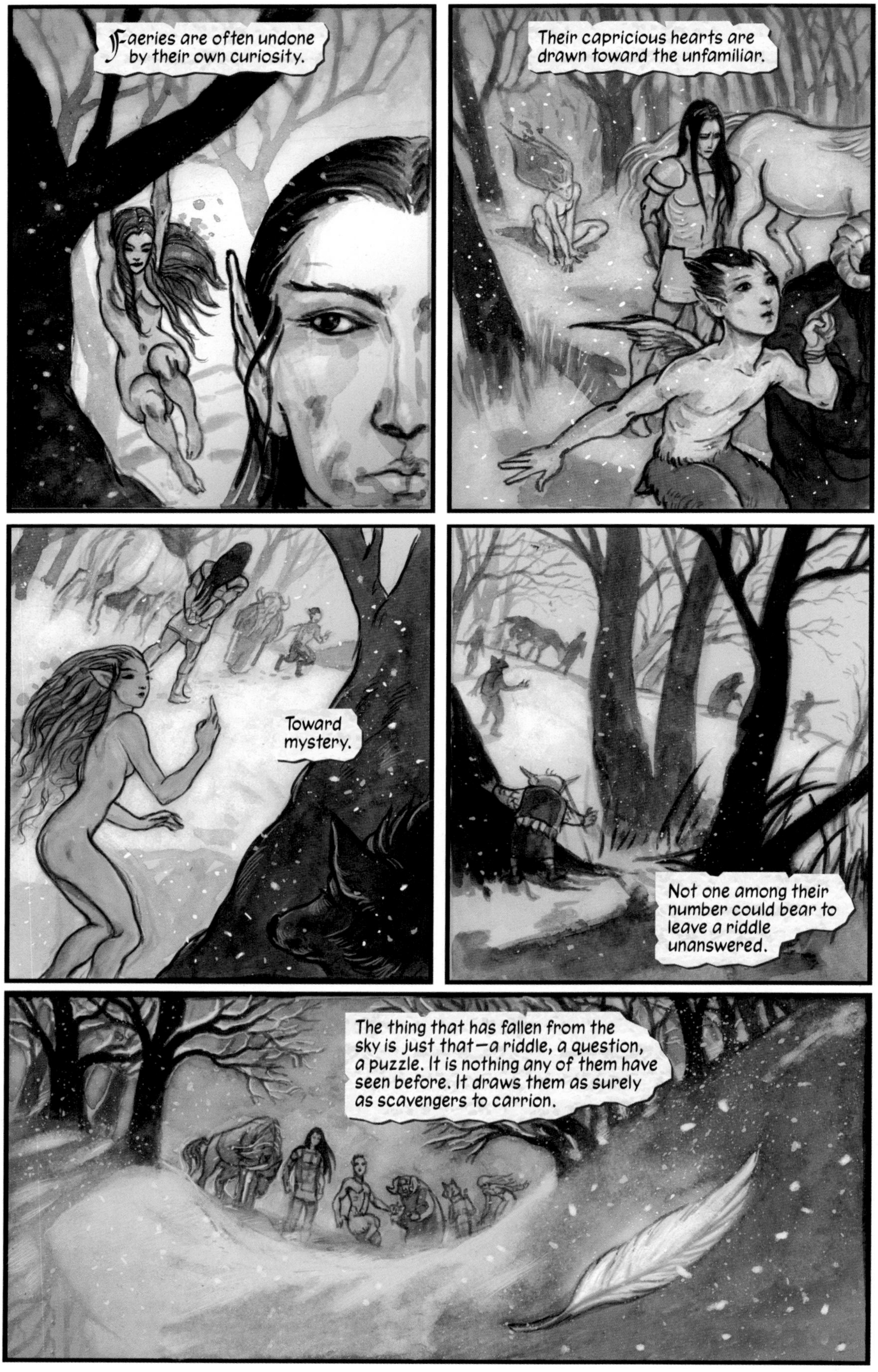
Faeries are often undone by their own curiosity.
Their capricious hearts are drawn toward the unfamiliar.
Toward mystery.
Not one among their number could bear to leave a riddle unanswered.
The thing that has fallen from the sky is just that—a riddle, a question, a puzzle. It is nothing any of them have seen before. It draws them as surely as scavengers to carrion.

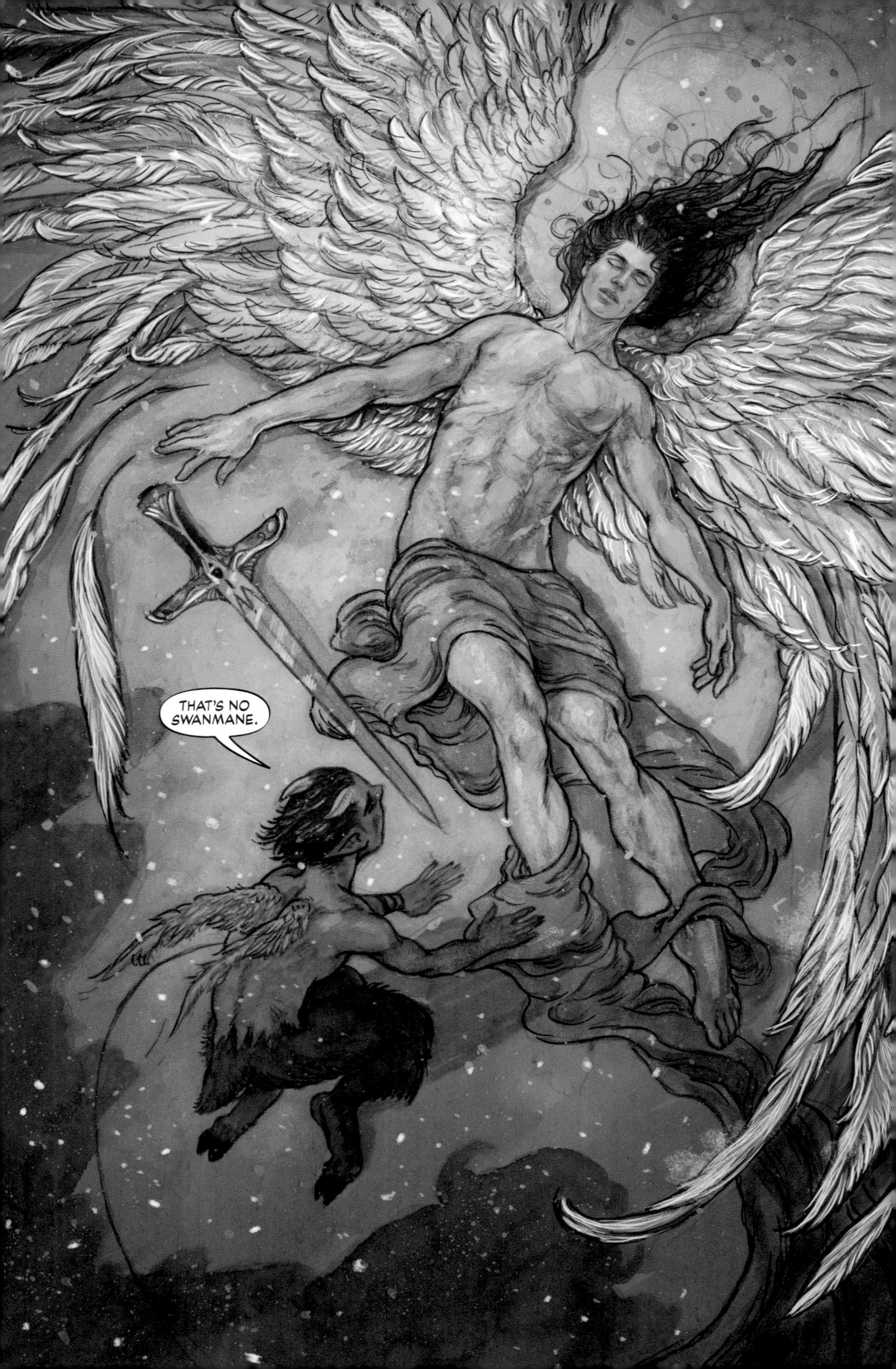
THAT'S NO SWANMANE.

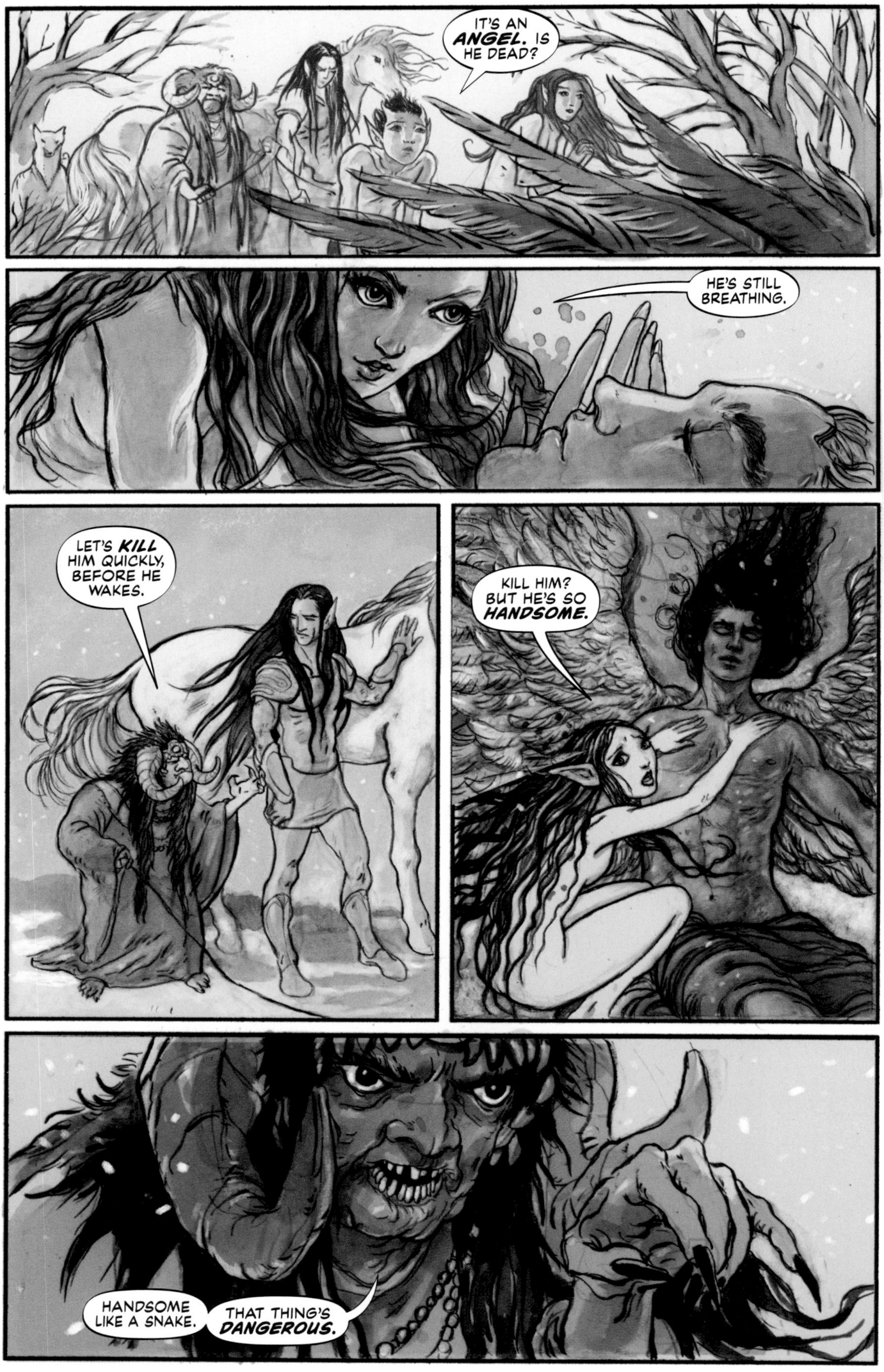
IT'S AN ANGEL. IS HE DEAD?
HE'S STILL BREATHING.
LET'S KILL HIM QUICKLY, BEFORE HE WAKES.
KILL HIM? BUT HE'S SO HANDSOME.
HANDSOME LIKE A SNAKE.
THAT THING'S DANGEROUS.

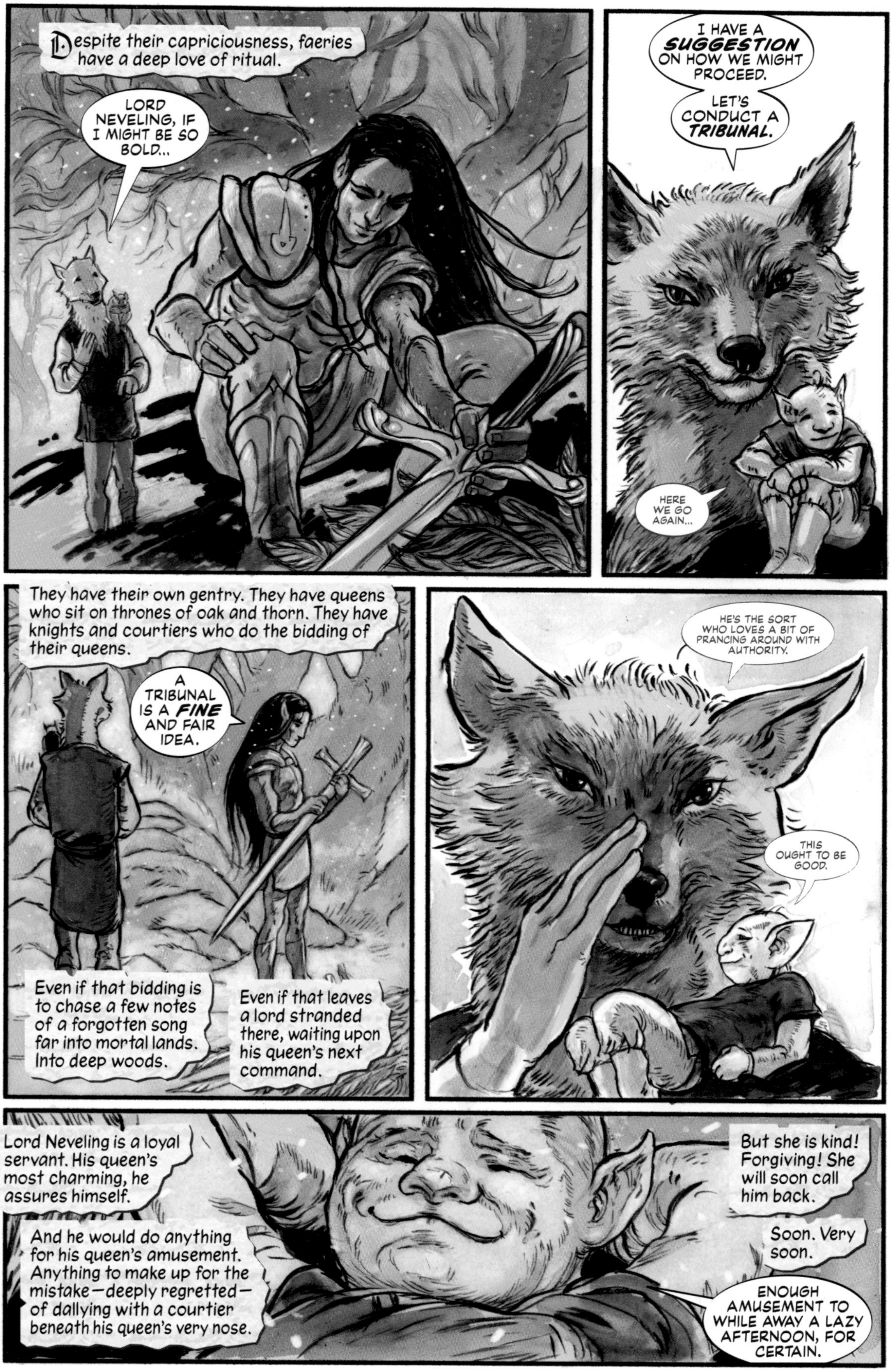
Despite their capriciousness, faeries have a deep love of ritual.
LORD NEVELING, IF I MIGHT BE SO BOLD...
I HAVE A SUGGESTION ON HOW WE MIGHT PROCEED.
LET'S CONDUCT A TRIBUNAL.
HERE WE GO AGAIN...
They have their own gentry. They have queens who sit on thrones of oak and thorn. They have knights and courtiers who do the bidding of their queens.
A TRIBUNAL IS A FINE AND FAIR IDEA.
Even if that bidding is to chase a few notes of a forgotten song far into mortal lands. Into deep woods.
Even if that leaves a lord stranded there, waiting upon his queen's next command.
HE'S THE SORT WHO LOVES A BIT OF PRANCING AROUND WITH AUTHORITY.
THIS OUGHT TO BE GOOD.
Lord Neveling is a loyal servant. His queen's most charming, he assures himself.
And he would do anything for his queen's amusement. Anything to make up for the mistake—deeply regretted—of dallying with a courtier beneath his queen's very nose.
But she is kind! Forgiving! She will soon call him back.
Soon. Very soon.
ENOUGH AMUSEMENT TO WHILE AWAY A LAZY AFTERNOON, FOR CERTAIN.

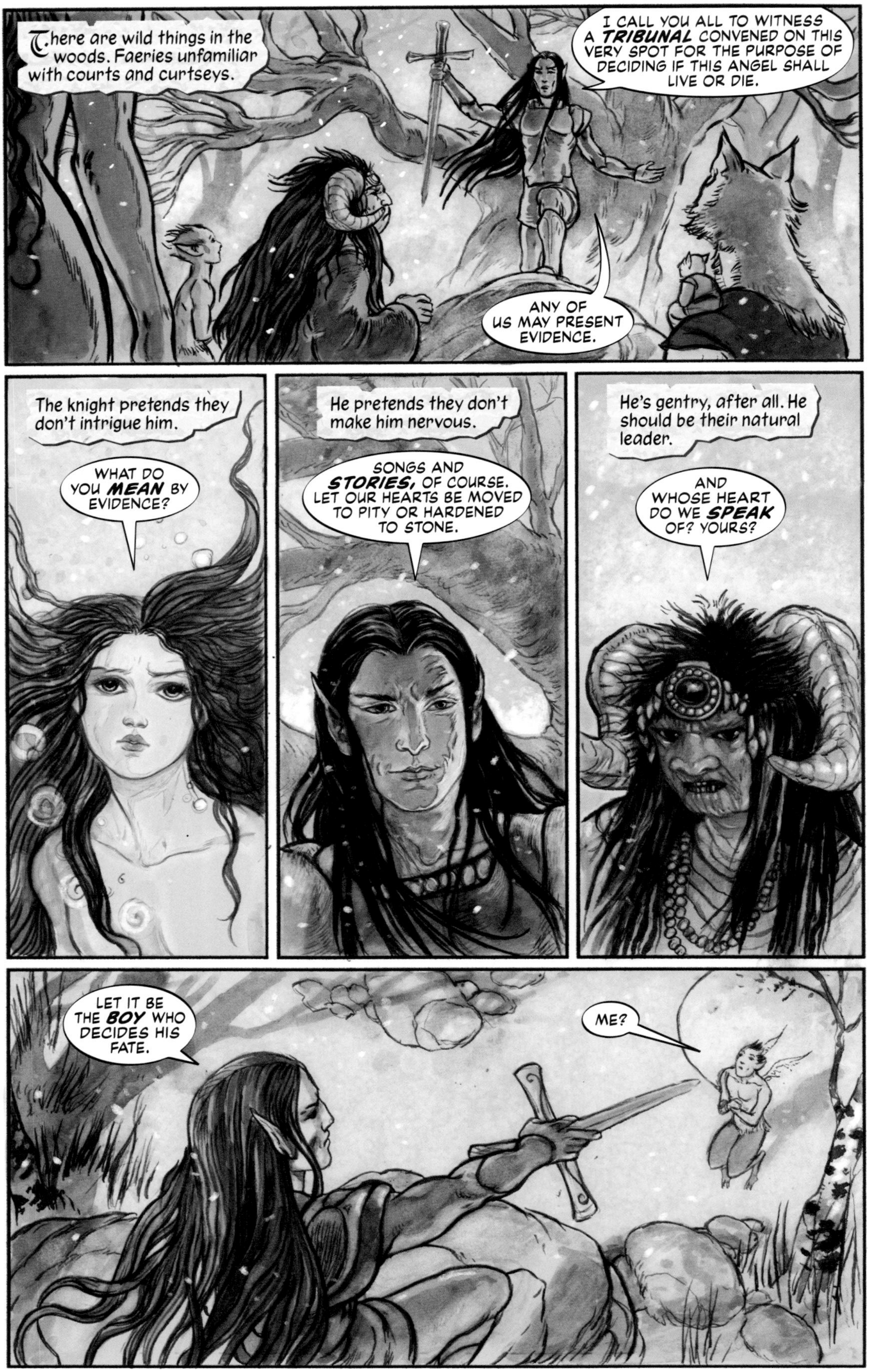
There are wild things in the woods. Faeries unfamiliar with courts and curtseys.
I CALL YOU ALL TO WITNESS A TRIBUNAL CONVENED ON THIS VERY SPOT FOR THE PURPOSE OF DECIDING IF THIS ANGEL SHALL LIVE OR DIE.
ANY OF US MAY PRESENT EVIDENCE.
The knight pretends they don't intrigue him.
WHAT DO YOU MEAN BY EVIDENCE?
He pretends they don't make him nervous.
SONGS AND STORIES, OF COURSE. LET OUR HEARTS BE MOVED TO PITY OR HARDENED TO STONE.
He's gentry, after all. He should be their natural leader.
AND WHOSE HEART DO WE SPEAK OF? YOURS?
LET IT BE THE BOY WHO DECIDES HIS FATE.
ME?

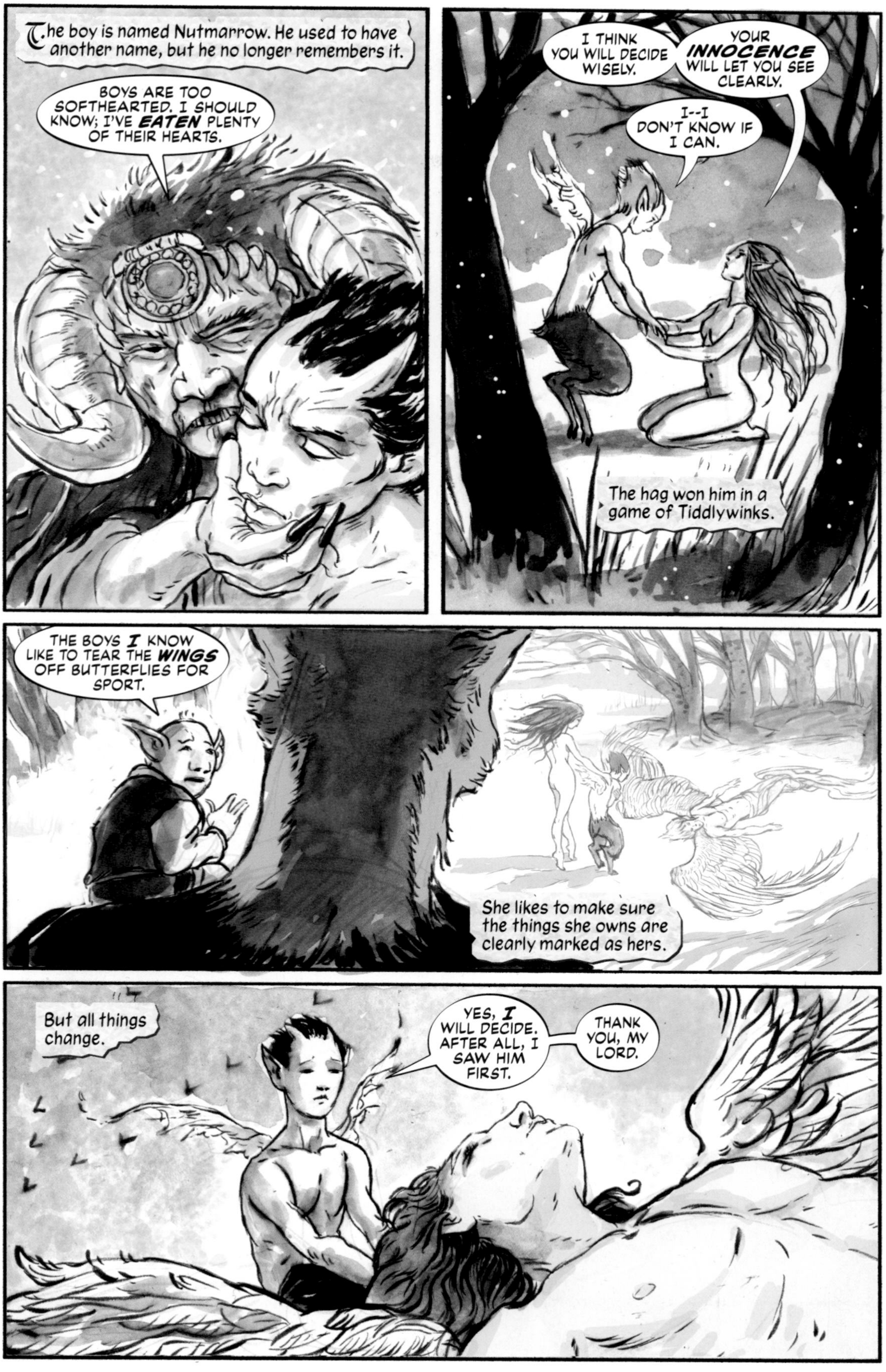
The boy is named Nutmarrow. He used to have another name, but he no longer remembers it.
BOYS ARE TOO SOFTHEARTED. I SHOULD KNOW; I'VE EATEN PLENTY OF THEIR HEARTS.
I THINK YOU WILL DECIDE WISELY.
YOUR INNOCENCE WILL LET YOU SEE CLEARLY.
I--I DON'T KNOW IF I CAN.
The hag won him in a game of Tiddlywinks.
THE BOYS I KNOW LIKE TO TEAR THE WINGS OFF BUTTERFLIES FOR SPORT.
She likes to make sure the things she owns are clearly marked as hers.
But all things change.
YES, I WILL DECIDE. AFTER ALL, I SAW HIM FIRST.
THANK YOU, MY LORD.

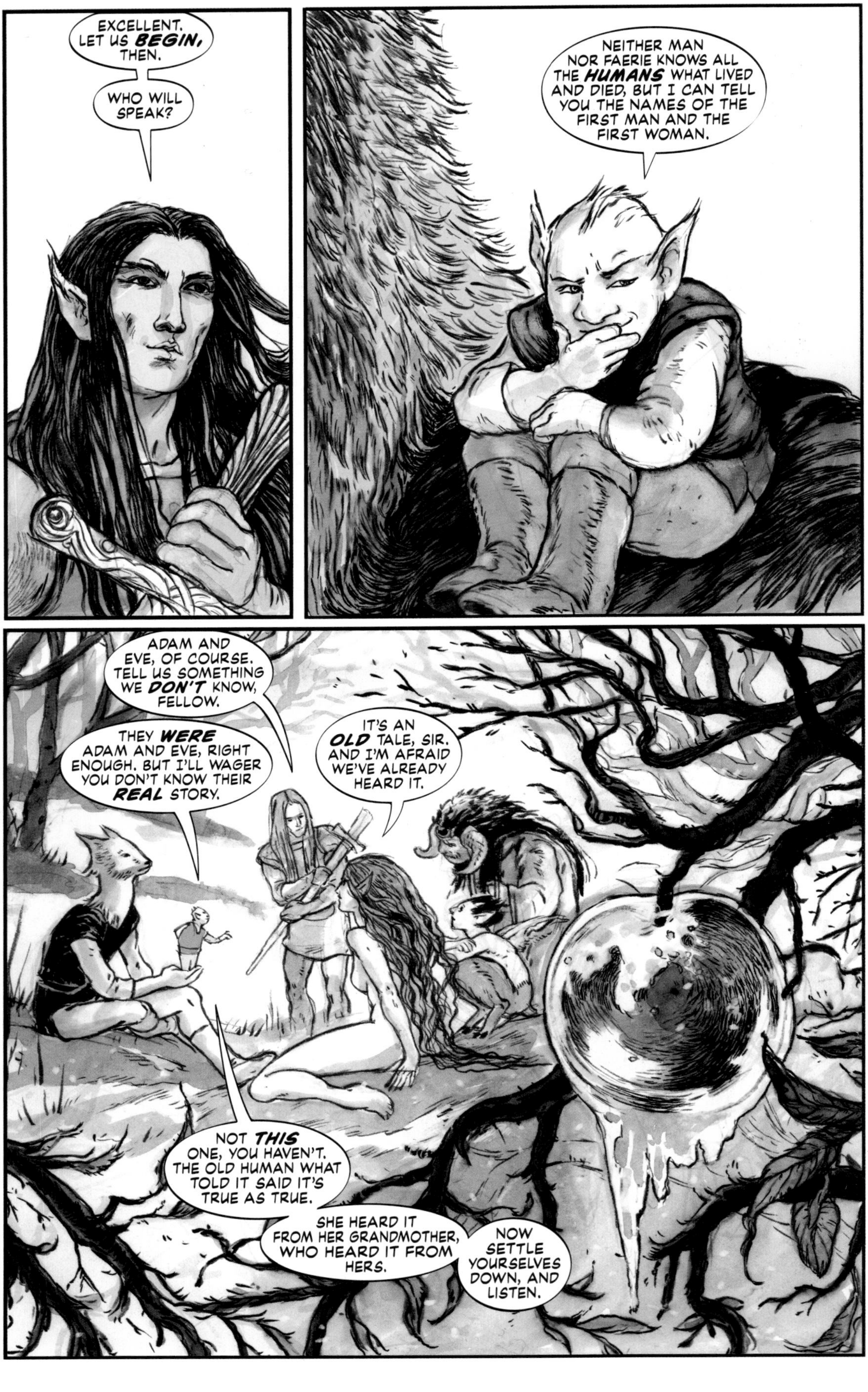
EXCELLENT. LET US BEGIN, THEN.
WHO WILL SPEAK?
NEITHER MAN NOR FAERIE KNOWS ALL THE HUMANS WHAT LIVED AND DIED, BUT I CAN TELL YOU THE NAMES OF THE FIRST MAN AND THE FIRST WOMAN.
ADAM AND EVE, OF COURSE. TELL US SOMETHING WE DON'T KNOW, FELLOW.
THEY WERE ADAM AND EVE, RIGHT ENOUGH. BUT I'LL WAGER YOU DON'T KNOW THEIR REAL STORY.
IT'S AN OLD TALE, SIR. AND I'M AFRAID WE'VE ALREADY HEARD IT.
NOT THIS ONE, YOU HAVEN'T. THE OLD HUMAN WHAT TOLD IT SAID IT'S TRUE AS TRUE.
SHE HEARD IT FROM HER GRANDMOTHER, WHO HEARD IT FROM HERS.
NOW SETTLE YOURSELVES DOWN, AND LISTEN.

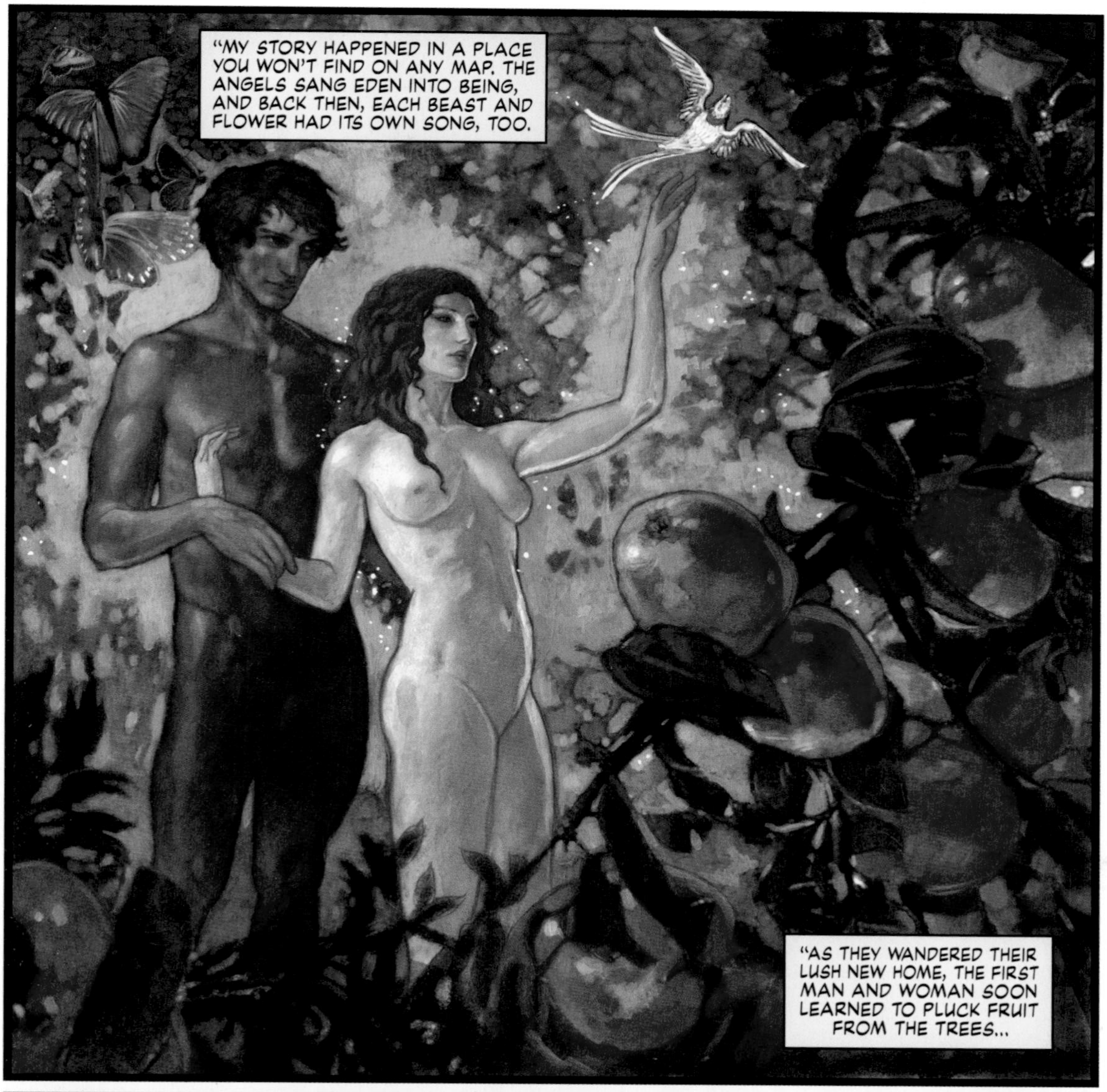
"MY STORY HAPPENED IN A PLACE YOU WON'T FIND ON ANY MAP. THE ANGELS SANG EDEN INTO BEING, AND BACK THEN, EACH BEAST AND FLOWER HAD ITS OWN SONG, TOO.
"AS THEY WANDERED THEIR LUSH NEW HOME, THE FIRST MAN AND WOMAN SOON LEARNED TO PLUCK FRUIT FROM THE TREES...

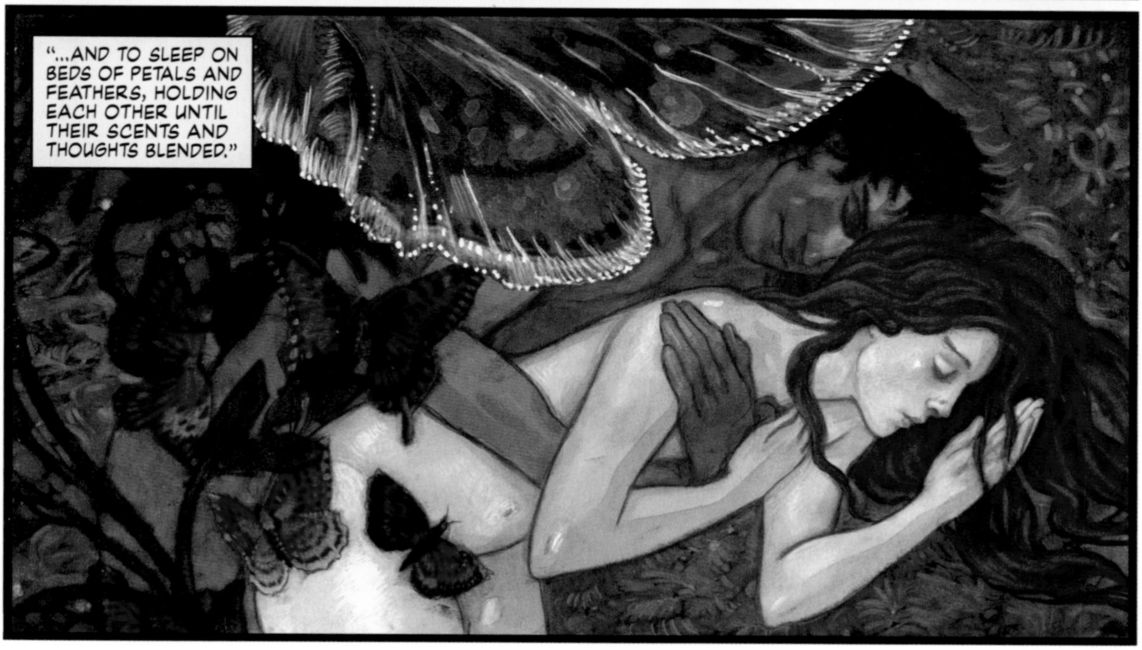
"...AND TO SLEEP ON BEDS OF PETALS AND FEATHERS, HOLDING EACH OTHER UNTIL THEIR SCENTS AND THOUGHTS BLENDED."

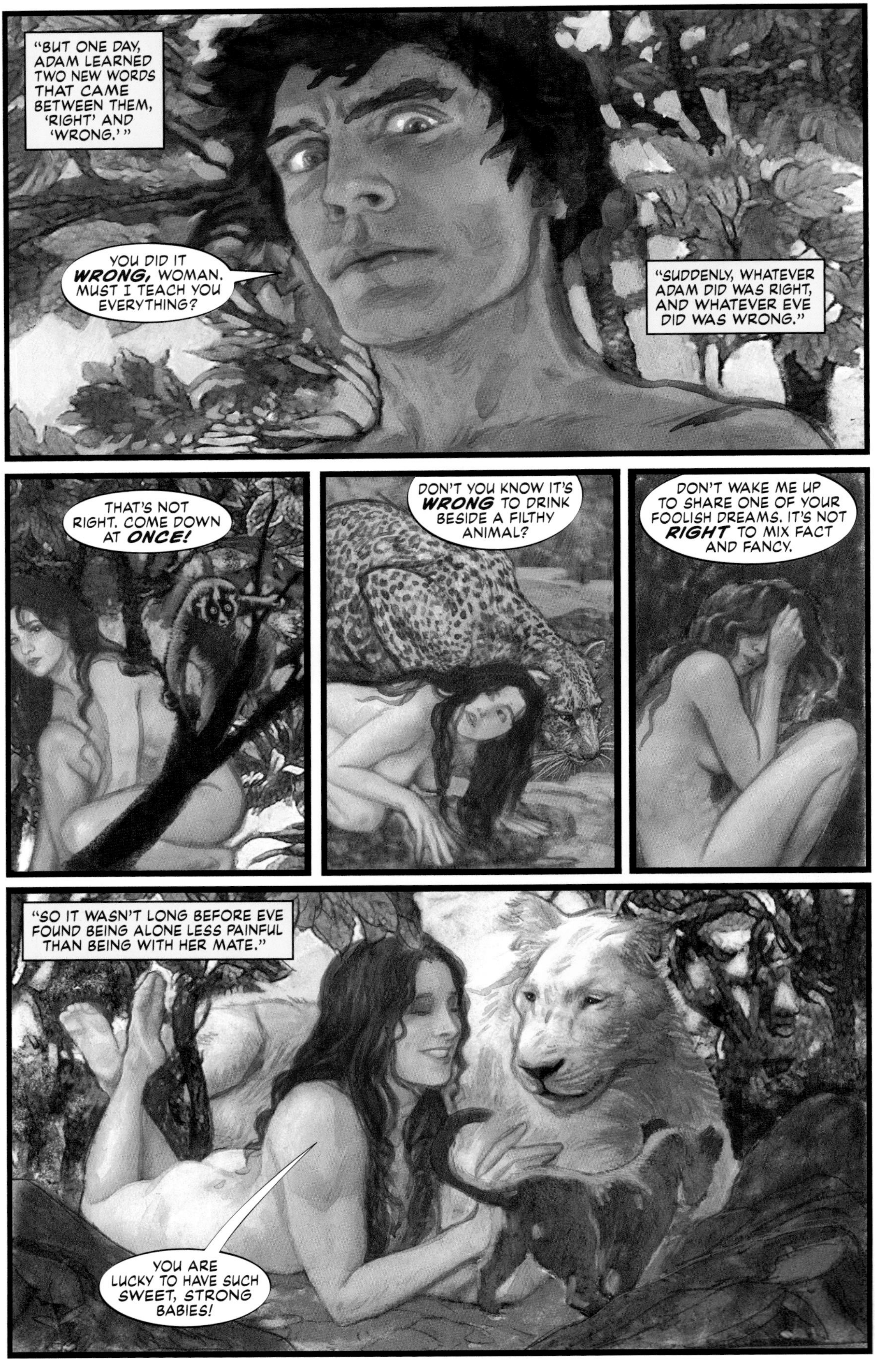
"BUT ONE DAY, ADAM LEARNED TWO NEW WORDS THAT CAME BETWEEN THEM, 'RIGHT' AND 'WRONG.'"
YOU DID IT WRONG, WOMAN. MUST I TEACH YOU EVERYTHING?
"SUDDENLY, WHATEVER ADAM DID WAS RIGHT, AND WHATEVER EVE DID WAS WRONG."
THAT'S NOT RIGHT. COME DOWN AT ONCE!
DON'T YOU KNOW IT'S WRONG TO DRINK BESIDE A FILTHY ANIMAL?
DON'T WAKE ME UP TO SHARE ONE OF YOUR FOOLISH DREAMS. IT'S NOT RIGHT TO MIX FACT AND FANCY.
"SO IT WASN'T LONG BEFORE EVE FOUND BEING ALONE LESS PAINFUL THAN BEING WITH HER MATE."
YOU ARE LUCKY TO HAVE SUCH SWEET, STRONG BABIES!

"EACH DAY EDEN OFFERED SOME FRESH DELIGHT THAT HELPED HER FORGET THE LOOK IN ADAM'S EYES, THE LOOK THAT SAID 'WRONG.'"

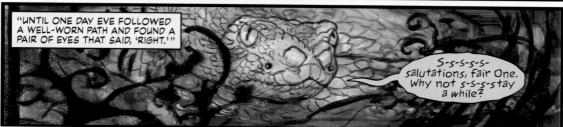

"UNTIL ONE DAY EVE FOLLOWED A WELL-WORN PATH AND FOUND A PAIR OF EYES THAT SAID, 'RIGHT.'"

S-s-s-s-s-salutations, fair One. Why not s-s-s-stay a while?

S-s-s-suppose you tell me what's troubling you?

"EVE STEPPED CLOSER, AND AS SHE DID, SHE FELT HERSELF FALLING INTO THE GLASSY DEPTHS OF THE SERPENT'S EYES.

"SOON SHE HAD POURED OUT HER HEART TO HER NEW FRIEND."

MY MATE NEVER SPEAKS TO ME EXCEPT TO SCOLD. HE SAYS I AM NOT **MODEST.**

Modes-s-st? What is-s-s modes-s-st?

ADAM SAYS I AM WORSE THAN THE ANIMALS, WITH NO FUR TO COVER MY BODY.

Perhaps-s-s-s you could pleas-s-se him by shedding s-s-skins?

Watch clos-s-s-sely, pleas-s-se.

MY EYES! THE LIGHT!

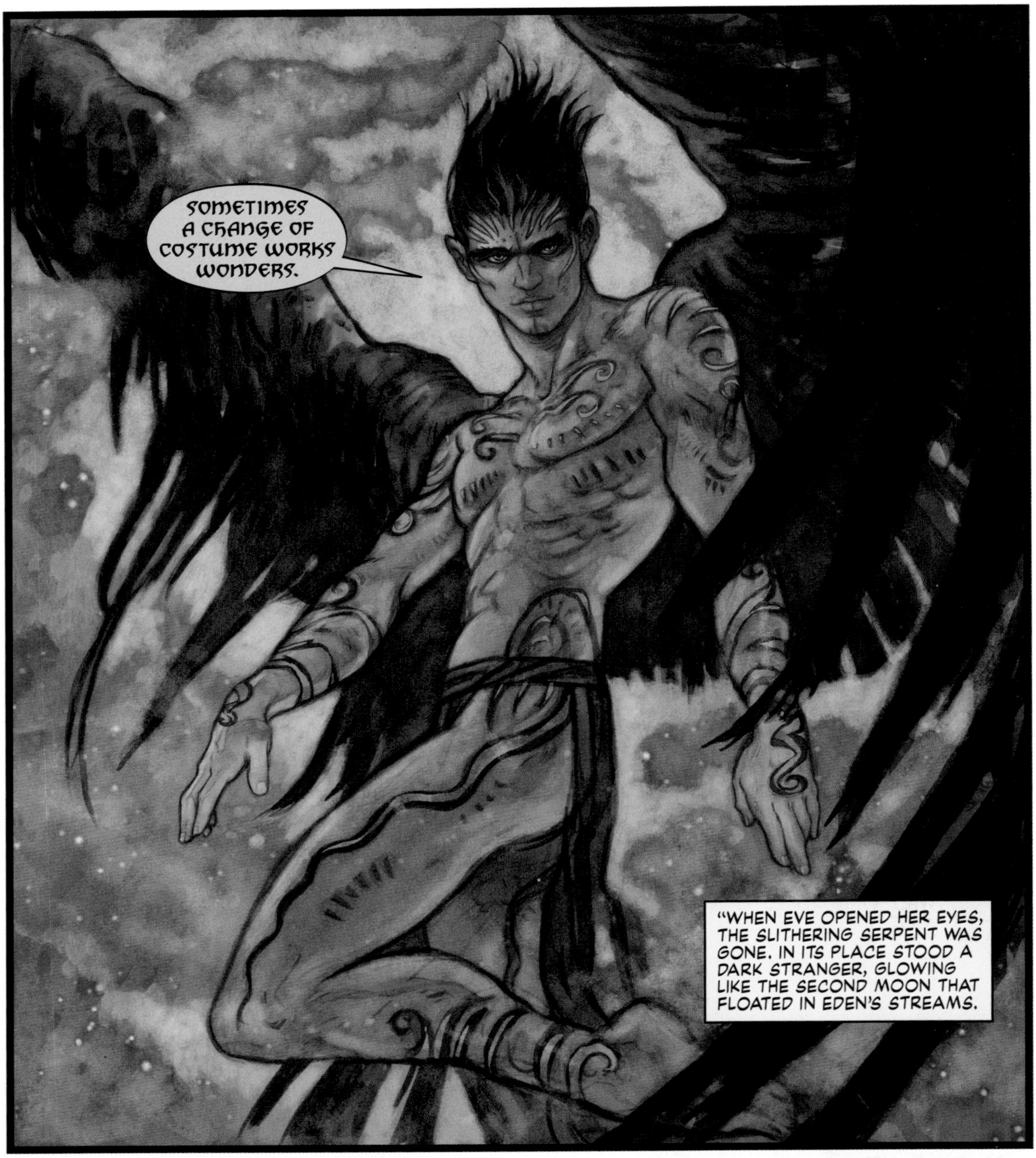
SOMETIMES A CHANGE OF COSTUME WORKS WONDERS.
"WHEN EVE OPENED HER EYES, THE SLITHERING SERPENT WAS GONE. IN ITS PLACE STOOD A DARK STRANGER, GLOWING LIKE THE SECOND MOON THAT FLOATED IN EDEN'S STREAMS.
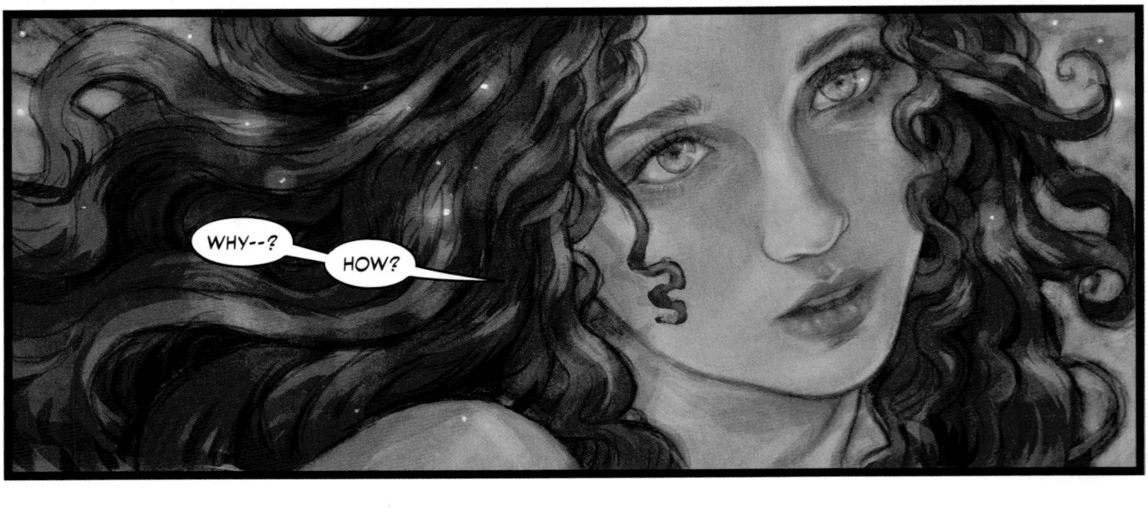
WHY--?
HOW?

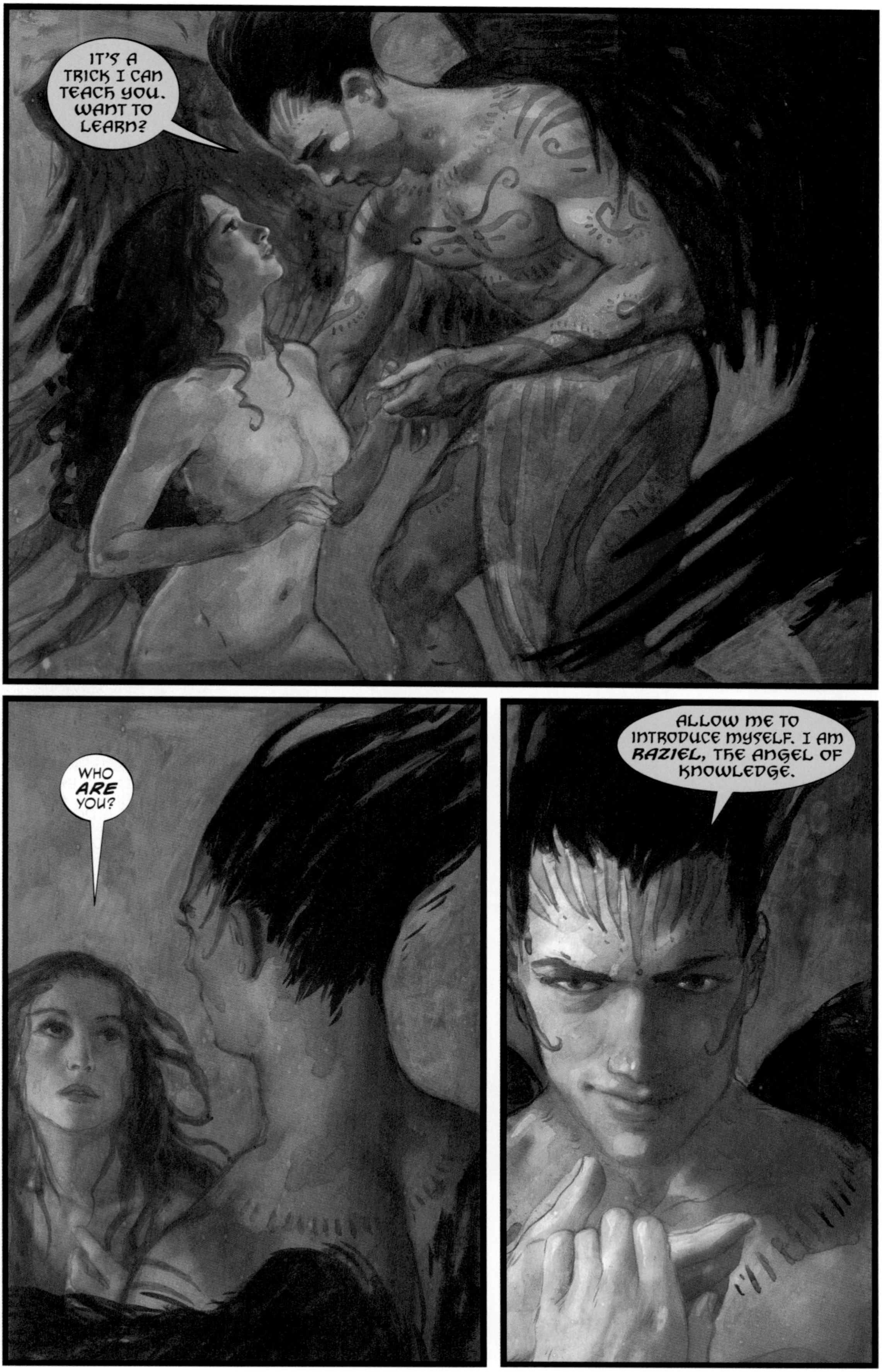
IT'S A TRICK I CAN TEACH YOU. WANT TO LEARN?
WHO *ARE* YOU?
ALLOW ME TO INTRODUCE MYSELF. I AM *RAZIEL*, THE ANGEL OF KNOWLEDGE.

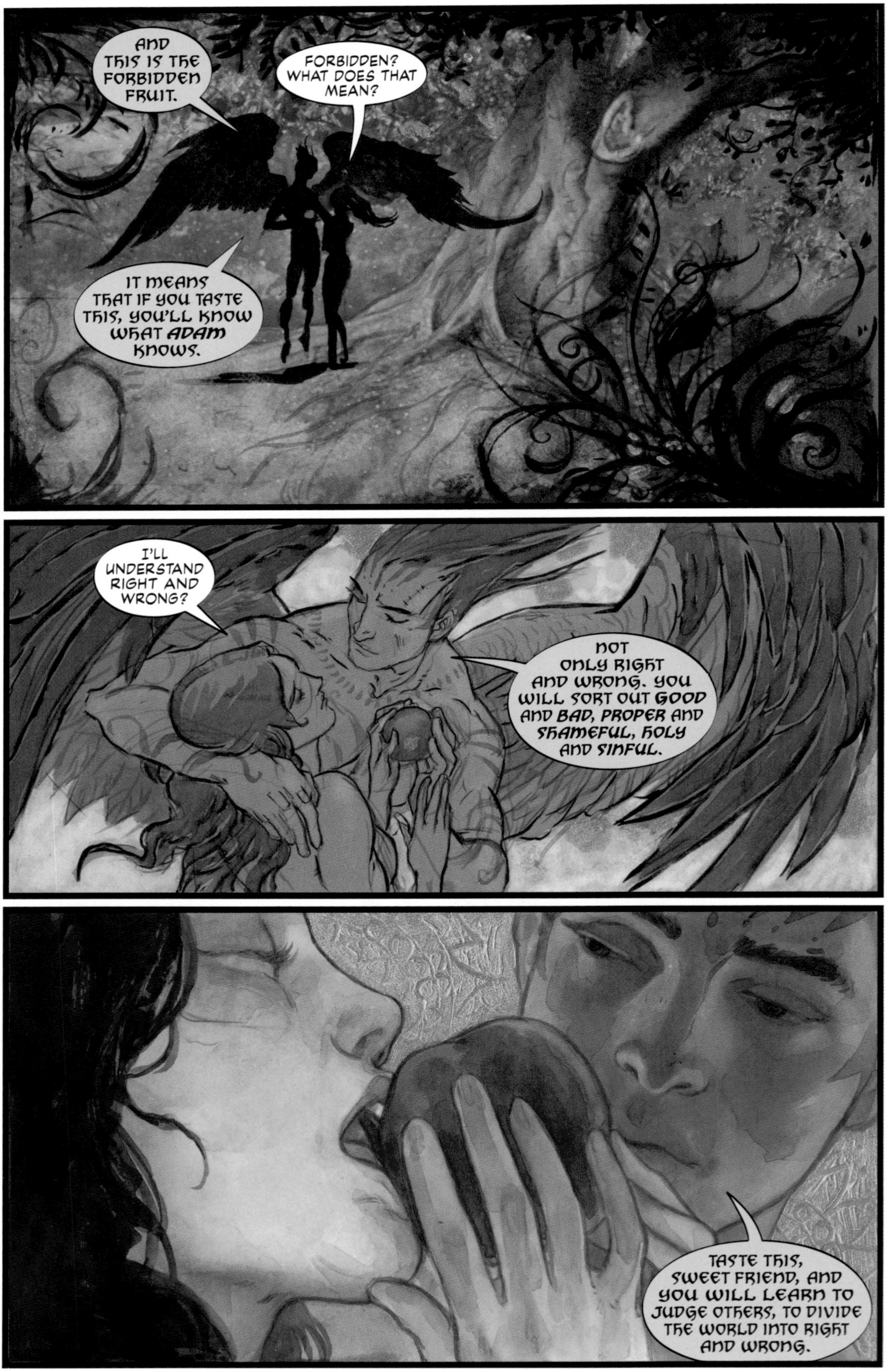
AND THIS IS THE FORBIDDEN FRUIT.
FORBIDDEN? WHAT DOES THAT MEAN?
IT MEANS THAT IF YOU TASTE THIS, YOU'LL KNOW WHAT *ADAM* KNOWS.
I'LL UNDERSTAND RIGHT AND WRONG?
NOT ONLY RIGHT AND WRONG. YOU WILL SORT OUT **GOOD** AND ***BAD***, ***PROPER*** AND ***SHAMEFUL***, ***HOLY*** AND ***SINFUL***.
TASTE THIS, SWEET FRIEND, AND YOU WILL LEARN TO JUDGE OTHERS, TO DIVIDE THE WORLD INTO RIGHT AND WRONG.

NOW *JUDGMENT* WILL SEPARATE YOU FROM ALL THE OTHER ANIMALS, EVEN FROM ANGELS. ONLY *HUMANS* WILL WORRY ABOUT GOOD AND BAD.

"WITH THE LAST BITE, EVE WAS DIFFERENT. AND SO WAS EVERYTHING SHE SAW."

IT'S A SHAME ANGELS HAVE NO SENSE OF WHAT'S PROPER. WHY, JUST *LOOK* AT THE WAY YOU'RE DRESSED! THAT CLOAK IS SCANDALOUS-- I CAN SEE RIGHT THROUGH IT!

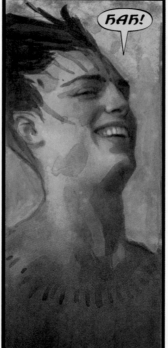

HAH!

WHAT'S SO FUNNY?

YOU *DARE* TO SCOLD ME FOR MY CLOAK? YOU, WHO ARE WEARING *NOTHING* AT ALL?!

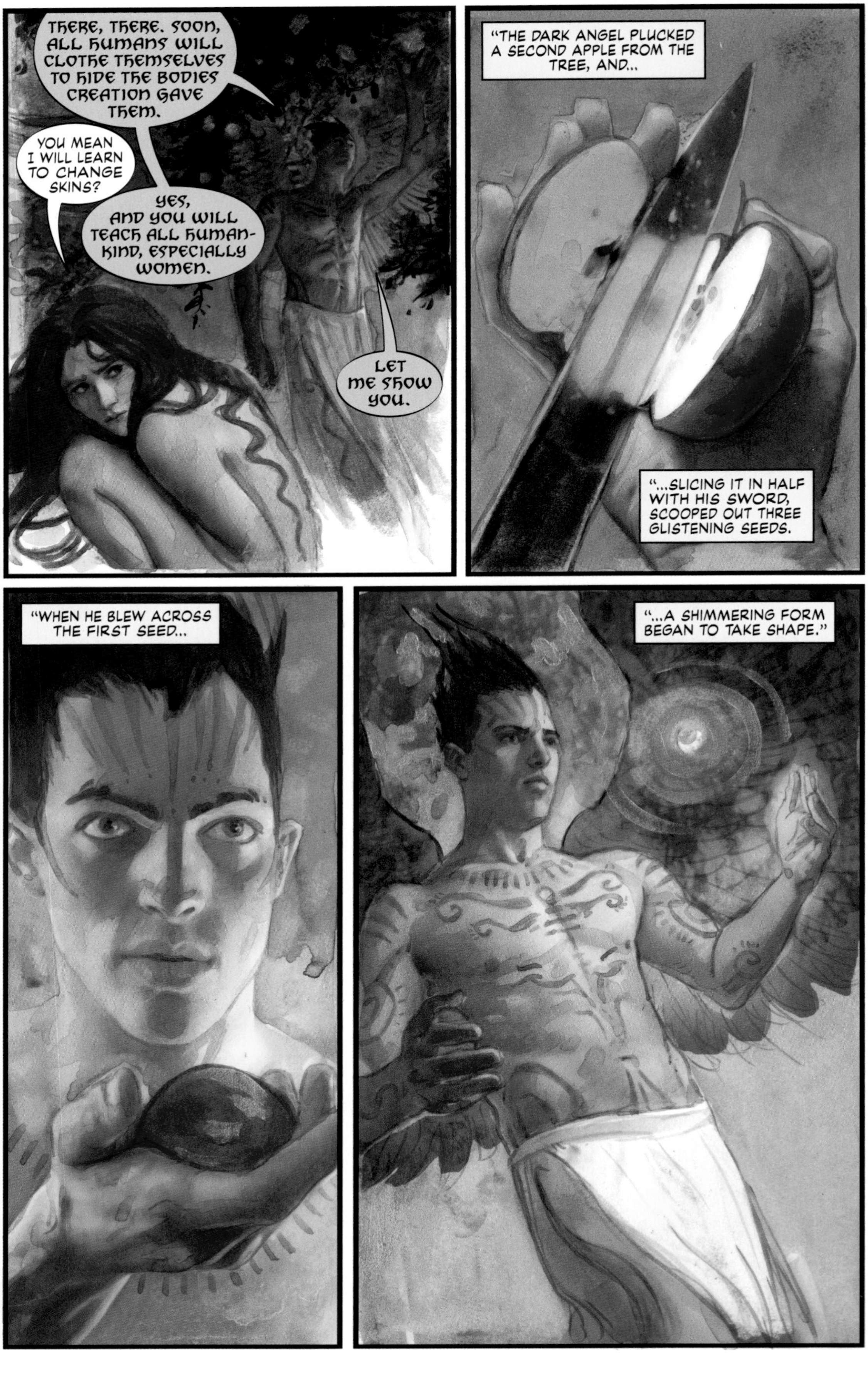
THERE, THERE. SOON, ALL HUMANS WILL CLOTHE THEMSELVES TO HIDE THE BODIES CREATION GAVE THEM.
YOU MEAN I WILL LEARN TO CHANGE SKINS?
YES, AND YOU WILL TEACH ALL HUMAN-KIND, ESPECIALLY WOMEN.
LET ME SHOW YOU.
"THE DARK ANGEL PLUCKED A SECOND APPLE FROM THE TREE, AND...
"...SLICING IT IN HALF WITH HIS SWORD, SCOOPED OUT THREE GLISTENING SEEDS.
"WHEN HE BLEW ACROSS THE FIRST SEED...
"...A SHIMMERING FORM BEGAN TO TAKE SHAPE."

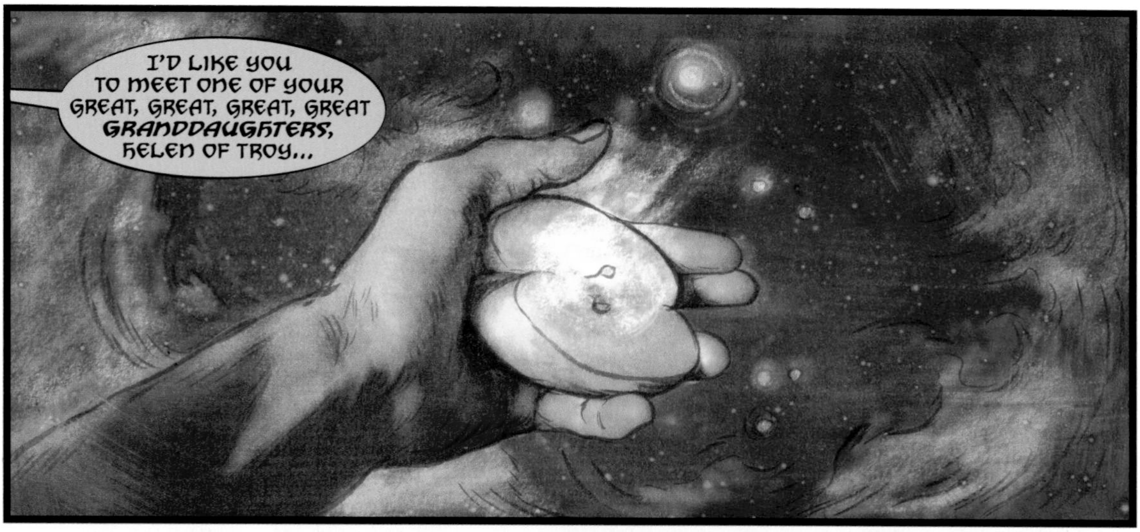
I'D LIKE YOU TO MEET ONE OF YOUR GREAT, GREAT, GREAT, GREAT GRANDDAUGHTERS, HELEN OF TROY...

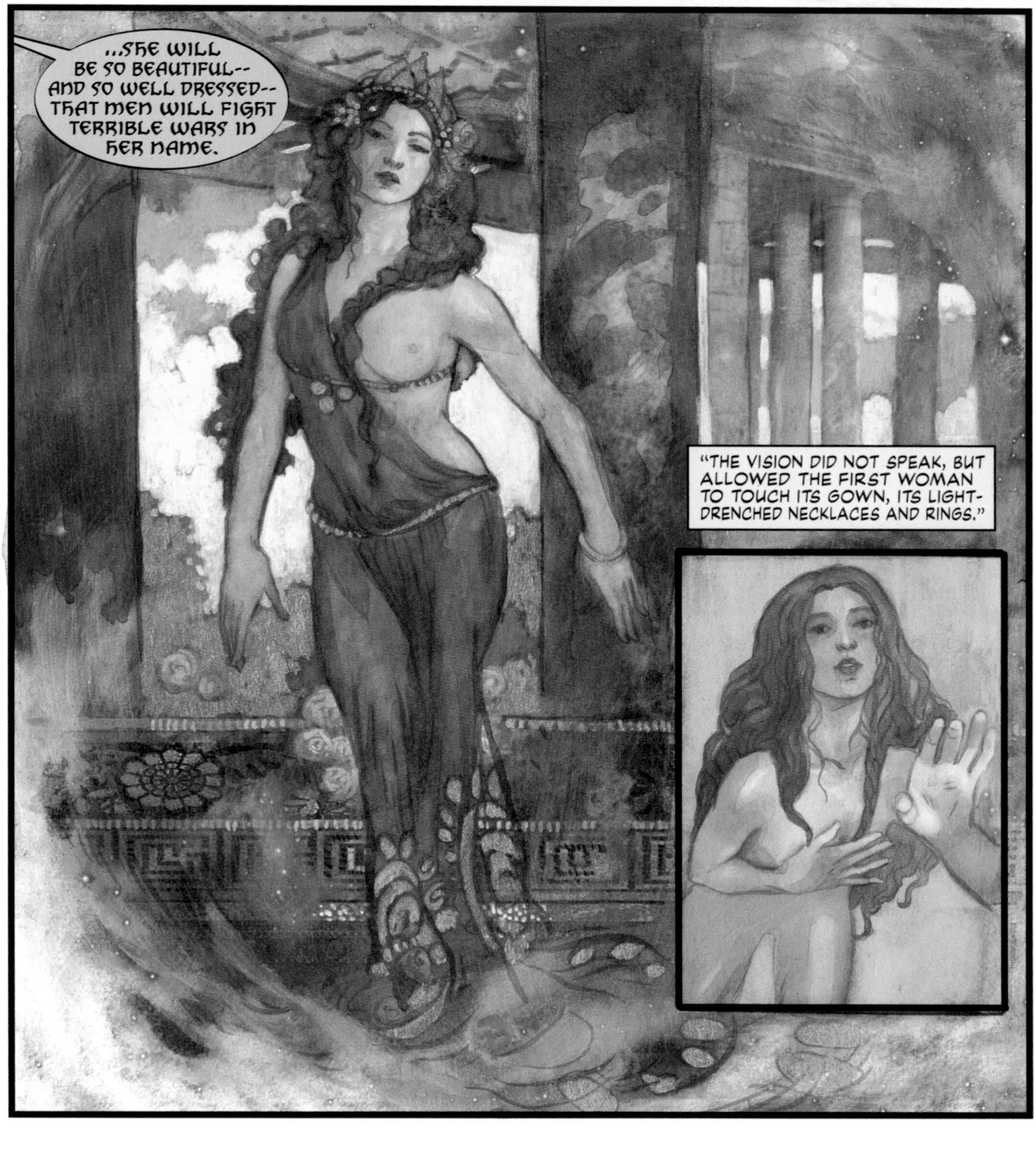
...SHE WILL BE SO BEAUTIFUL-- AND SO WELL DRESSED-- THAT MEN WILL FIGHT TERRIBLE WARS IN HER NAME.
"THE VISION DID NOT SPEAK, BUT ALLOWED THE FIRST WOMAN TO TOUCH ITS GOWN, ITS LIGHT-DRENCHED NECKLACES AND RINGS."

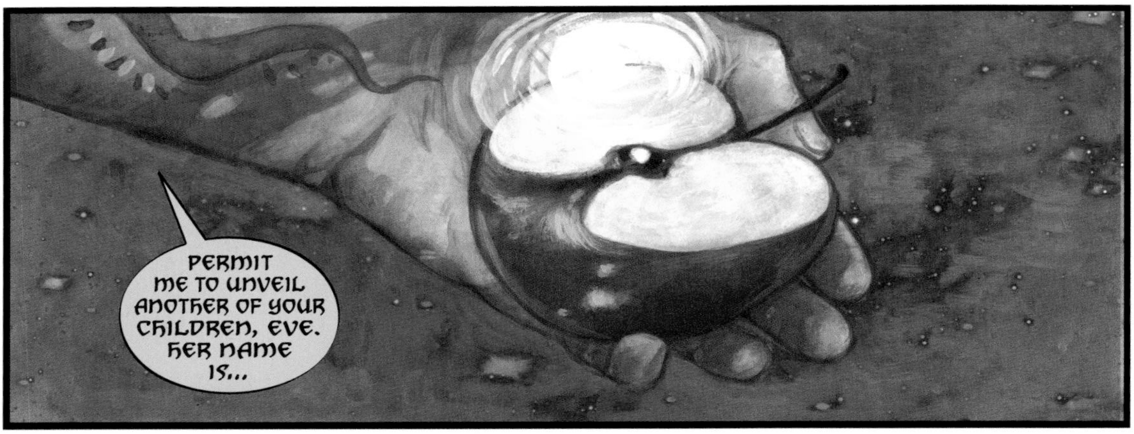
PERMIT ME TO UNVEIL ANOTHER OF YOUR CHILDREN, EVE. HER NAME IS...

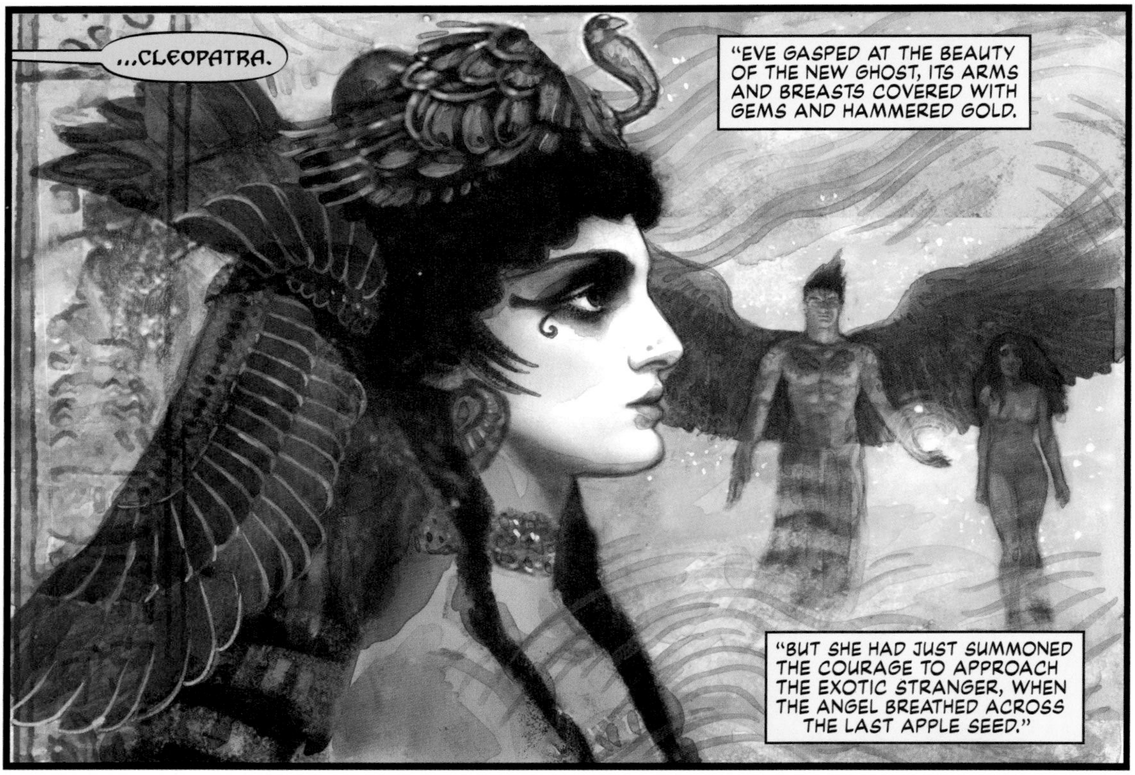
...CLEOPATRA.
"EVE GASPED AT THE BEAUTY OF THE NEW GHOST, ITS ARMS AND BREASTS COVERED WITH GEMS AND HAMMERED GOLD.
"BUT SHE HAD JUST SUMMONED THE COURAGE TO APPROACH THE EXOTIC STRANGER, WHEN THE ANGEL BREATHED ACROSS THE LAST APPLE SEED."

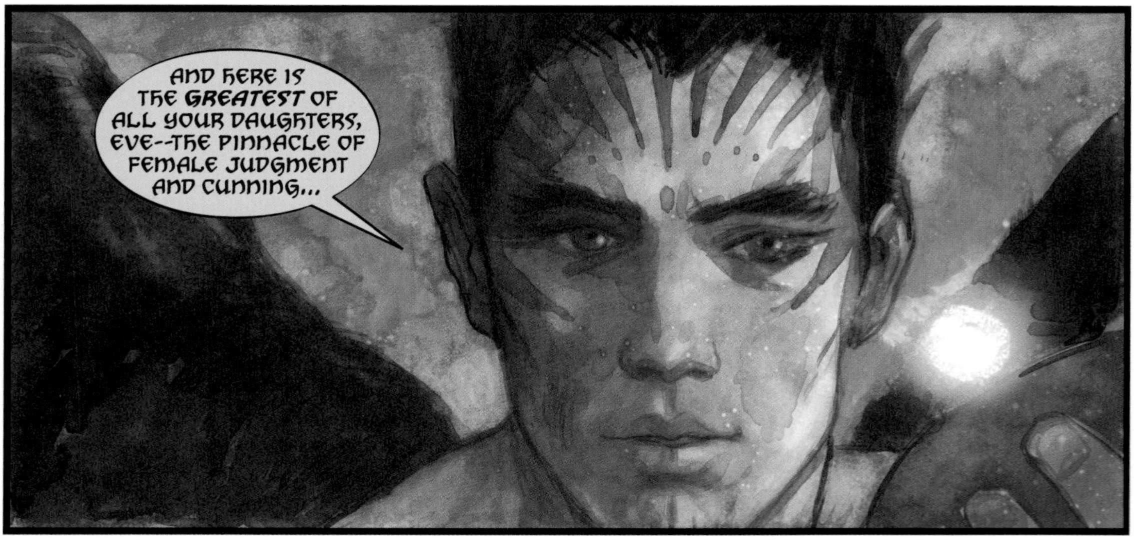
AND HERE IS THE *GREATEST* OF ALL YOUR DAUGHTERS, EVE--THE PINNACLE OF FEMALE JUDGMENT AND CUNNING...

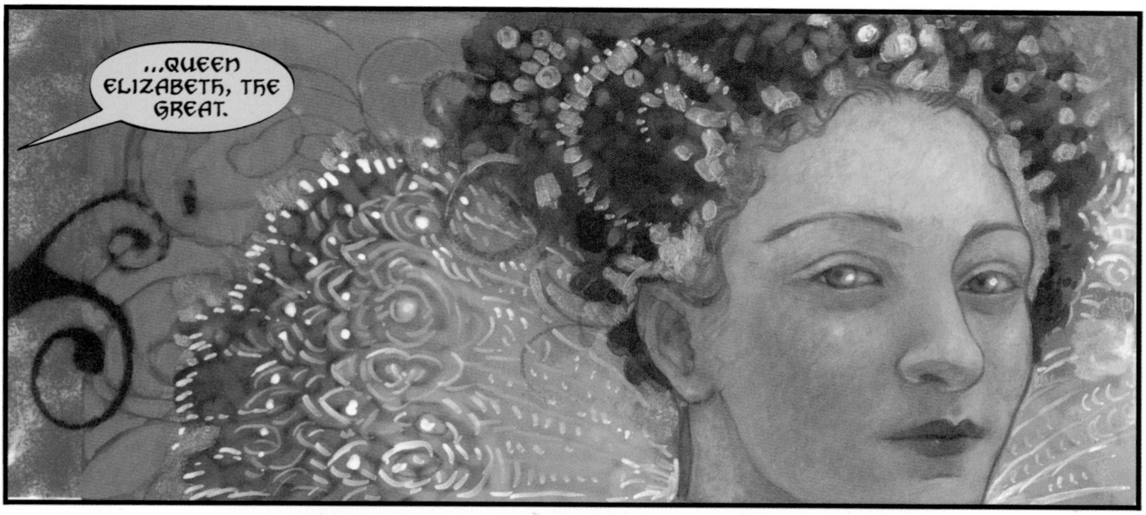
...QUEEN ELIZABETH, THE GREAT.

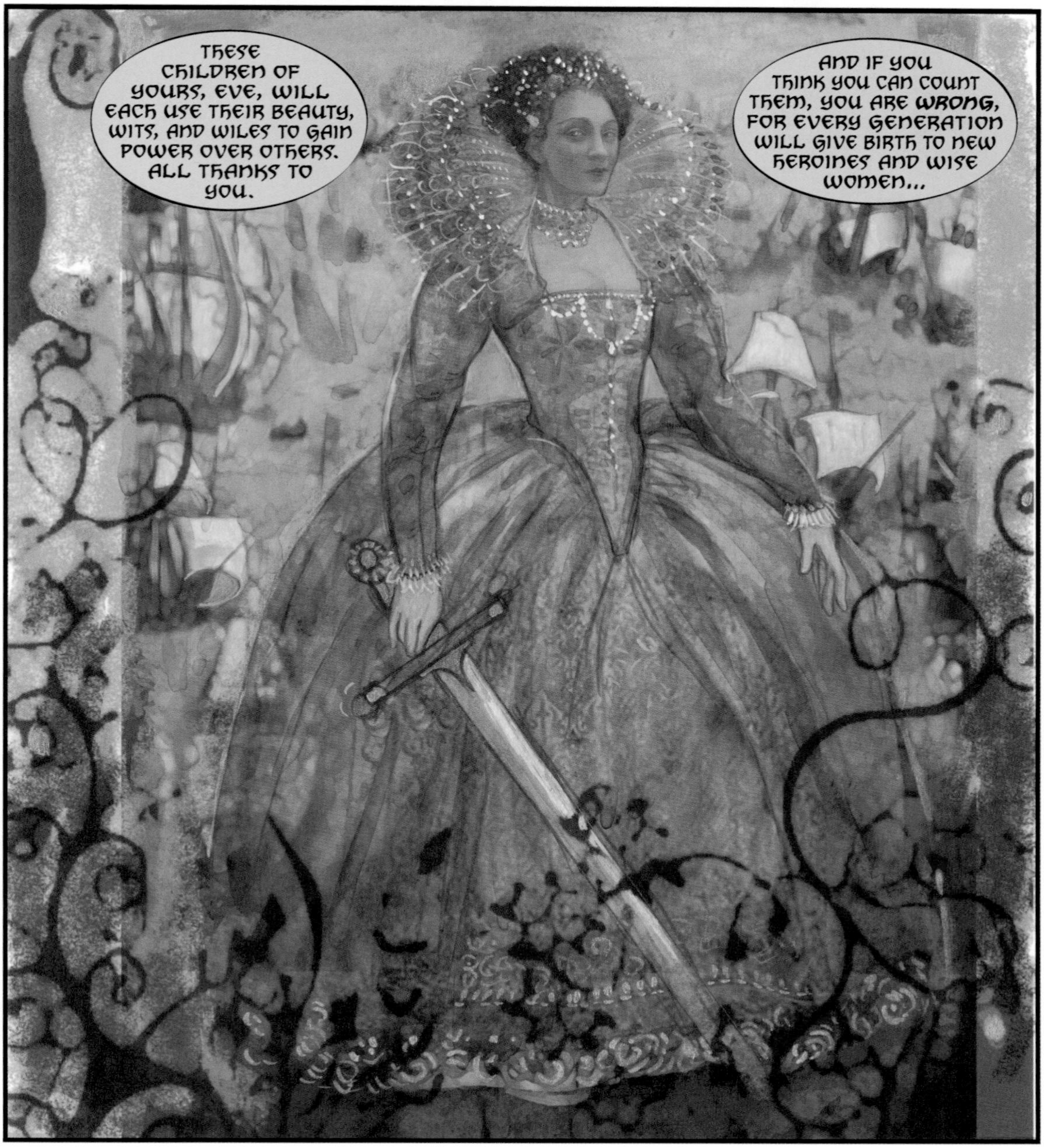
THESE CHILDREN OF YOURS, EVE, WILL EACH USE THEIR BEAUTY, WITS, AND WILES TO GAIN POWER OVER OTHERS. ALL THANKS TO YOU.
AND IF YOU THINK YOU CAN COUNT THEM, YOU ARE *WRONG*, FOR EVERY GENERATION WILL GIVE BIRTH TO NEW HEROINES AND WISE WOMEN...

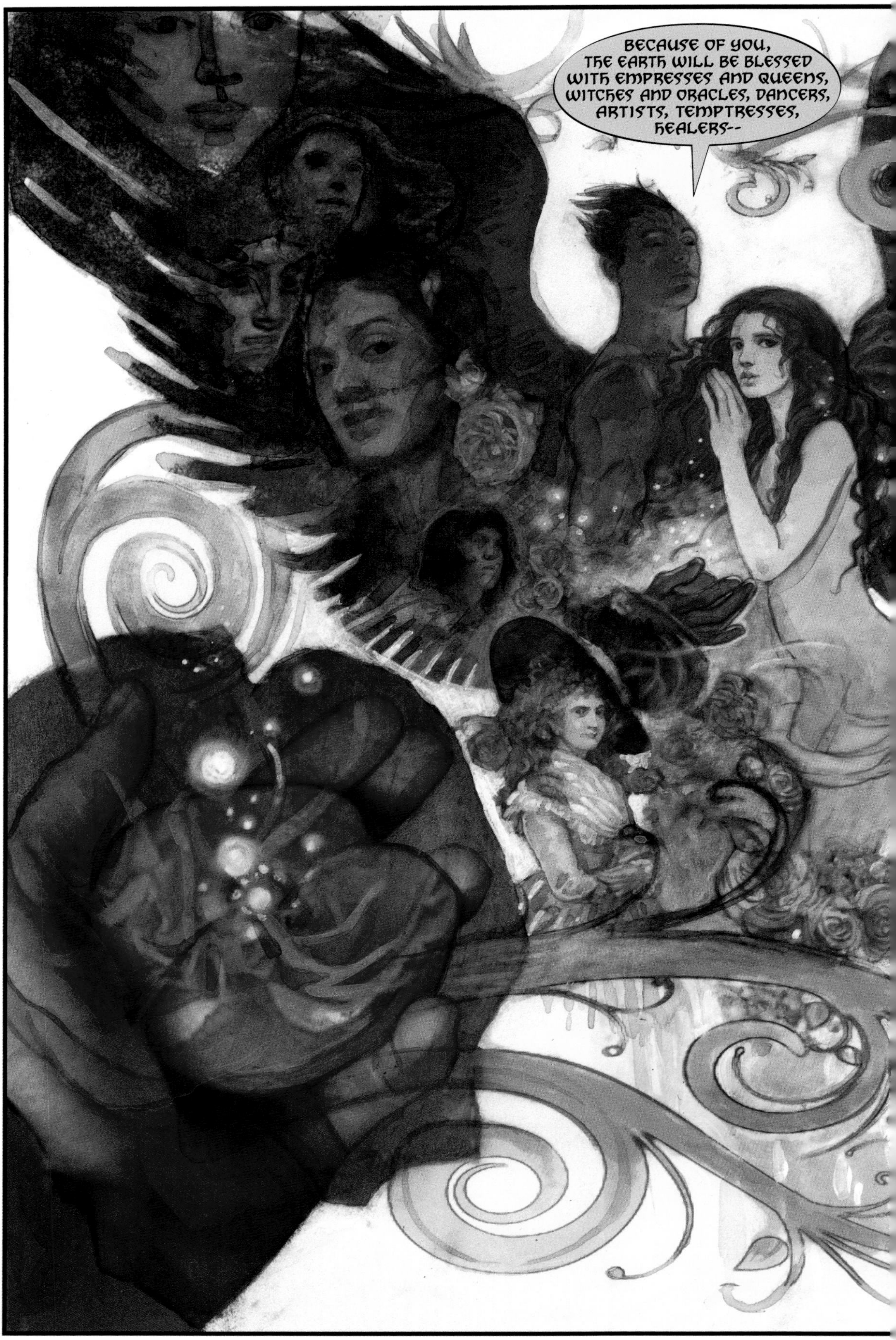
BECAUSE OF YOU, THE EARTH WILL BE BLESSED WITH EMPRESSES AND QUEENS, WITCHES AND ORACLES, DANCERS, ARTISTS, TEMPTRESSES, HEALERS--

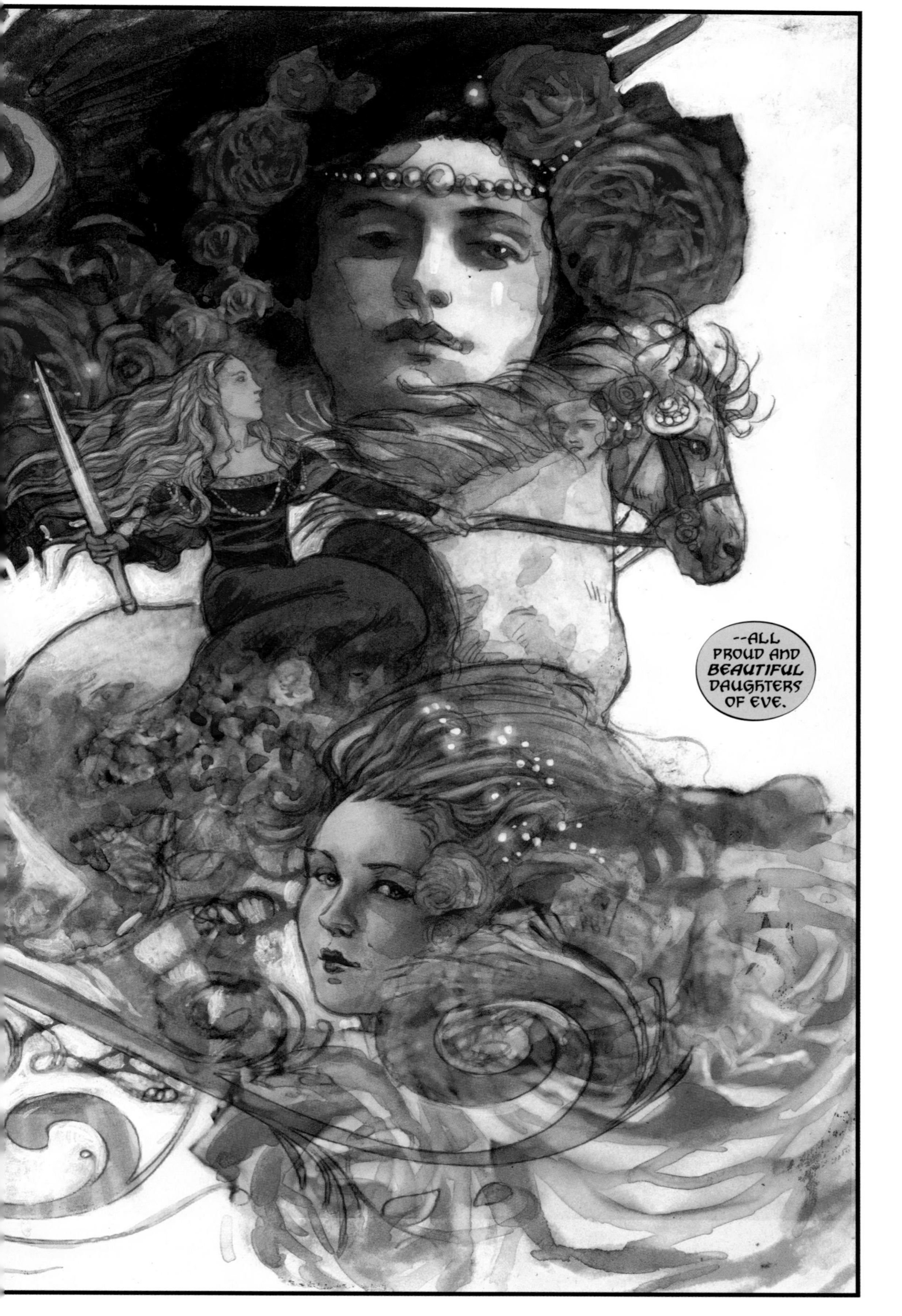
--ALL PROUD AND BEAUTIFUL DAUGHTERS OF EVE.

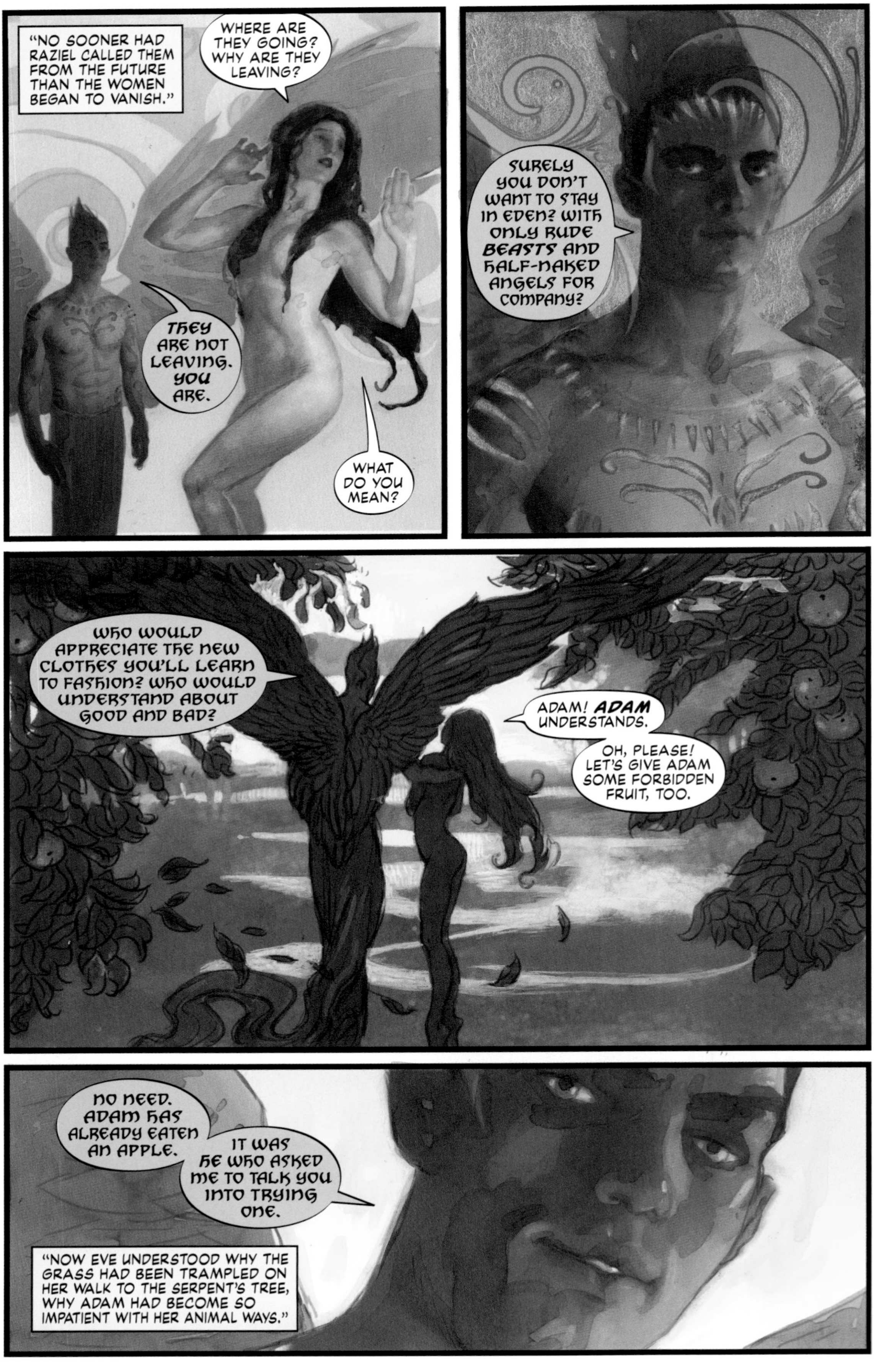
"NO SOONER HAD RAZIEL CALLED THEM FROM THE FUTURE THAN THE WOMEN BEGAN TO VANISH."
WHERE ARE THEY GOING? WHY ARE THEY LEAVING?
THEY ARE NOT LEAVING. YOU ARE.
WHAT DO YOU MEAN?
SURELY YOU DON'T WANT TO STAY IN EDEN? WITH ONLY RUDE BEASTS AND HALF-NAKED ANGELS FOR COMPANY?
WHO WOULD APPRECIATE THE NEW CLOTHES YOU'LL LEARN TO FASHION? WHO WOULD UNDERSTAND ABOUT GOOD AND BAD?
ADAM! ADAM UNDERSTANDS.
OH, PLEASE! LET'S GIVE ADAM SOME FORBIDDEN FRUIT, TOO.
NO NEED. ADAM HAS ALREADY EATEN AN APPLE.
IT WAS HE WHO ASKED ME TO TALK YOU INTO TRYING ONE.
"NOW EVE UNDERSTOOD WHY THE GRASS HAD BEEN TRAMPLED ON HER WALK TO THE SERPENT'S TREE, WHY ADAM HAD BECOME SO IMPATIENT WITH HER ANIMAL WAYS."

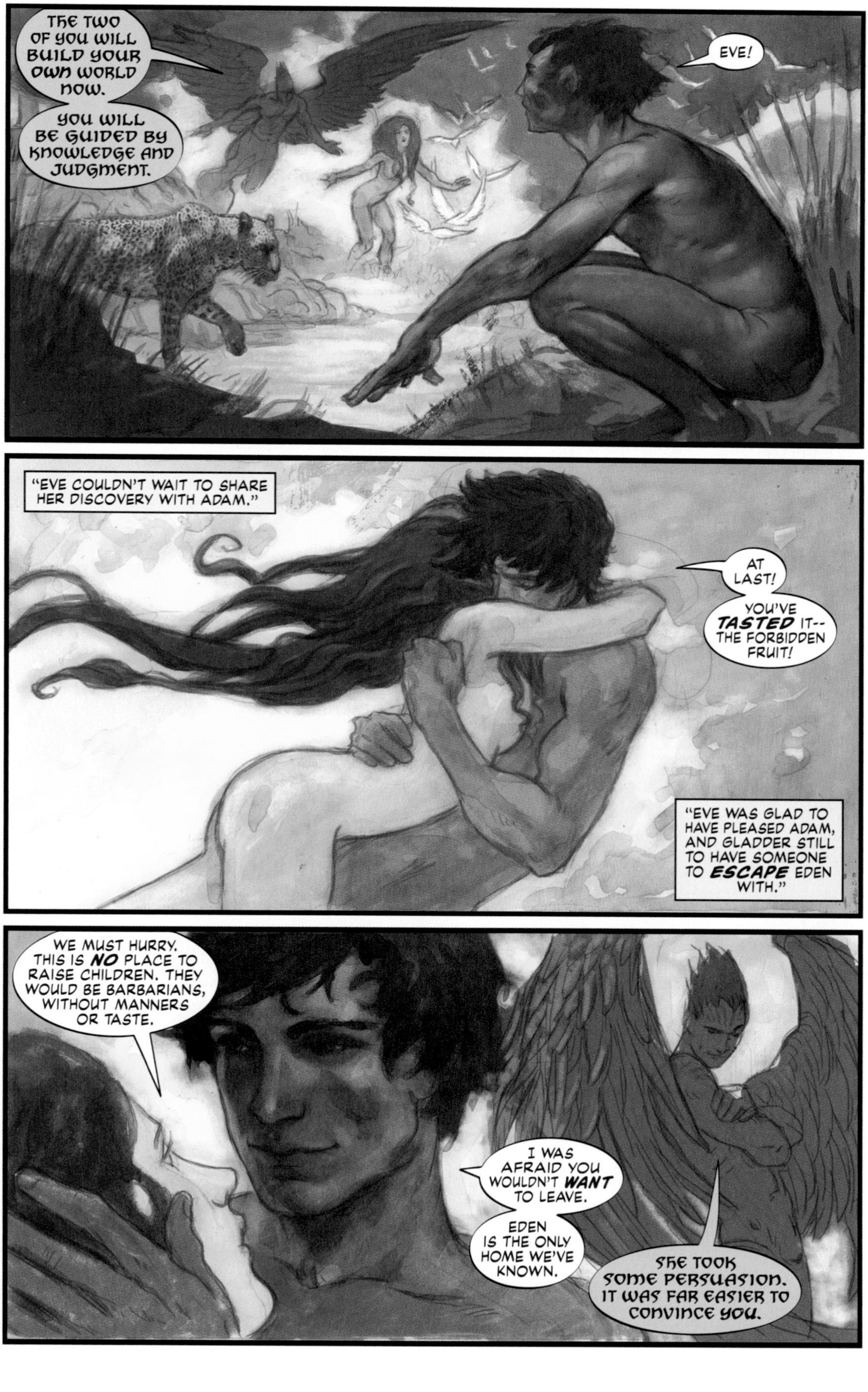
THE TWO OF YOU WILL BUILD YOUR OWN WORLD NOW.
YOU WILL BE GUIDED BY KNOWLEDGE AND JUDGMENT.
EVE!
"EVE COULDN'T WAIT TO SHARE HER DISCOVERY WITH ADAM."
AT LAST!
YOU'VE TASTED IT-- THE FORBIDDEN FRUIT!
"EVE WAS GLAD TO HAVE PLEASED ADAM, AND GLADDER STILL TO HAVE SOMEONE TO ESCAPE EDEN WITH."
WE MUST HURRY. THIS IS NO PLACE TO RAISE CHILDREN. THEY WOULD BE BARBARIANS, WITHOUT MANNERS OR TASTE.
I WAS AFRAID YOU WOULDN'T WANT TO LEAVE.
EDEN IS THE ONLY HOME WE'VE KNOWN.
SHE TOOK SOME PERSUASION. IT WAS FAR EASIER TO CONVINCE YOU.

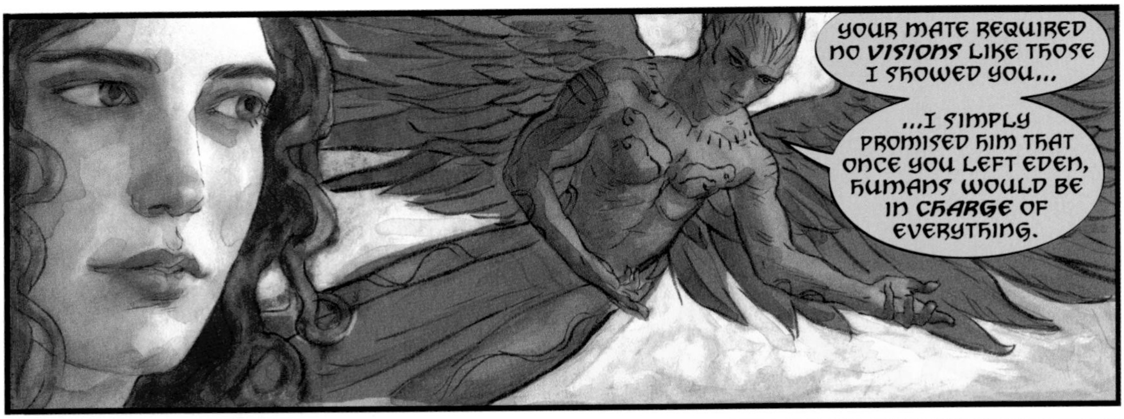
YOUR MATE REQUIRED NO VISIONS LIKE THOSE I SHOWED YOU...
...I SIMPLY PROMISED HIM THAT ONCE YOU LEFT EDEN, HUMANS WOULD BE IN CHARGE OF EVERYTHING.

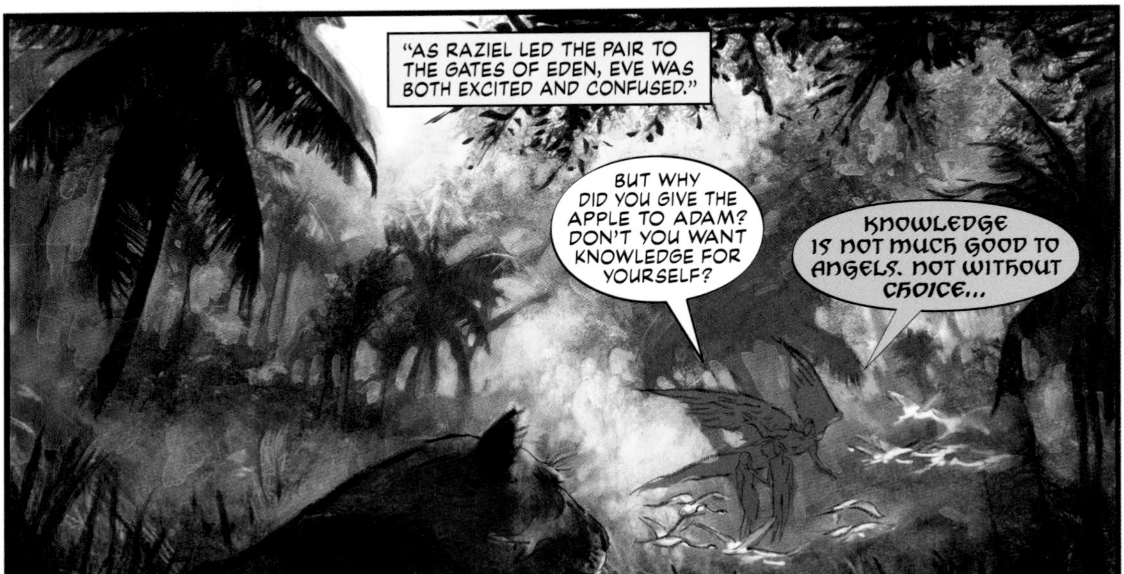
"AS RAZIEL LED THE PAIR TO THE GATES OF EDEN, EVE WAS BOTH EXCITED AND CONFUSED."
BUT WHY DID YOU GIVE THE APPLE TO ADAM? DON'T YOU WANT KNOWLEDGE FOR YOURSELF?
KNOWLEDGE IS NOT MUCH GOOD TO ANGELS. NOT WITHOUT CHOICE...

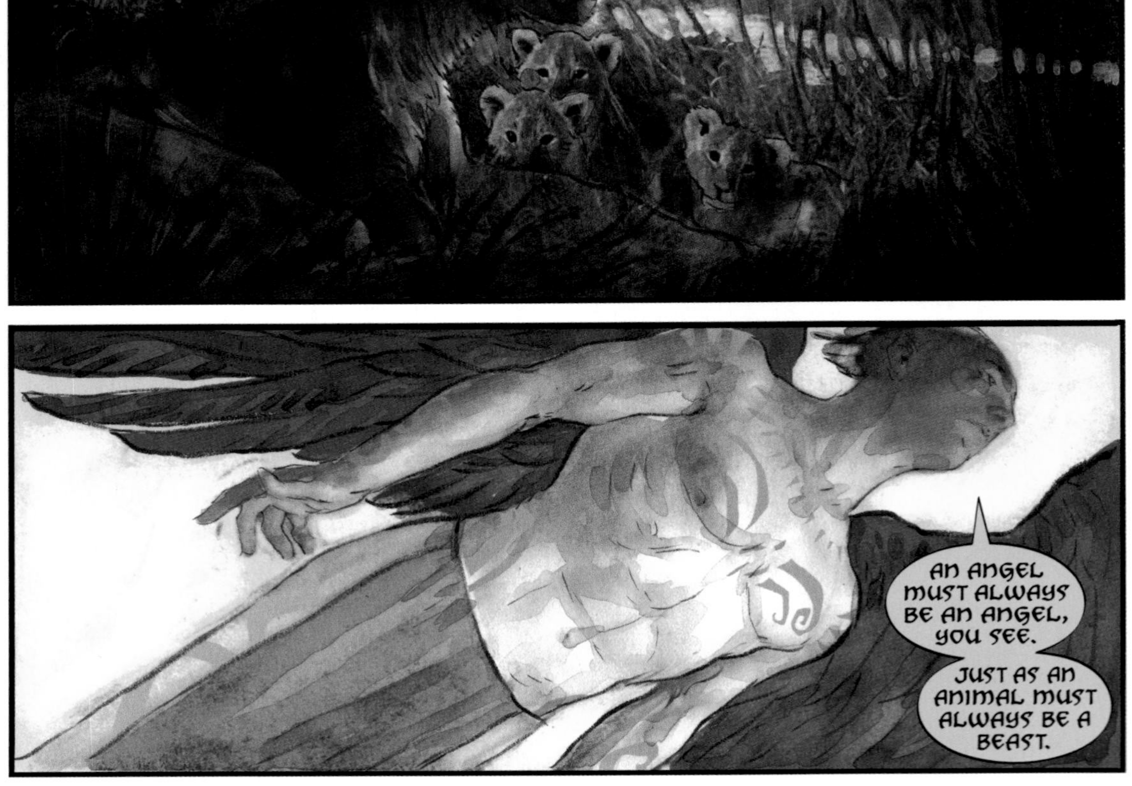
AN ANGEL MUST ALWAYS BE AN ANGEL, YOU SEE.
JUST AS AN ANIMAL MUST ALWAYS BE A BEAST.

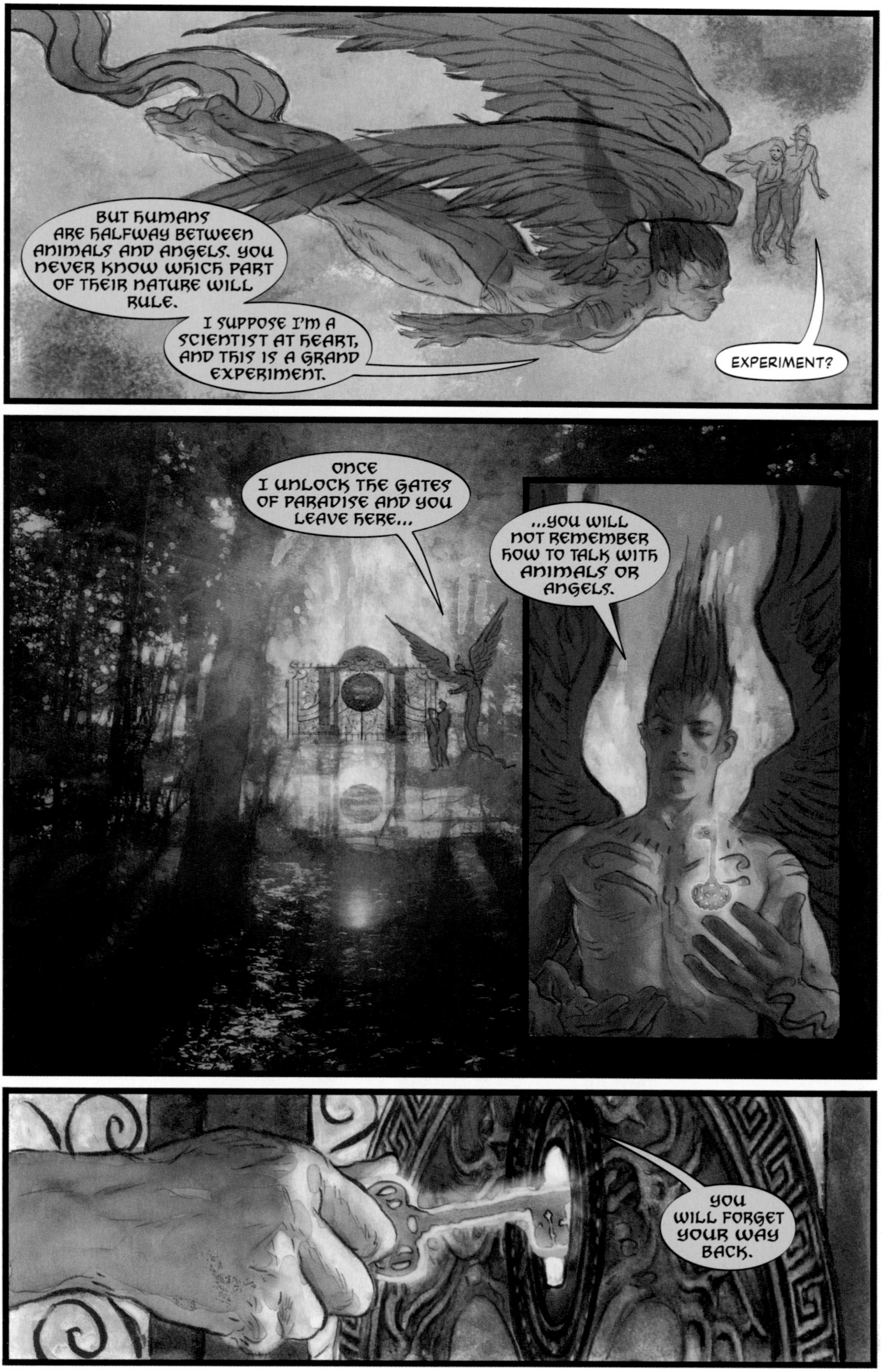
BUT HUMANS ARE HALFWAY BETWEEN ANIMALS AND ANGELS. YOU NEVER KNOW WHICH PART OF THEIR NATURE WILL RULE.
I SUPPOSE I'M A SCIENTIST AT HEART, AND THIS IS A GRAND EXPERIMENT.
EXPERIMENT?
ONCE I UNLOCK THE GATES OF PARADISE AND YOU LEAVE HERE...
...YOU WILL NOT REMEMBER HOW TO TALK WITH ANIMALS OR ANGELS.
YOU WILL FORGET YOUR WAY BACK.

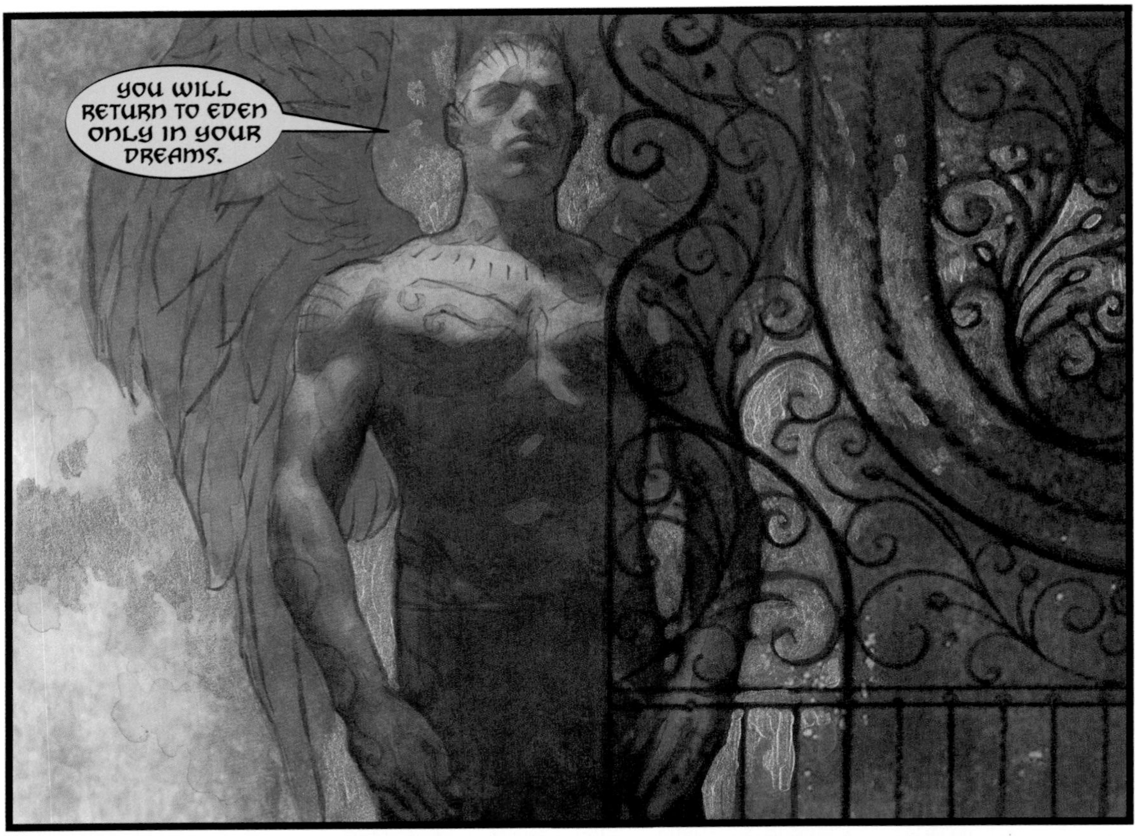
YOU WILL RETURN TO EDEN ONLY IN YOUR DREAMS.

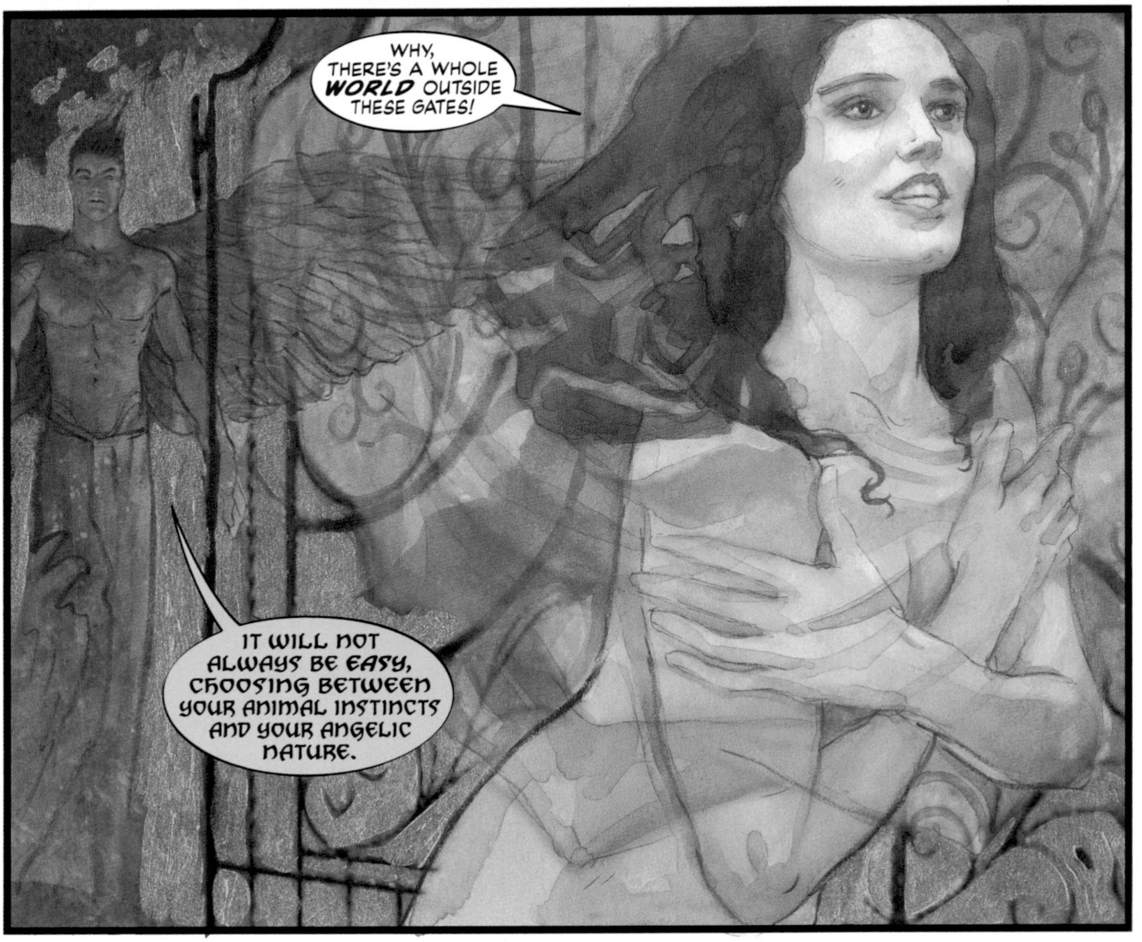
WHY, THERE'S A WHOLE **WORLD** OUTSIDE THESE GATES!
IT WILL NOT ALWAYS BE **EASY**, CHOOSING BETWEEN YOUR ANIMAL INSTINCTS AND YOUR ANGELIC NATURE.

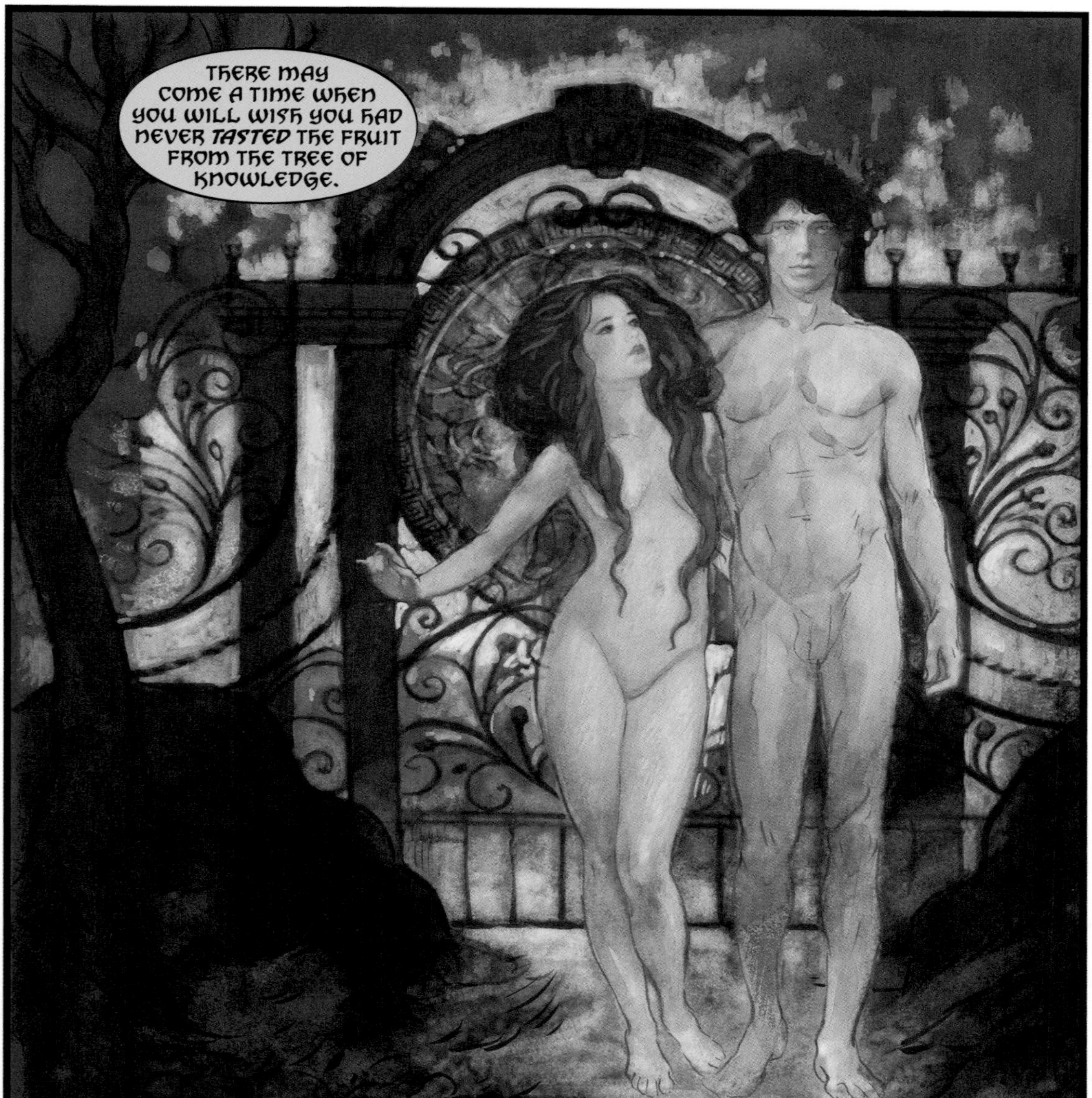
THERE MAY COME A TIME WHEN YOU WILL WISH YOU HAD NEVER *TASTED* THE FRUIT FROM THE TREE OF KNOWLEDGE.

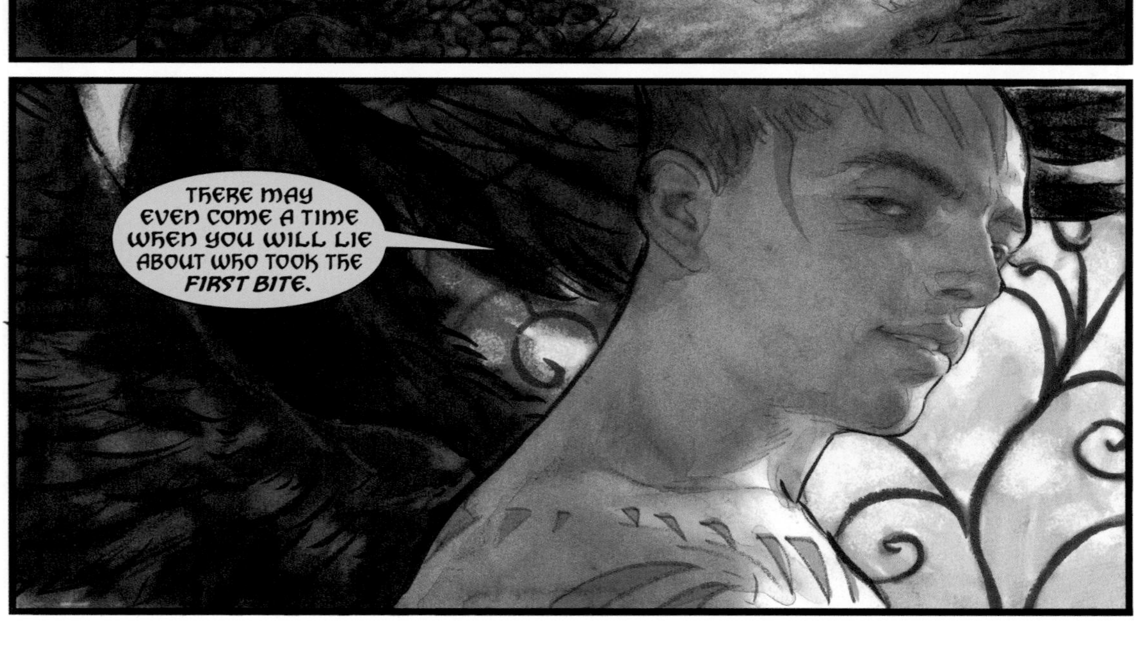
THERE MAY EVEN COME A TIME WHEN YOU WILL LIE ABOUT WHO TOOK THE *FIRST BITE*.

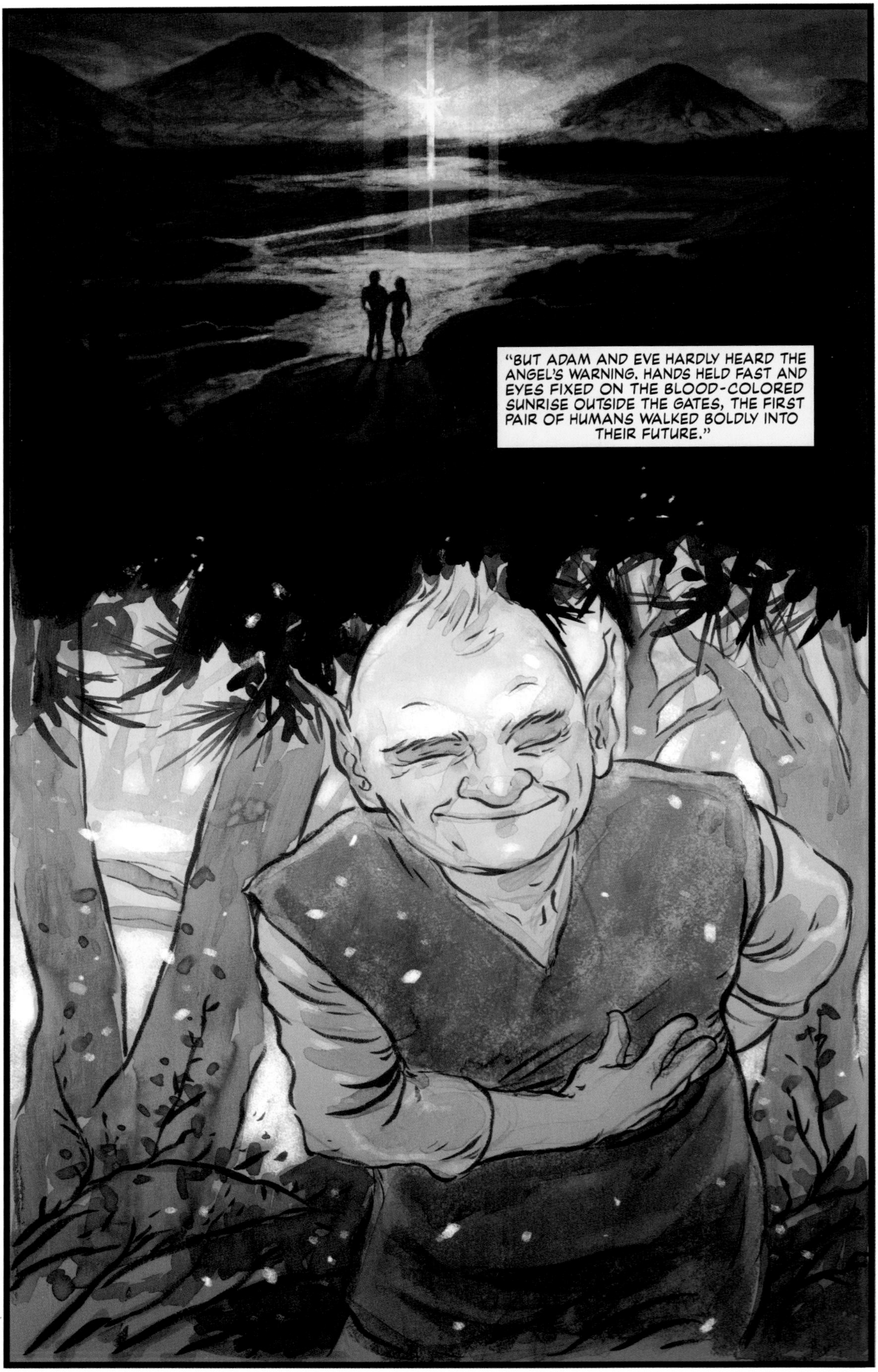
"BUT ADAM AND EVE HARDLY HEARD THE ANGEL'S WARNING. HANDS HELD FAST AND EYES FIXED ON THE BLOOD-COLORED SUNRISE OUTSIDE THE GATES, THE FIRST PAIR OF HUMANS WALKED BOLDLY INTO THEIR FUTURE."

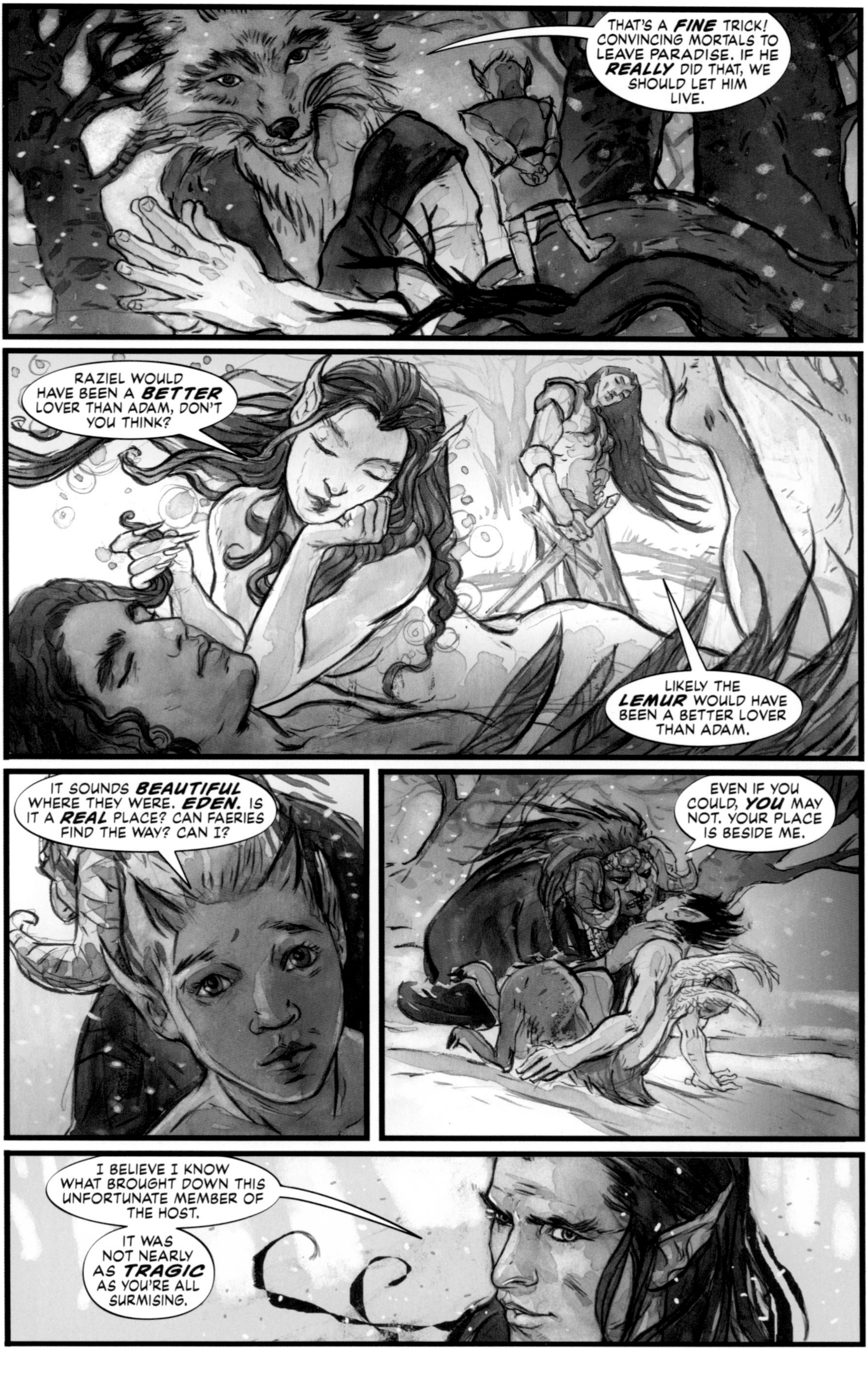
THAT'S A FINE TRICK! CONVINCING MORTALS TO LEAVE PARADISE. IF HE REALLY DID THAT, WE SHOULD LET HIM LIVE.
RAZIEL WOULD HAVE BEEN A BETTER LOVER THAN ADAM, DON'T YOU THINK?
LIKELY THE LEMUR WOULD HAVE BEEN A BETTER LOVER THAN ADAM.
IT SOUNDS BEAUTIFUL WHERE THEY WERE. EDEN. IS IT A REAL PLACE? CAN FAERIES FIND THE WAY? CAN I?
EVEN IF YOU COULD, YOU MAY NOT. YOUR PLACE IS BESIDE ME.
I BELIEVE I KNOW WHAT BROUGHT DOWN THIS UNFORTUNATE MEMBER OF THE HOST.
IT WAS NOT NEARLY AS TRAGIC AS YOU'RE ALL SURMISING.

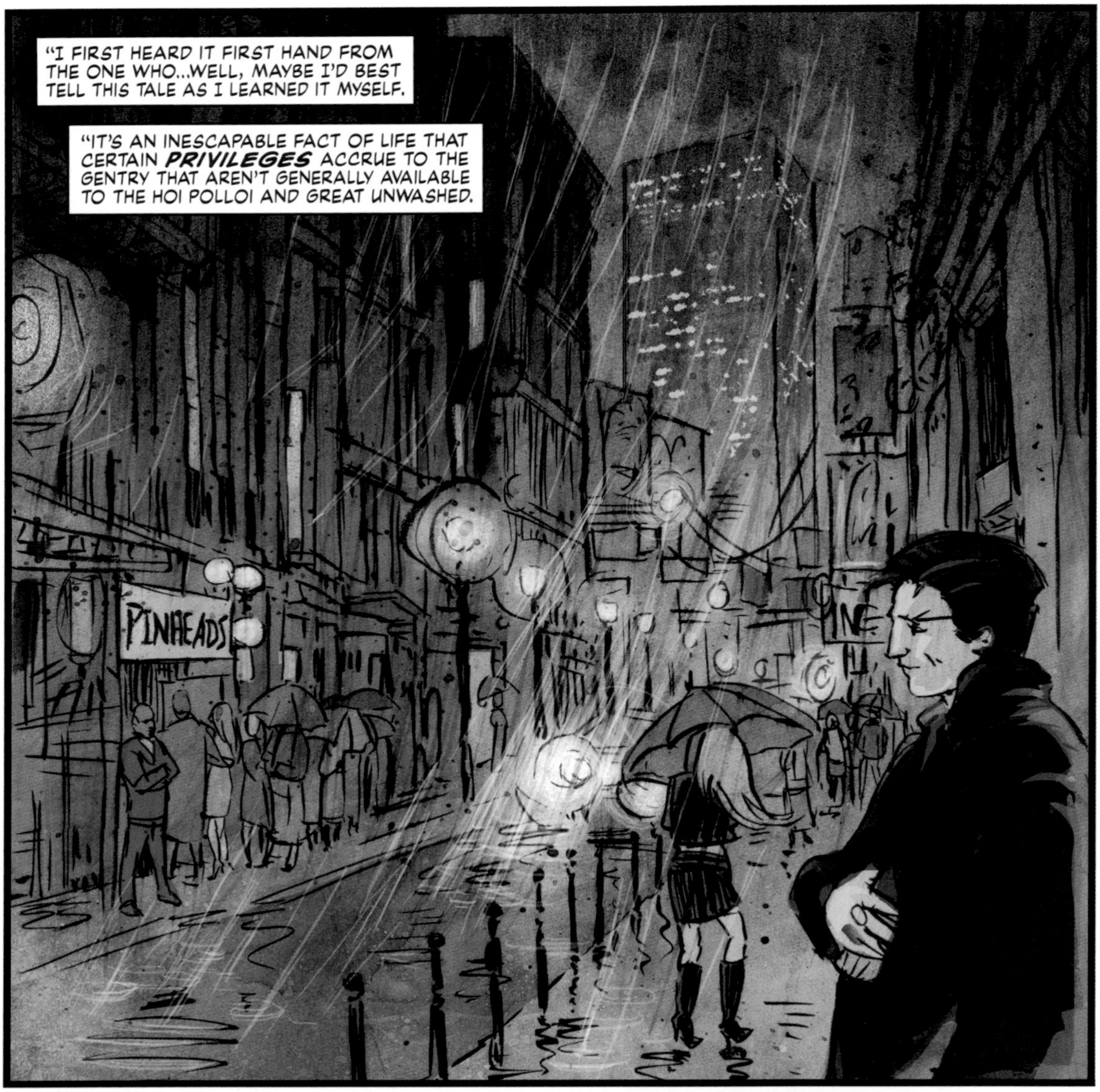
"I FIRST HEARD IT FIRST HAND FROM THE ONE WHO...WELL, MAYBE I'D BEST TELL THIS TALE AS I LEARNED IT MYSELF.
"IT'S AN INESCAPABLE FACT OF LIFE THAT CERTAIN **PRIVILEGES** ACCRUE TO THE GENTRY THAT AREN'T GENERALLY AVAILABLE TO THE HOI POLLOI AND GREAT UNWASHED.
PINHEADS

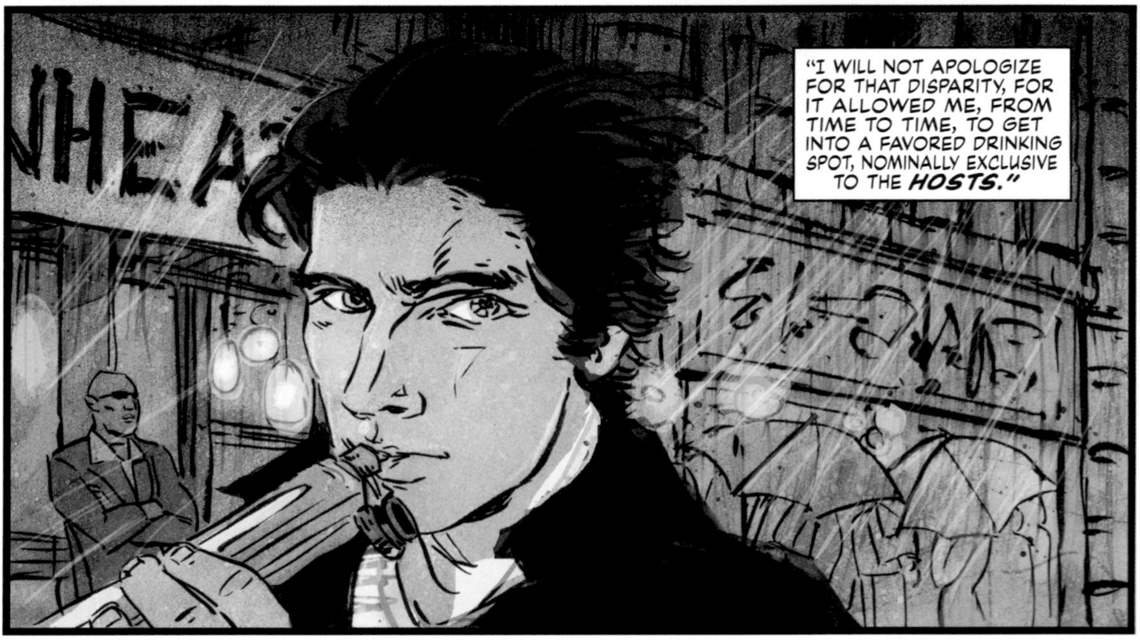
"I WILL NOT APOLOGIZE FOR THAT DISPARITY, FOR IT ALLOWED ME, FROM TIME TO TIME, TO GET INTO A FAVORED DRINKING SPOT, NOMINALLY EXCLUSIVE TO THE **HOSTS.**"

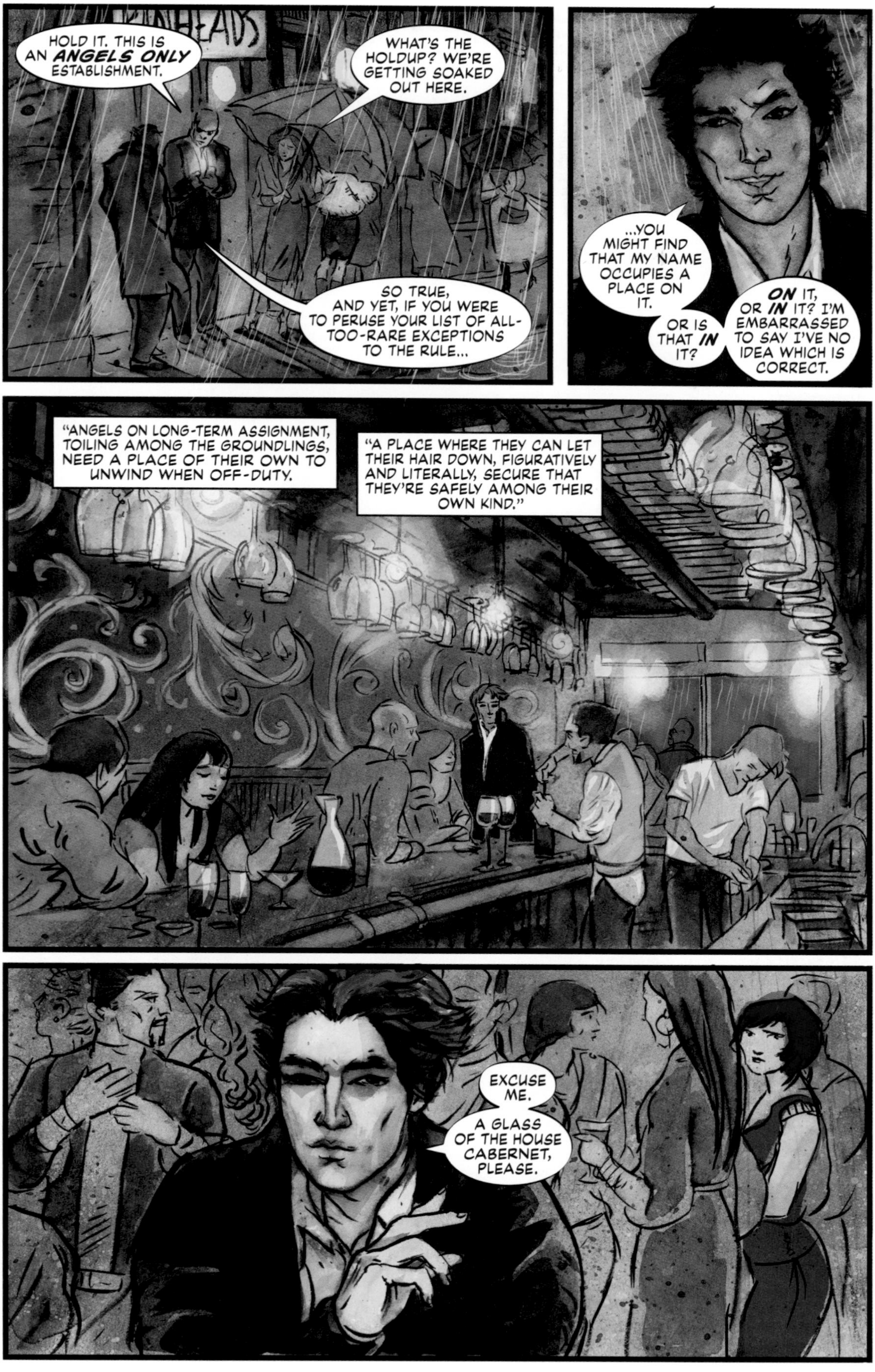
HOLD IT. THIS IS AN ANGELS ONLY ESTABLISHMENT.
WHAT'S THE HOLDUP? WE'RE GETTING SOAKED OUT HERE.
SO TRUE, AND YET, IF YOU WERE TO PERUSE YOUR LIST OF ALL-TOO-RARE EXCEPTIONS TO THE RULE...
...YOU MIGHT FIND THAT MY NAME OCCUPIES A PLACE ON IT.
OR IS THAT IN IT?
ON IT, OR IN IT? I'M EMBARRASSED TO SAY I'VE NO IDEA WHICH IS CORRECT.
"ANGELS ON LONG-TERM ASSIGNMENT, TOILING AMONG THE GROUNDLINGS, NEED A PLACE OF THEIR OWN TO UNWIND WHEN OFF-DUTY.
"A PLACE WHERE THEY CAN LET THEIR HAIR DOWN, FIGURATIVELY AND LITERALLY, SECURE THAT THEY'RE SAFELY AMONG THEIR OWN KIND."
EXCUSE ME.
A GLASS OF THE HOUSE CABERNET, PLEASE.

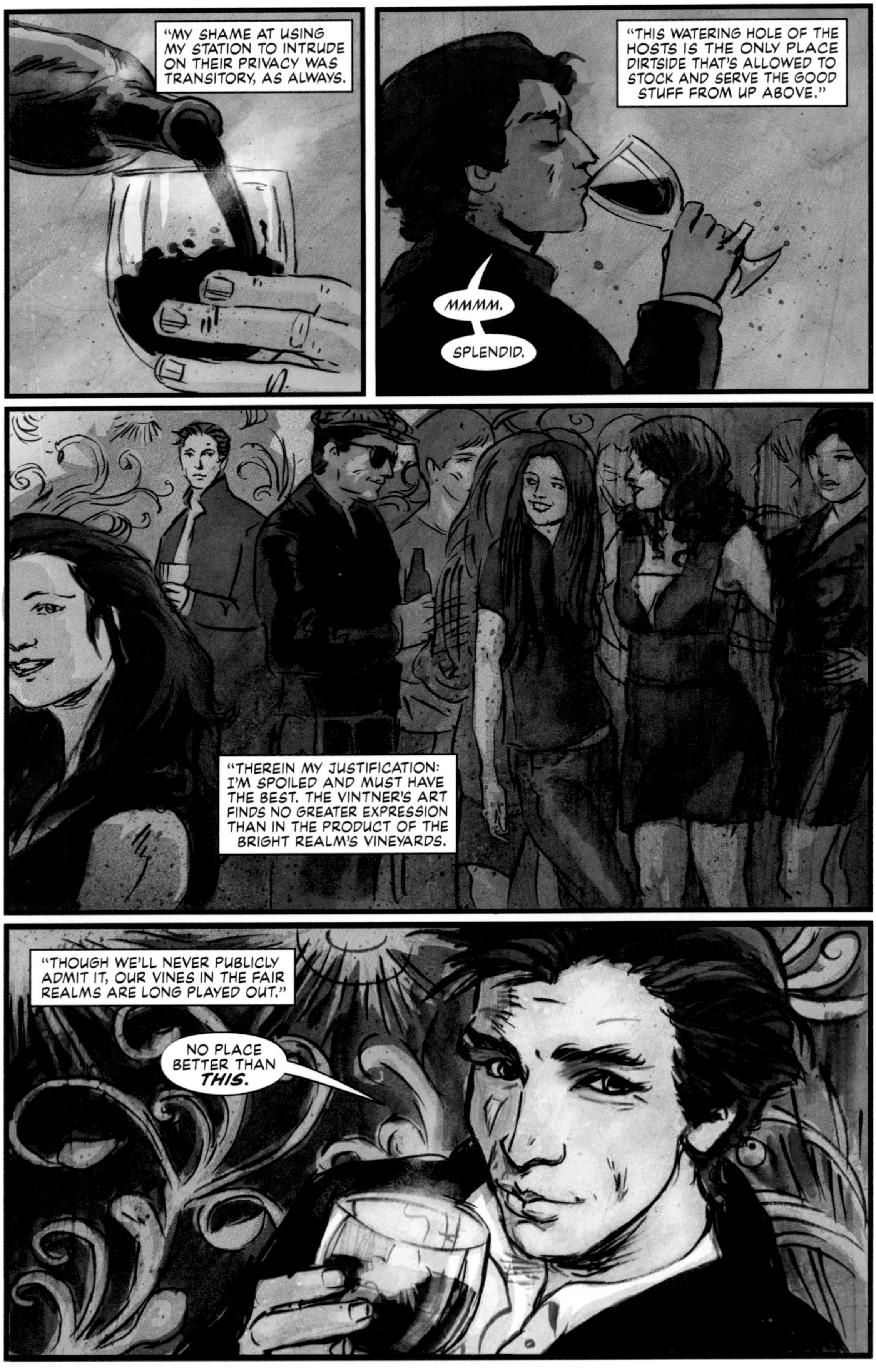
"MY SHAME AT USING MY STATION TO INTRUDE ON THEIR PRIVACY WAS TRANSITORY, AS ALWAYS.
"THIS WATERING HOLE OF THE HOSTS IS THE ONLY PLACE DIRTSIDE THAT'S ALLOWED TO STOCK AND SERVE THE GOOD STUFF FROM UP ABOVE."
MMMM.
SPLENDID.
"THEREIN MY JUSTIFICATION: I'M SPOILED AND MUST HAVE THE BEST. THE VINTNER'S ART FINDS NO GREATER EXPRESSION THAN IN THE PRODUCT OF THE BRIGHT REALM'S VINEYARDS.
"THOUGH WE'LL NEVER PUBLICLY ADMIT IT, OUR VINES IN THE FAIR REALMS ARE LONG PLAYED OUT."
NO PLACE BETTER THAN *THIS*.

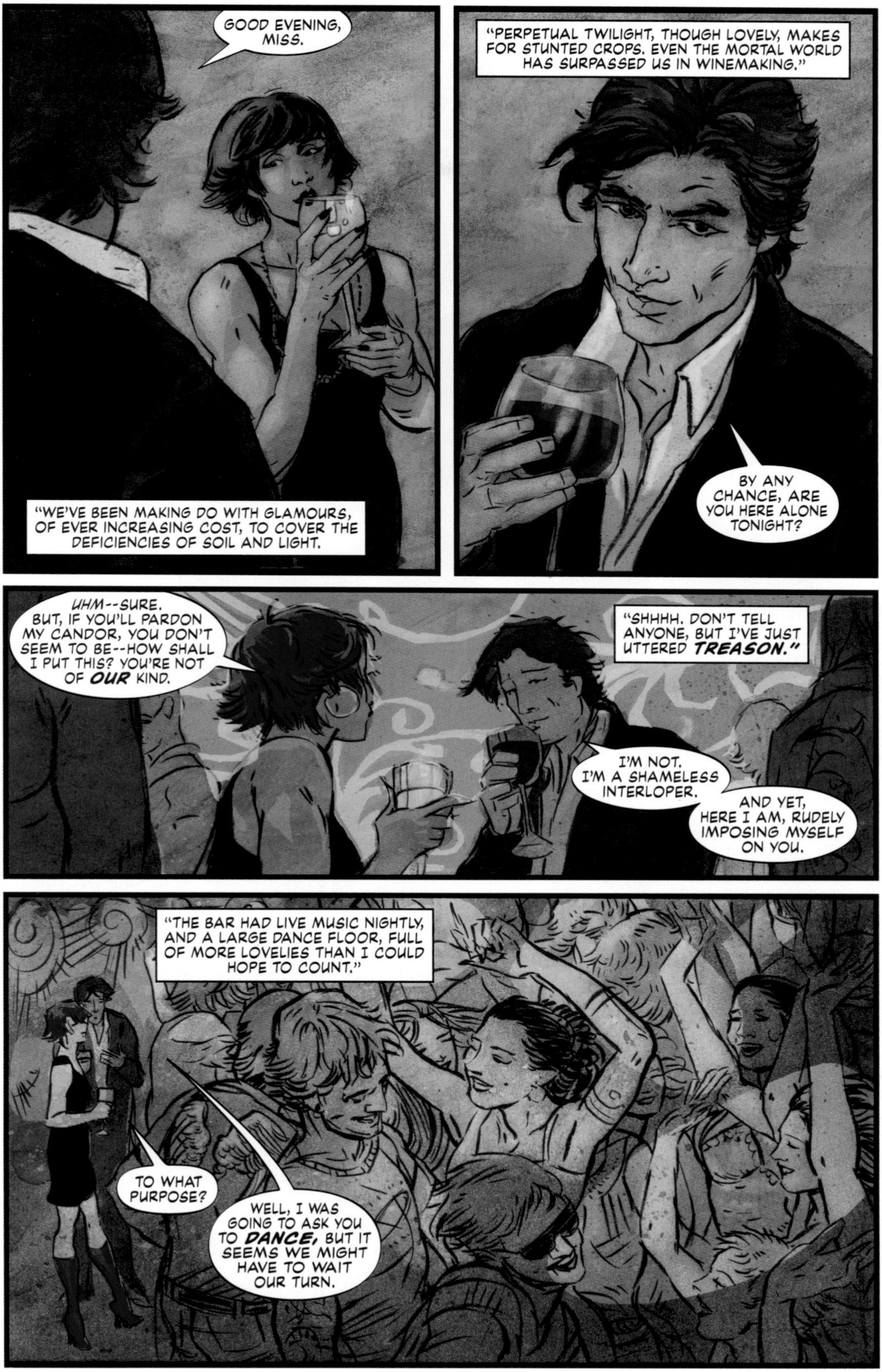
GOOD EVENING, MISS.
"WE'VE BEEN MAKING DO WITH GLAMOURS, OF EVER INCREASING COST, TO COVER THE DEFICIENCIES OF SOIL AND LIGHT.
"PERPETUAL TWILIGHT, THOUGH LOVELY, MAKES FOR STUNTED CROPS. EVEN THE MORTAL WORLD HAS SURPASSED US IN WINEMAKING."
BY ANY CHANCE, ARE YOU HERE ALONE TONIGHT?
UHM--SURE. BUT, IF YOU'LL PARDON MY CANDOR, YOU DON'T SEEM TO BE--HOW SHALL I PUT THIS? YOU'RE NOT OF OUR KIND.
"SHHHH. DON'T TELL ANYONE, BUT I'VE JUST UTTERED TREASON."
I'M NOT. I'M A SHAMELESS INTERLOPER.
AND YET, HERE I AM, RUDELY IMPOSING MYSELF ON YOU.
"THE BAR HAD LIVE MUSIC NIGHTLY, AND A LARGE DANCE FLOOR, FULL OF MORE LOVELIES THAN I COULD HOPE TO COUNT."
TO WHAT PURPOSE?
WELL, I WAS GOING TO ASK YOU TO DANCE, BUT IT SEEMS WE MIGHT HAVE TO WAIT OUR TURN.

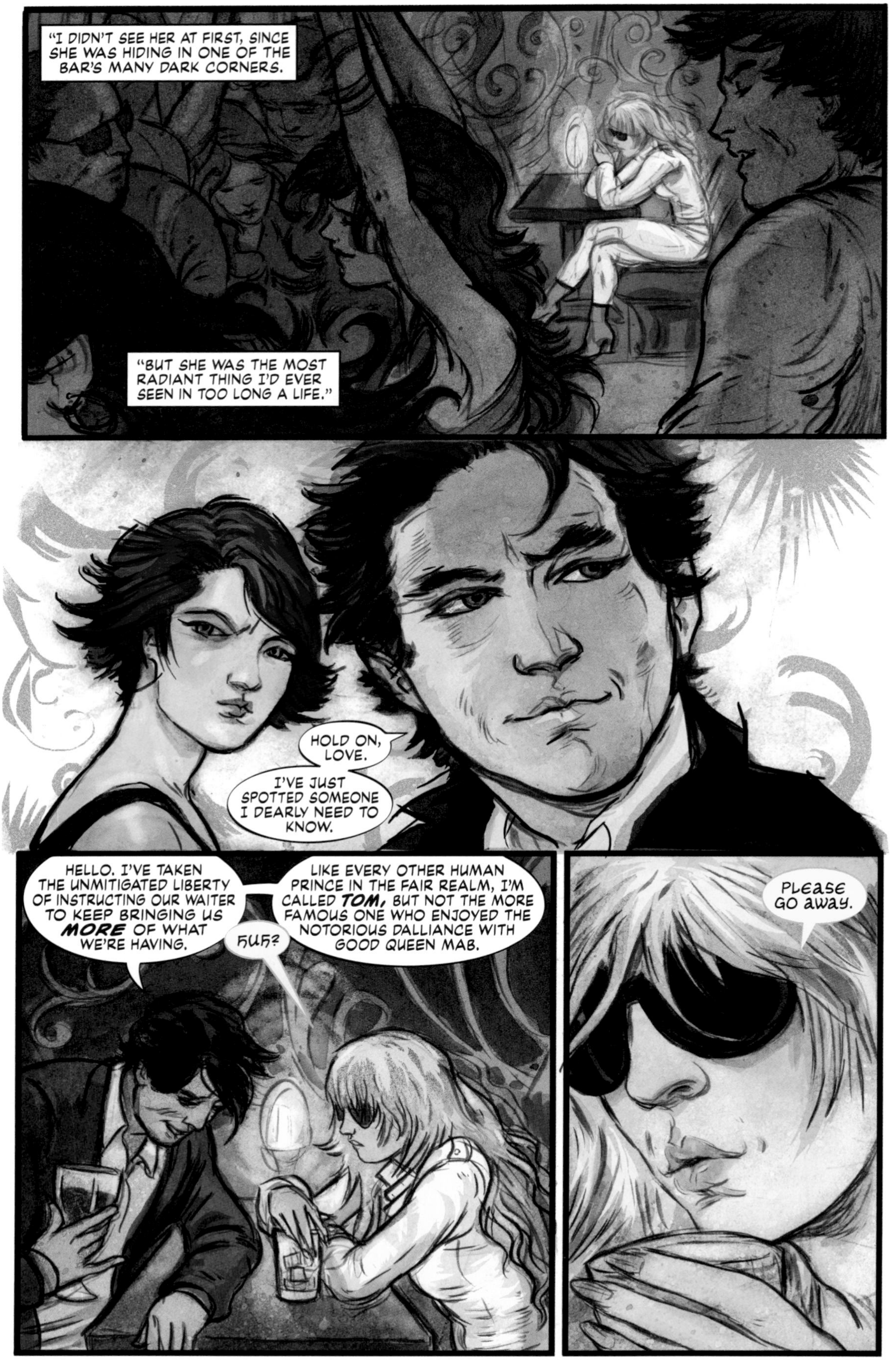
"I DIDN'T SEE HER AT FIRST, SINCE SHE WAS HIDING IN ONE OF THE BAR'S MANY DARK CORNERS.
"BUT SHE WAS THE MOST RADIANT THING I'D EVER SEEN IN TOO LONG A LIFE."
HOLD ON, LOVE.
I'VE JUST SPOTTED SOMEONE I DEARLY NEED TO KNOW.
HELLO. I'VE TAKEN THE UNMITIGATED LIBERTY OF INSTRUCTING OUR WAITER TO KEEP BRINGING US MORE OF WHAT WE'RE HAVING.
HUH?
LIKE EVERY OTHER HUMAN PRINCE IN THE FAIR REALM, I'M CALLED TOM, BUT NOT THE MORE FAMOUS ONE WHO ENJOYED THE NOTORIOUS DALLIANCE WITH GOOD QUEEN MAB.
PLEASE GO AWAY.

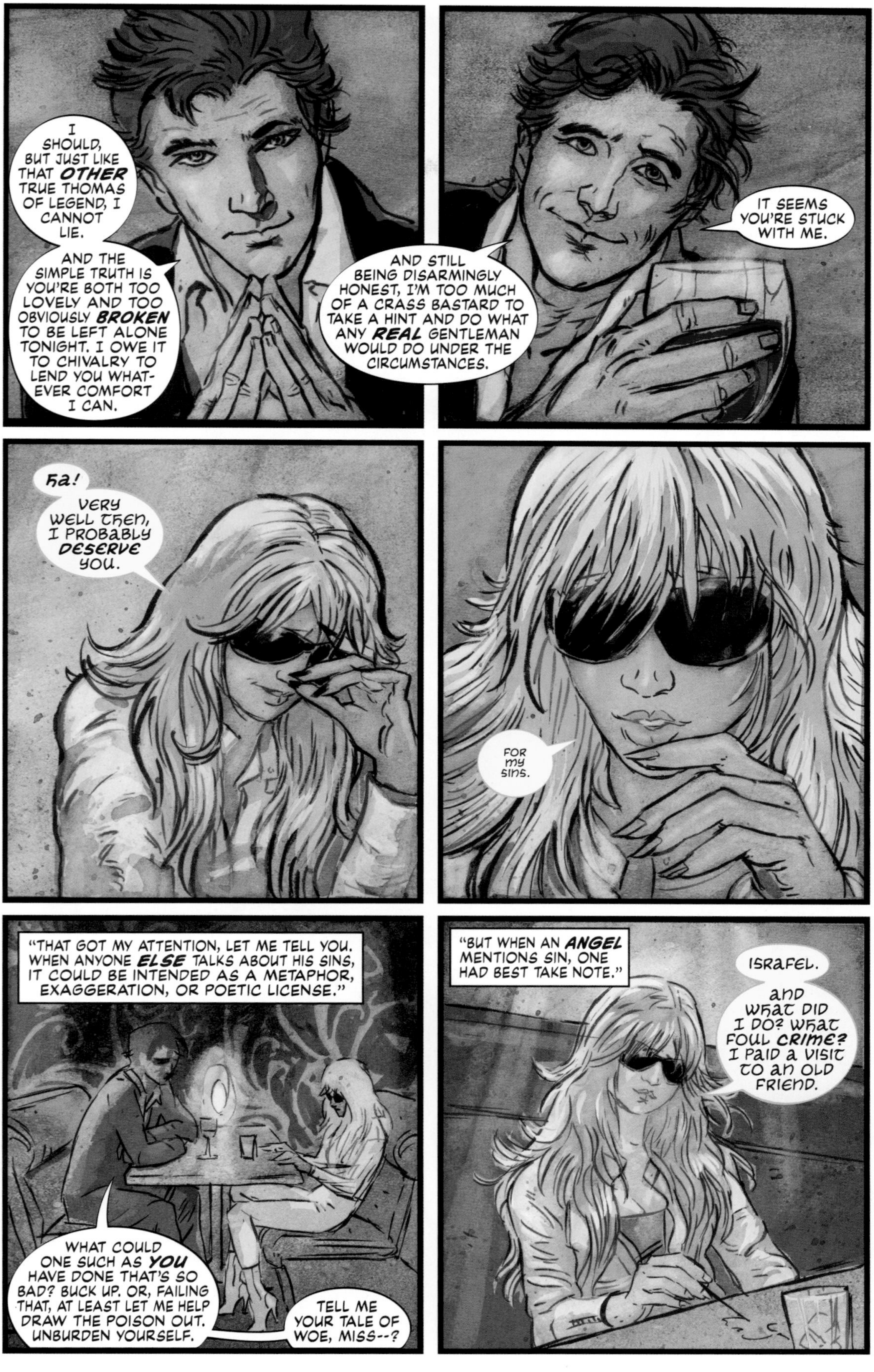
I SHOULD, BUT JUST LIKE THAT OTHER TRUE THOMAS OF LEGEND, I CANNOT LIE.
AND THE SIMPLE TRUTH IS YOU'RE BOTH TOO LOVELY AND TOO OBVIOUSLY BROKEN TO BE LEFT ALONE TONIGHT. I OWE IT TO CHIVALRY TO LEND YOU WHAT-EVER COMFORT I CAN.
AND STILL BEING DISARMINGLY HONEST, I'M TOO MUCH OF A CRASS BASTARD TO TAKE A HINT AND DO WHAT ANY REAL GENTLEMAN WOULD DO UNDER THE CIRCUMSTANCES.
IT SEEMS YOU'RE STUCK WITH ME.
HA!
VERY WELL THEN, I PROBABLY DESERVE YOU.
FOR MY SINS.
"THAT GOT MY ATTENTION, LET ME TELL YOU. WHEN ANYONE ELSE TALKS ABOUT HIS SINS, IT COULD BE INTENDED AS A METAPHOR, EXAGGERATION, OR POETIC LICENSE."
WHAT COULD ONE SUCH AS YOU HAVE DONE THAT'S SO BAD? BUCK UP. OR, FAILING THAT, AT LEAST LET ME HELP DRAW THE POISON OUT. UNBURDEN YOURSELF.
TELL ME YOUR TALE OF WOE, MISS--?
"BUT WHEN AN ANGEL MENTIONS SIN, ONE HAD BEST TAKE NOTE."
ISRAFEL.
AND WHAT DID I DO? WHAT FOUL CRIME? I PAID A VISIT TO AN OLD FRIEND.

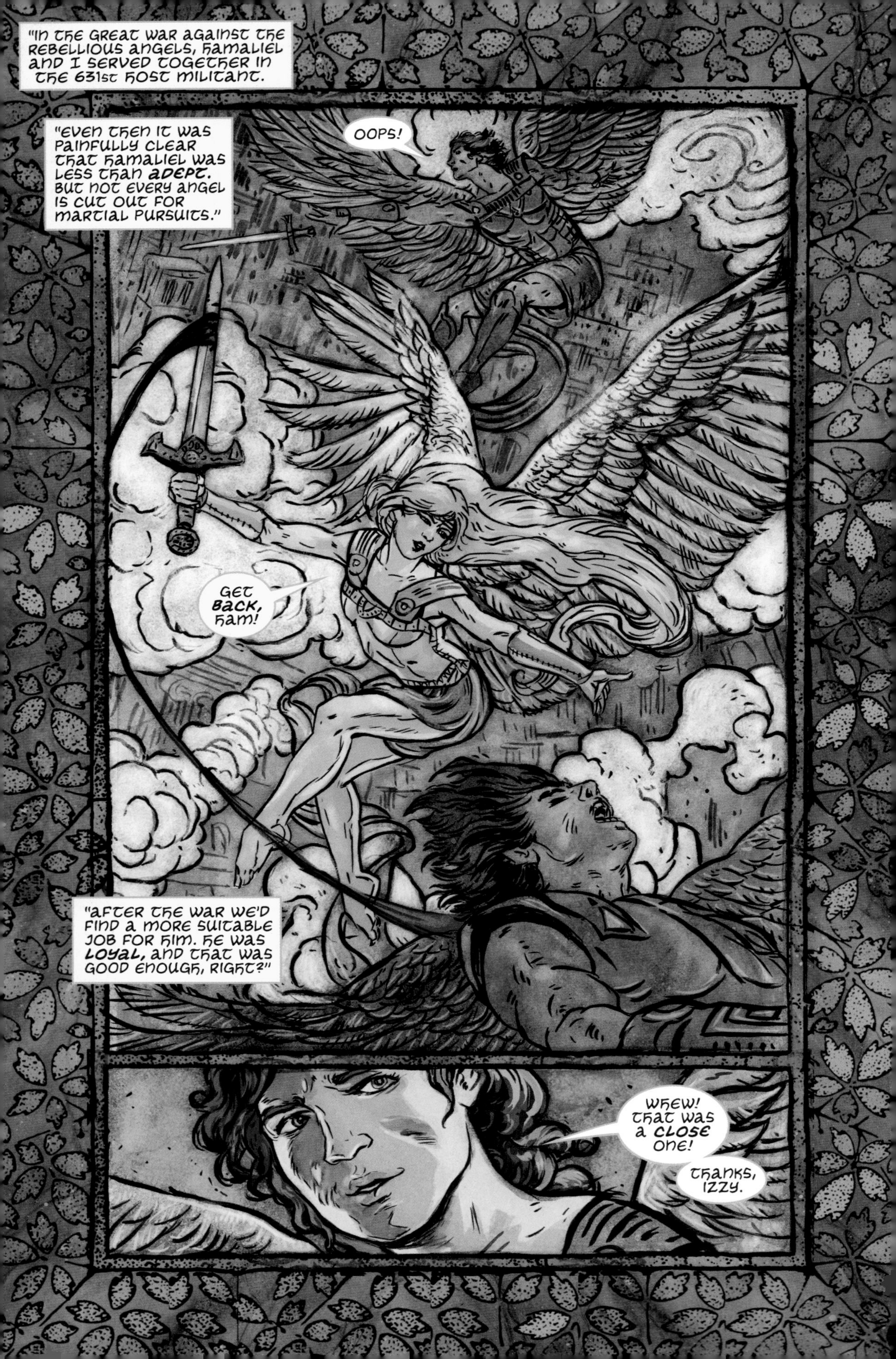
"In the great war against the rebellious angels, Hamaliel and I served together in the 631st Host Militant.
"Even then it was painfully clear that Hamaliel was less than adept. But not every angel is cut out for martial pursuits."
OOPS!
GET BACK, HAM!
"After the war we'd find a more suitable job for him. He was loyal, and that was good enough, right?"
WHEW! THAT WAS A CLOSE ONE!
THANKS, IZZY.

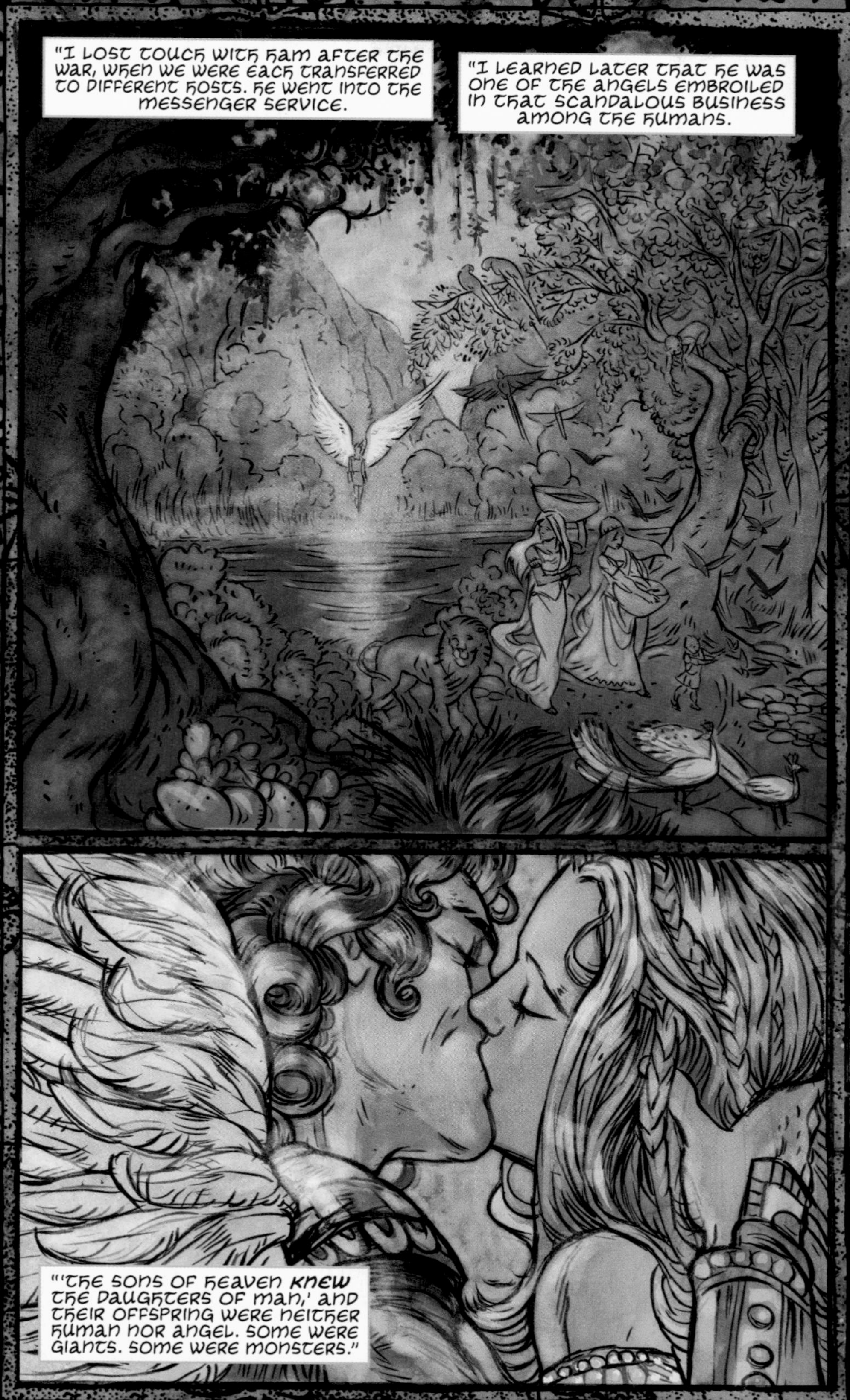
"I LOST TOUCH WITH HAM AFTER THE WAR, WHEN WE WERE EACH TRANSFERRED TO DIFFERENT HOSTS. HE WENT INTO THE MESSENGER SERVICE.
"I LEARNED LATER THAT HE WAS ONE OF THE ANGELS EMBROILED IN THAT SCANDALOUS BUSINESS AMONG THE HUMANS.
"'THE SONS OF HEAVEN **KNEW** THE DAUGHTERS OF MAN,' AND THEIR OFFSPRING WERE NEITHER HUMAN NOR ANGEL. SOME WERE GIANTS. SOME WERE MONSTERS."

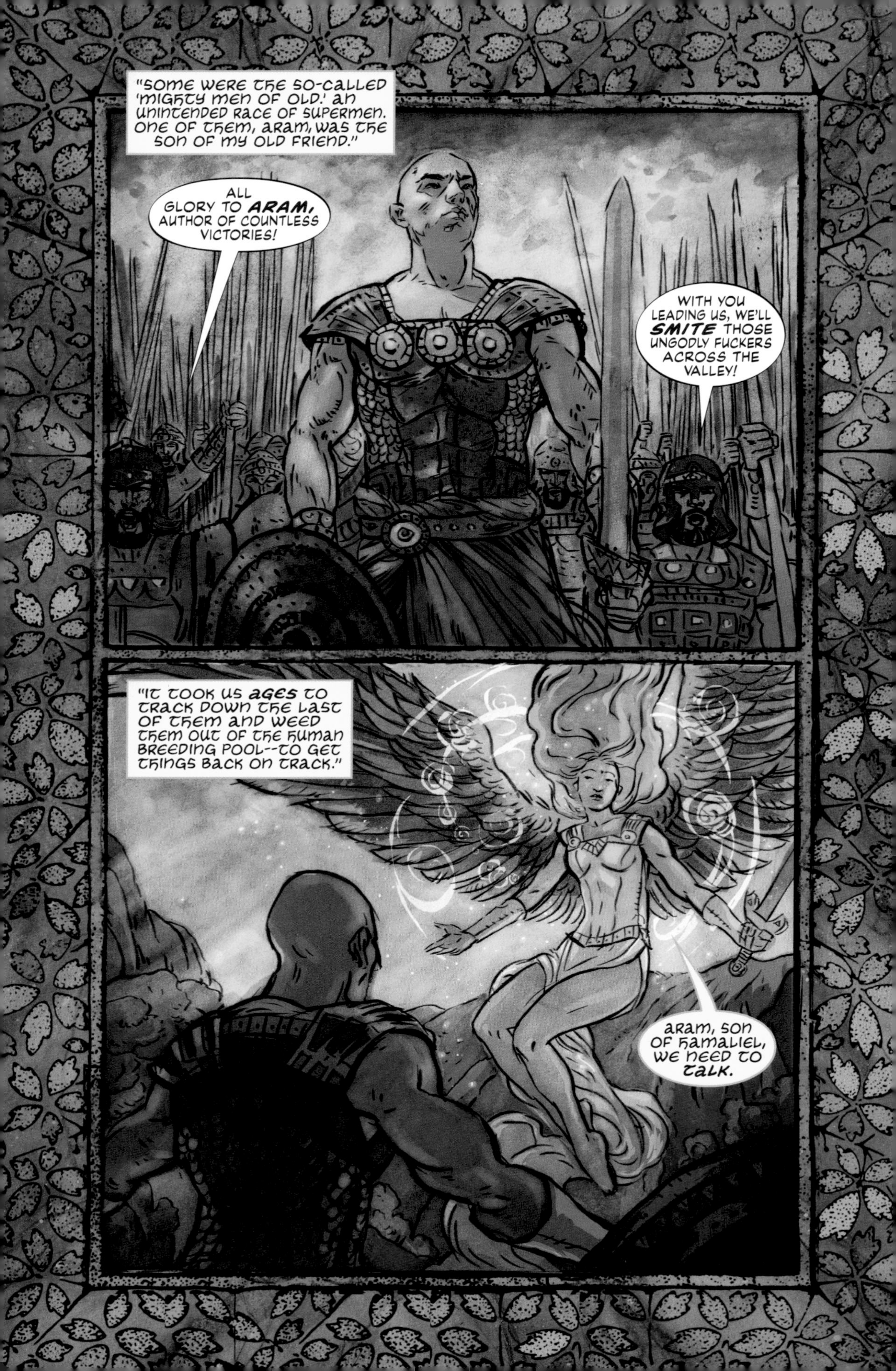
"SOME WERE THE SO-CALLED 'MIGHTY MEN OF OLD,' AN UNINTENDED RACE OF SUPERMEN. ONE OF THEM, ARAM, WAS THE SON OF MY OLD FRIEND."
ALL GLORY TO **ARAM,** AUTHOR OF COUNTLESS VICTORIES!
WITH YOU LEADING US, WE'LL **SMITE** THOSE UNGODLY FUCKERS ACROSS THE VALLEY!
"IT TOOK US **AGES** TO TRACK DOWN THE LAST OF THEM AND WEED THEM OUT OF THE HUMAN BREEDING POOL--TO GET THINGS BACK ON TRACK."
ARAM, SON OF HAMALIEL, WE NEED TO **TALK.**

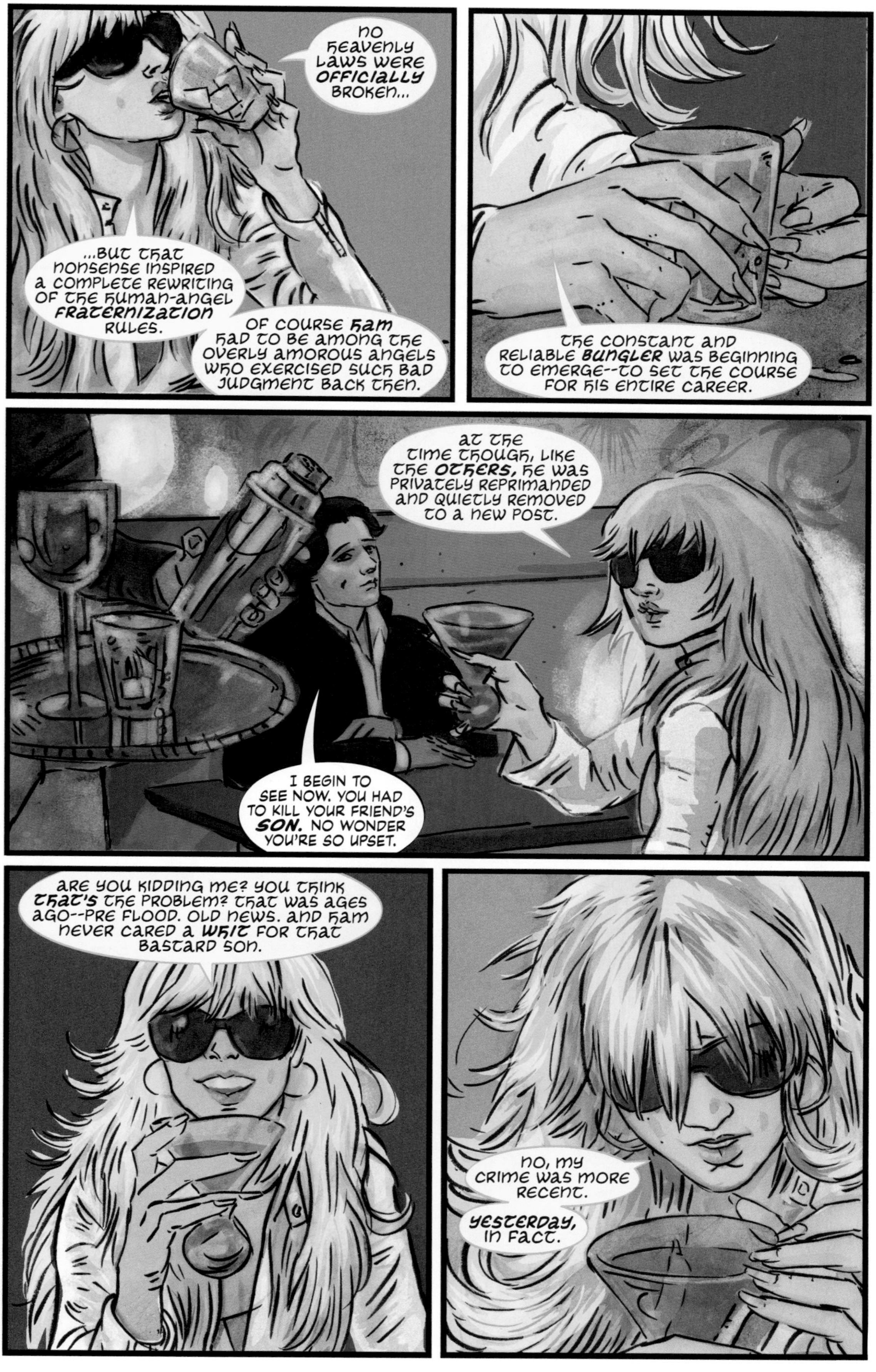
No heavenly laws were officially broken...
...but that nonsense inspired a complete rewriting of the human-angel fraternization rules.
Of course Ham had to be among the overly amorous angels who exercised such bad judgment back then.
The constant and reliable bungler was beginning to emerge--to set the course for his entire career.
At the time though, like the others, he was privately reprimanded and quietly removed to a new post.
I BEGIN TO SEE NOW. YOU HAD TO KILL YOUR FRIEND'S SON. NO WONDER YOU'RE SO UPSET.
Are you kidding me? You think that's the problem? That was ages ago--pre flood. Old news. And Ham never cared a whit for that bastard son.
No, my crime was more recent.
Yesterday, in fact.

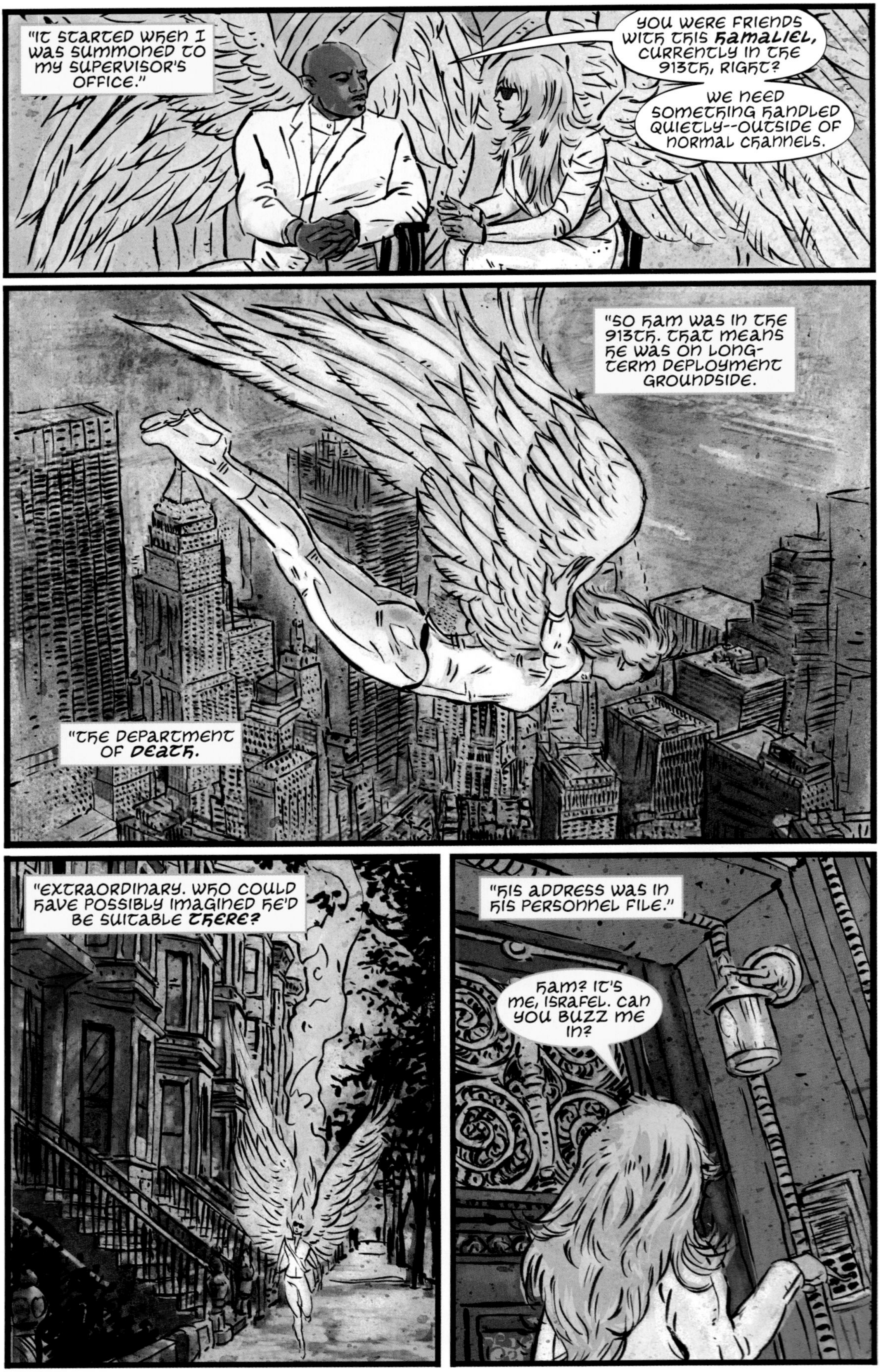
"IT STARTED WHEN I WAS SUMMONED TO MY SUPERVISOR'S OFFICE."
YOU WERE FRIENDS WITH THIS HAMALIEL, CURRENTLY IN THE 913TH, RIGHT?
WE NEED SOMETHING HANDLED QUIETLY--OUTSIDE OF NORMAL CHANNELS.
"SO HAM WAS IN THE 913TH. THAT MEANS HE WAS ON LONG-TERM DEPLOYMENT GROUNDSIDE.
"THE DEPARTMENT OF DEATH.
"EXTRAORDINARY. WHO COULD HAVE POSSIBLY IMAGINED HE'D BE SUITABLE THERE?
"HIS ADDRESS WAS IN HIS PERSONNEL FILE."
HAM? IT'S ME, ISRAFEL. CAN YOU BUZZ ME IN?

IT'S SO *GOOD* TO SEE YOU, IZZY! HOW LONG HAS IT BEEN? WHAT DO THEY HAVE YOU DOING NOW?

AGES. I'M STILL IN WEAPONS DEVELOPMENT, WITH THE 308TH.

YOU WERE ALWAYS THE *STABLE* ONE. OLD RELIABLE.

IT'S IMPORTANT WORK. NO ONE KNOWS WHEN THE OLD MAN'S GOING TO CALL US OUT FOR THE FINAL BATTLE AGAINST THE FALLEN.

WE NEED TO BE *READY*.

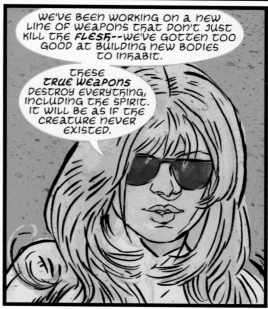

WE'VE BEEN WORKING ON A NEW LINE OF WEAPONS THAT DON'T JUST KILL THE *FLESH*--WE'VE GOTTEN TOO GOOD AT BUILDING NEW BODIES TO INHABIT.

THESE *TRUE WEAPONS* DESTROY EVERYTHING, INCLUDING THE SPIRIT. IT WILL BE AS IF THE CREATURE NEVER EXISTED.

BUT I DIDN'T COME HERE TO TALK *SHOP*. I'M ON A THREE-DAY PASS.

I WANTED TO STOP BY AND CATCH UP BEFORE HEADING OVER TO *PINHEADS* FOR A FULL AND DETAILED *EXPLORATION* OF THE ALLOWED VICES.

TELL ME WHAT YOU'VE BEEN UP TO SINCE WE LAST SAW EACH OTHER.

OH, YOU KNOW. THE *USUAL*. I SCREW UP IN ONE DEPARTMENT AND SO THEY SHIP ME OFF TO ANOTHER.

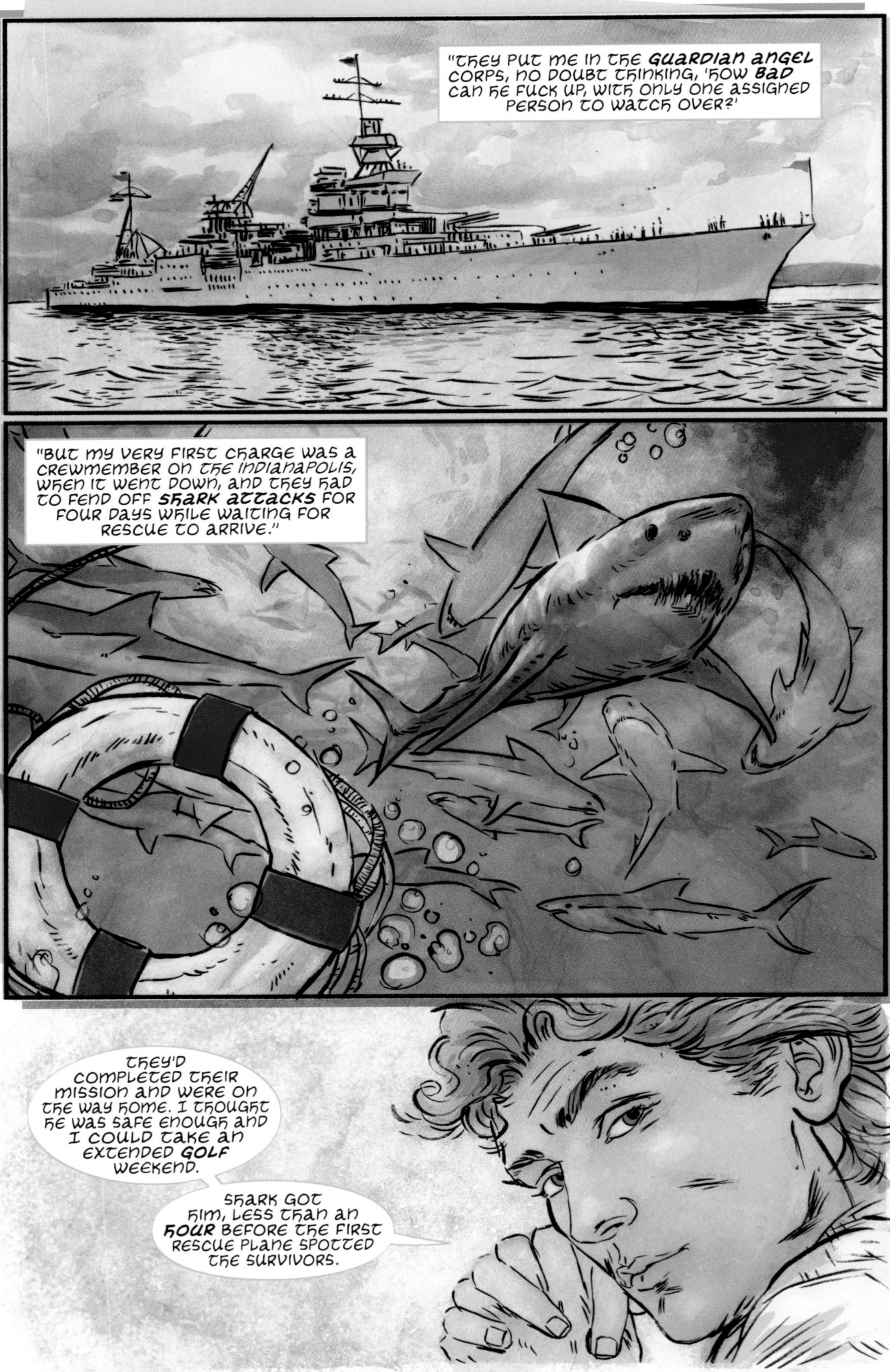
"THEY PUT ME IN THE GUARDIAN ANGEL CORPS, NO DOUBT THINKING, 'HOW BAD CAN HE FUCK UP, WITH ONLY ONE ASSIGNED PERSON TO WATCH OVER?'
"BUT MY VERY FIRST CHARGE WAS A CREWMEMBER ON THE INDIANAPOLIS, WHEN IT WENT DOWN, AND THEY HAD TO FEND OFF SHARK ATTACKS FOR FOUR DAYS WHILE WAITING FOR RESCUE TO ARRIVE."
THEY'D COMPLETED THEIR MISSION AND WERE ON THE WAY HOME. I THOUGHT HE WAS SAFE ENOUGH AND I COULD TAKE AN EXTENDED GOLF WEEKEND.
SHARK GOT HIM, LESS THAN AN HOUR BEFORE THE FIRST RESCUE PLANE SPOTTED THE SURVIVORS.

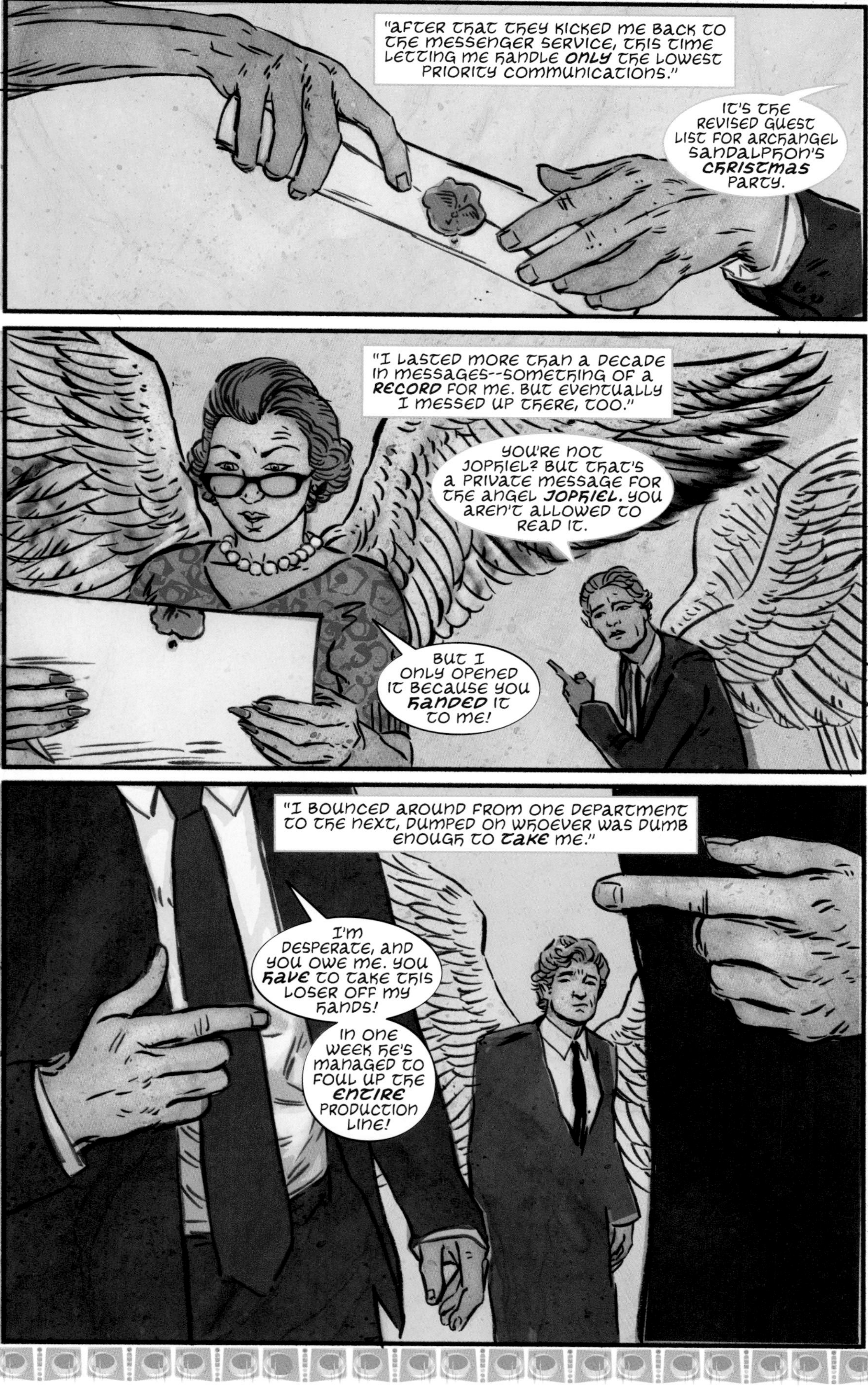
"AFTER THAT THEY KICKED ME BACK TO THE MESSENGER SERVICE, THIS TIME LETTING ME HANDLE ONLY THE LOWEST PRIORITY COMMUNICATIONS."
IT'S THE REVISED GUEST LIST FOR ARCHANGEL SANDALPHON'S CHRISTMAS PARTY.
"I LASTED MORE THAN A DECADE IN MESSAGES--SOMETHING OF A RECORD FOR ME. BUT EVENTUALLY I MESSED UP THERE, TOO."
YOU'RE NOT JOPHIEL? BUT THAT'S A PRIVATE MESSAGE FOR THE ANGEL JOPHIEL. YOU AREN'T ALLOWED TO READ IT.
BUT I ONLY OPENED IT BECAUSE YOU HANDED IT TO ME!
"I BOUNCED AROUND FROM ONE DEPARTMENT TO THE NEXT, DUMPED ON WHOEVER WAS DUMB ENOUGH TO TAKE ME."
I'M DESPERATE, AND YOU OWE ME. YOU HAVE TO TAKE THIS LOSER OFF MY HANDS!
IN ONE WEEK HE'S MANAGED TO FOUL UP THE ENTIRE PRODUCTION LINE!

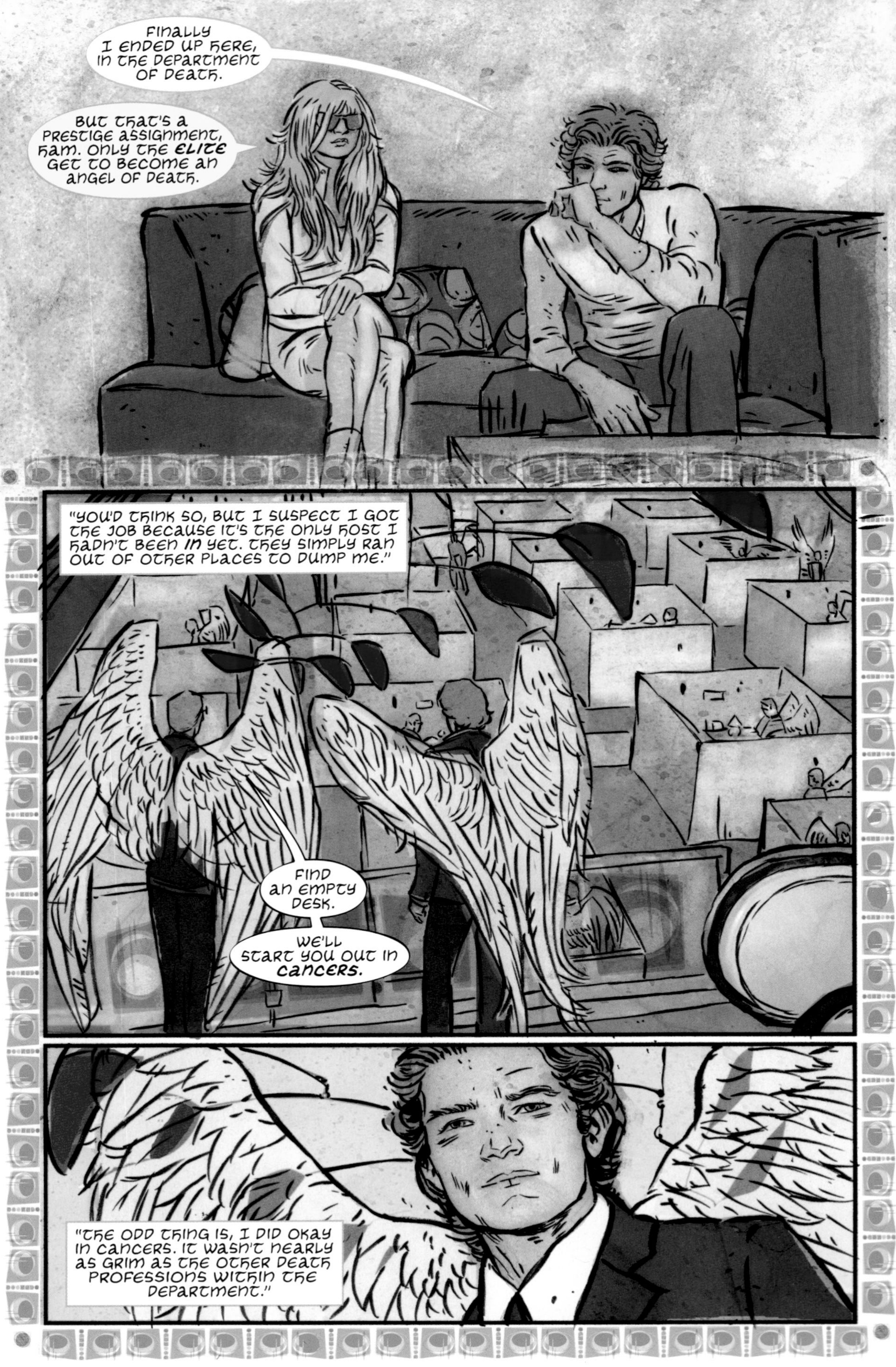
FINALLY I ENDED UP HERE, IN THE DEPARTMENT OF DEATH.
BUT THAT'S A PRESTIGE ASSIGNMENT, HAM. ONLY THE ELITE GET TO BECOME AN ANGEL OF DEATH.
"YOU'D THINK SO, BUT I SUSPECT I GOT THE JOB BECAUSE IT'S THE ONLY HOST I HADN'T BEEN IN YET. THEY SIMPLY RAN OUT OF OTHER PLACES TO DUMP ME."
FIND AN EMPTY DESK.
WE'LL START YOU OUT IN CANCERS.
"THE ODD THING IS, I DID OKAY IN CANCERS. IT WASN'T NEARLY AS GRIM AS THE OTHER DEATH PROFESSIONS WITHIN THE DEPARTMENT."

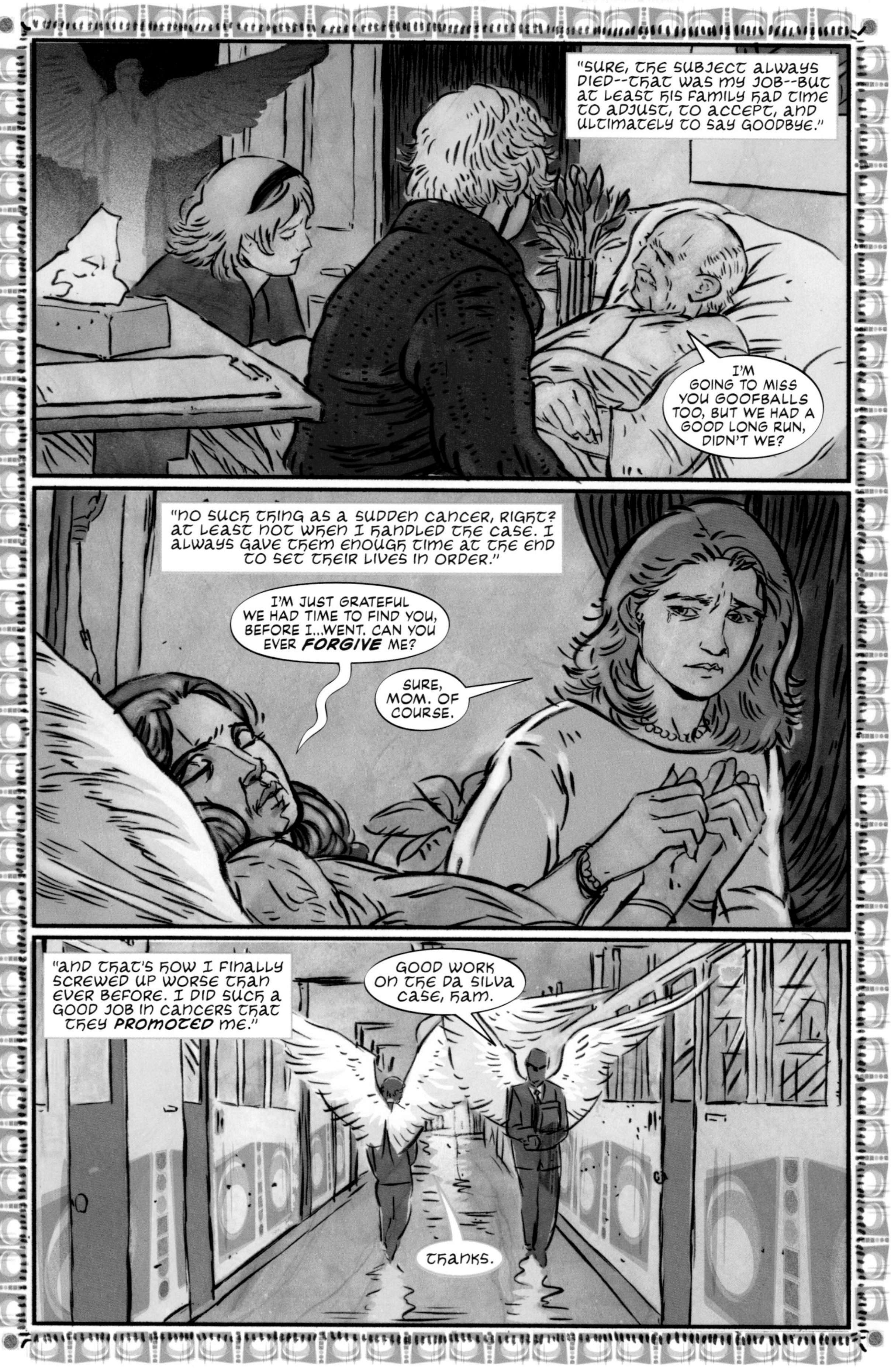
"SURE, THE SUBJECT ALWAYS DIED--THAT WAS MY JOB--BUT AT LEAST HIS FAMILY HAD TIME TO ADJUST, TO ACCEPT, AND ULTIMATELY TO SAY GOODBYE."
I'M GOING TO MISS YOU GOOFBALLS TOO, BUT WE HAD A GOOD LONG RUN, DIDN'T WE?
"NO SUCH THING AS A SUDDEN CANCER, RIGHT? AT LEAST NOT WHEN I HANDLED THE CASE. I ALWAYS GAVE THEM ENOUGH TIME AT THE END TO SET THEIR LIVES IN ORDER."
I'M JUST GRATEFUL WE HAD TIME TO FIND YOU, BEFORE I...WENT. CAN YOU EVER FORGIVE ME?
SURE, MOM. OF COURSE.
"AND THAT'S HOW I FINALLY SCREWED UP WORSE THAN EVER BEFORE. I DID SUCH A GOOD JOB IN CANCERS THAT THEY PROMOTED ME."
GOOD WORK ON THE DA SILVA CASE, HAM.
THANKS.

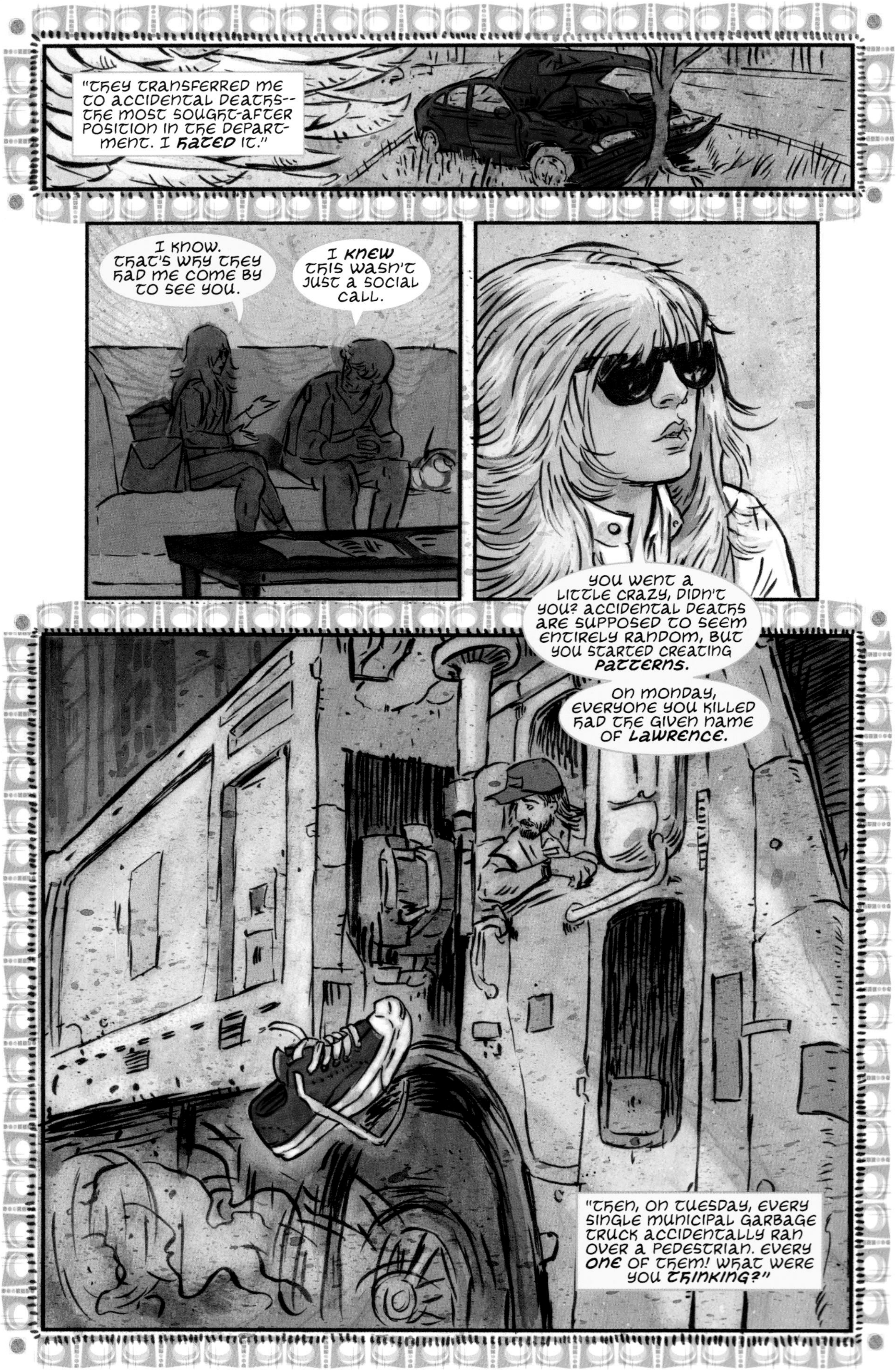
"THEY TRANSFERRED ME TO ACCIDENTAL DEATHS--THE MOST SOUGHT-AFTER POSITION IN THE DEPARTMENT. I HATED IT."
I KNOW. THAT'S WHY THEY HAD ME COME BY TO SEE YOU.
I KNEW THIS WASN'T JUST A SOCIAL CALL.
YOU WENT A LITTLE CRAZY, DIDN'T YOU? ACCIDENTAL DEATHS ARE SUPPOSED TO SEEM ENTIRELY RANDOM, BUT YOU STARTED CREATING PATTERNS.
ON MONDAY, EVERYONE YOU KILLED HAD THE GIVEN NAME OF LAWRENCE.
"THEN, ON TUESDAY, EVERY SINGLE MUNICIPAL GARBAGE TRUCK ACCIDENTALLY RAN OVER A PEDESTRIAN. EVERY ONE OF THEM! WHAT WERE YOU THINKING?"

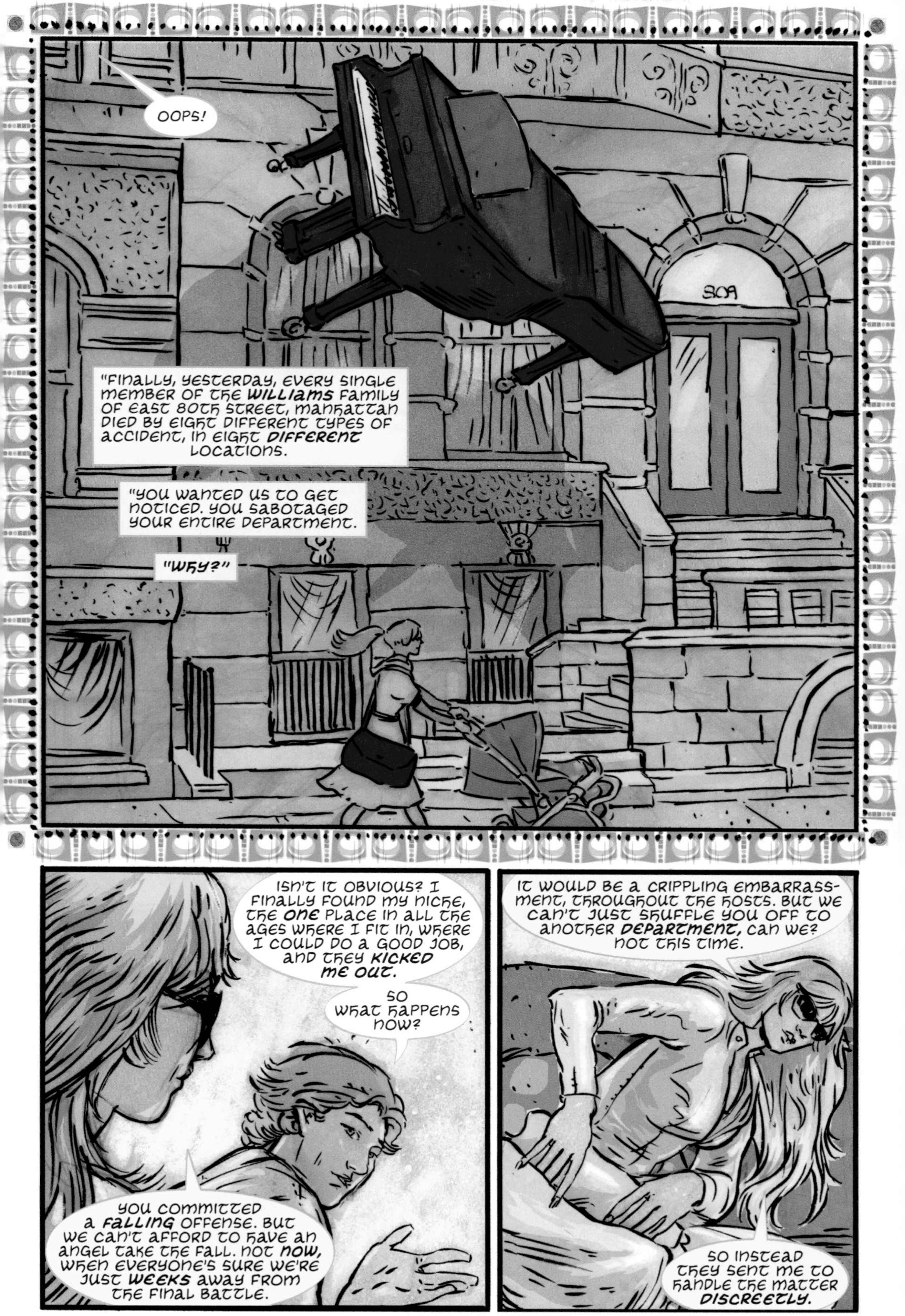
OOPS!
"FINALLY, YESTERDAY, EVERY SINGLE MEMBER OF THE WILLIAMS FAMILY OF EAST 80TH STREET, MANHATTAN DIED BY EIGHT DIFFERENT TYPES OF ACCIDENT, IN EIGHT DIFFERENT LOCATIONS.
"YOU WANTED US TO GET NOTICED. YOU SABOTAGED YOUR ENTIRE DEPARTMENT.
"WHY?"
ISN'T IT OBVIOUS? I FINALLY FOUND MY NICHE, THE ONE PLACE IN ALL THE AGES WHERE I FIT IN, WHERE I COULD DO A GOOD JOB, AND THEY KICKED ME OUT.
SO WHAT HAPPENS NOW?
YOU COMMITTED A FALLING OFFENSE. BUT WE CAN'T AFFORD TO HAVE AN ANGEL TAKE THE FALL. NOT NOW, WHEN EVERYONE'S SURE WE'RE JUST WEEKS AWAY FROM THE FINAL BATTLE.
IT WOULD BE A CRIPPLING EMBARRASSMENT, THROUGHOUT THE HOSTS. BUT WE CAN'T JUST SHUFFLE YOU OFF TO ANOTHER DEPARTMENT, CAN WE? NOT THIS TIME.
SO INSTEAD THEY SENT ME TO HANDLE THE MATTER DISCREETLY.

I MENTIONED THE NEW WEAPONS.

THIS IS *ONE* OF THEM. A PROTOTYPE READY FOR FINAL TESTING.

I SEE.

I GUESS THAT'S FAIR.

WILL YOU TELL EVERYONE I DIDN'T MEAN ANYTHING *PERSONAL?* IT WAS JUST ONE OF MY STANDARD SCREW-UPS. A SILLY TANTRUM.

SORRY, HAM, BUT I CAN'T DO THAT. YOU HAVE TO DISAPPEAR, *WITHOUT* EXPLANATION--A MYSTERY THAT NEVER GETS SOLVED.

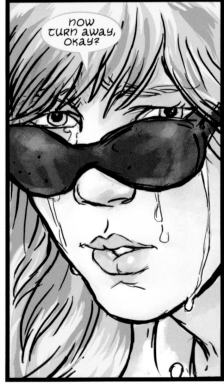

NOW TURN AWAY, OKAY?

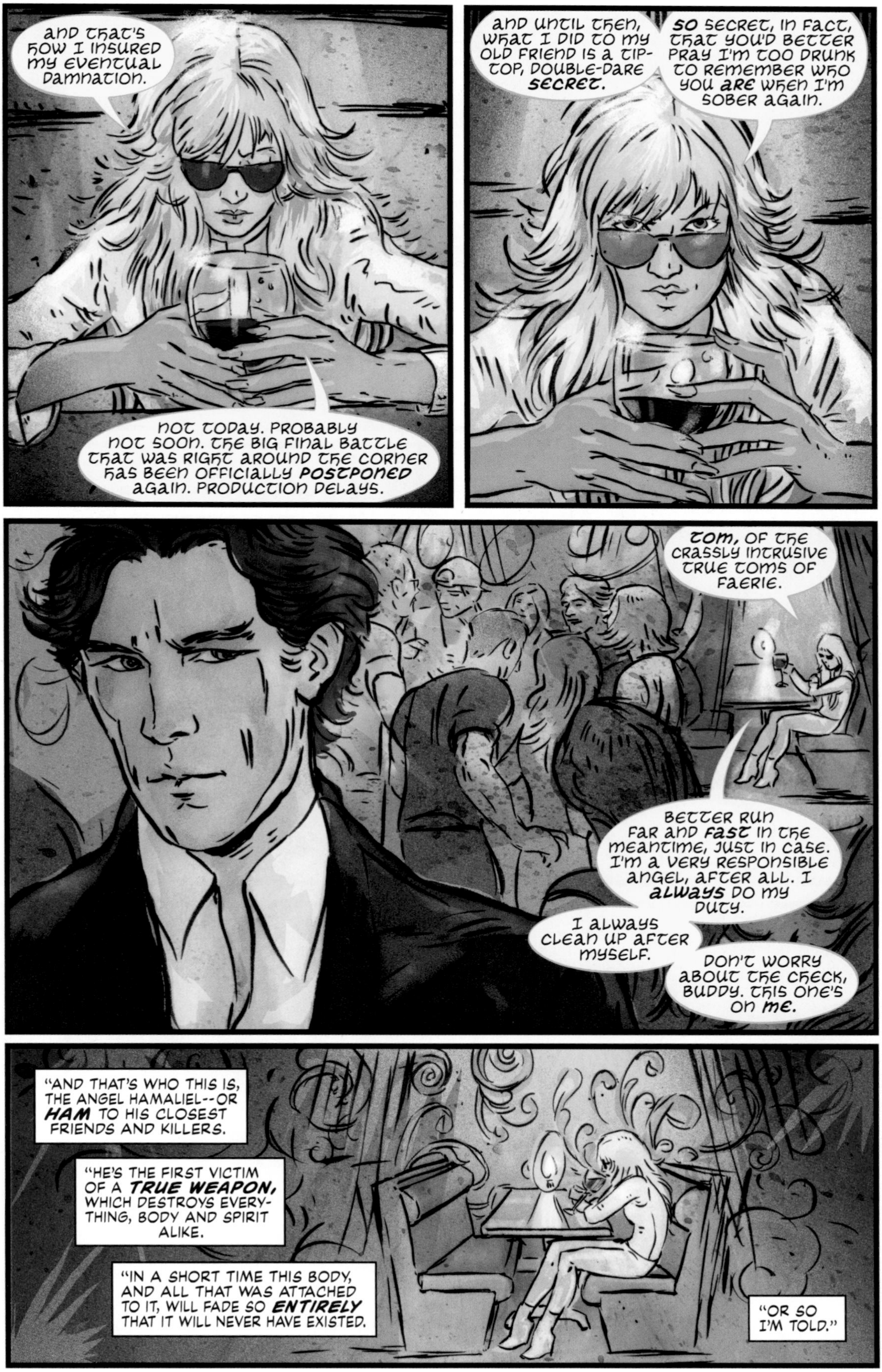
AND THAT'S HOW I INSURED MY EVENTUAL DAMNATION.
NOT TODAY. PROBABLY NOT SOON. THE BIG FINAL BATTLE THAT WAS RIGHT AROUND THE CORNER HAS BEEN OFFICIALLY POSTPONED AGAIN. PRODUCTION DELAYS.
AND UNTIL THEN, WHAT I DID TO MY OLD FRIEND IS A TIP-TOP, DOUBLE-DARE SECRET.
SO SECRET, IN FACT, THAT YOU'D BETTER PRAY I'M TOO DRUNK TO REMEMBER WHO YOU ARE WHEN I'M SOBER AGAIN.
TOM, OF THE CRASSLY INTRUSIVE TRUE TOMS OF FAERIE.
BETTER RUN FAR AND FAST IN THE MEANTIME, JUST IN CASE. I'M A VERY RESPONSIBLE ANGEL, AFTER ALL. I ALWAYS DO MY DUTY.
I ALWAYS CLEAN UP AFTER MYSELF.
DON'T WORRY ABOUT THE CHECK, BUDDY. THIS ONE'S ON ME.
"AND THAT'S WHO THIS IS, THE ANGEL HAMALIEL--OR HAM TO HIS CLOSEST FRIENDS AND KILLERS.
"HE'S THE FIRST VICTIM OF A TRUE WEAPON, WHICH DESTROYS EVERY-THING, BODY AND SPIRIT ALIKE.
"IN A SHORT TIME THIS BODY, AND ALL THAT WAS ATTACHED TO IT, WILL FADE SO ENTIRELY THAT IT WILL NEVER HAVE EXISTED.
"OR SO I'M TOLD."

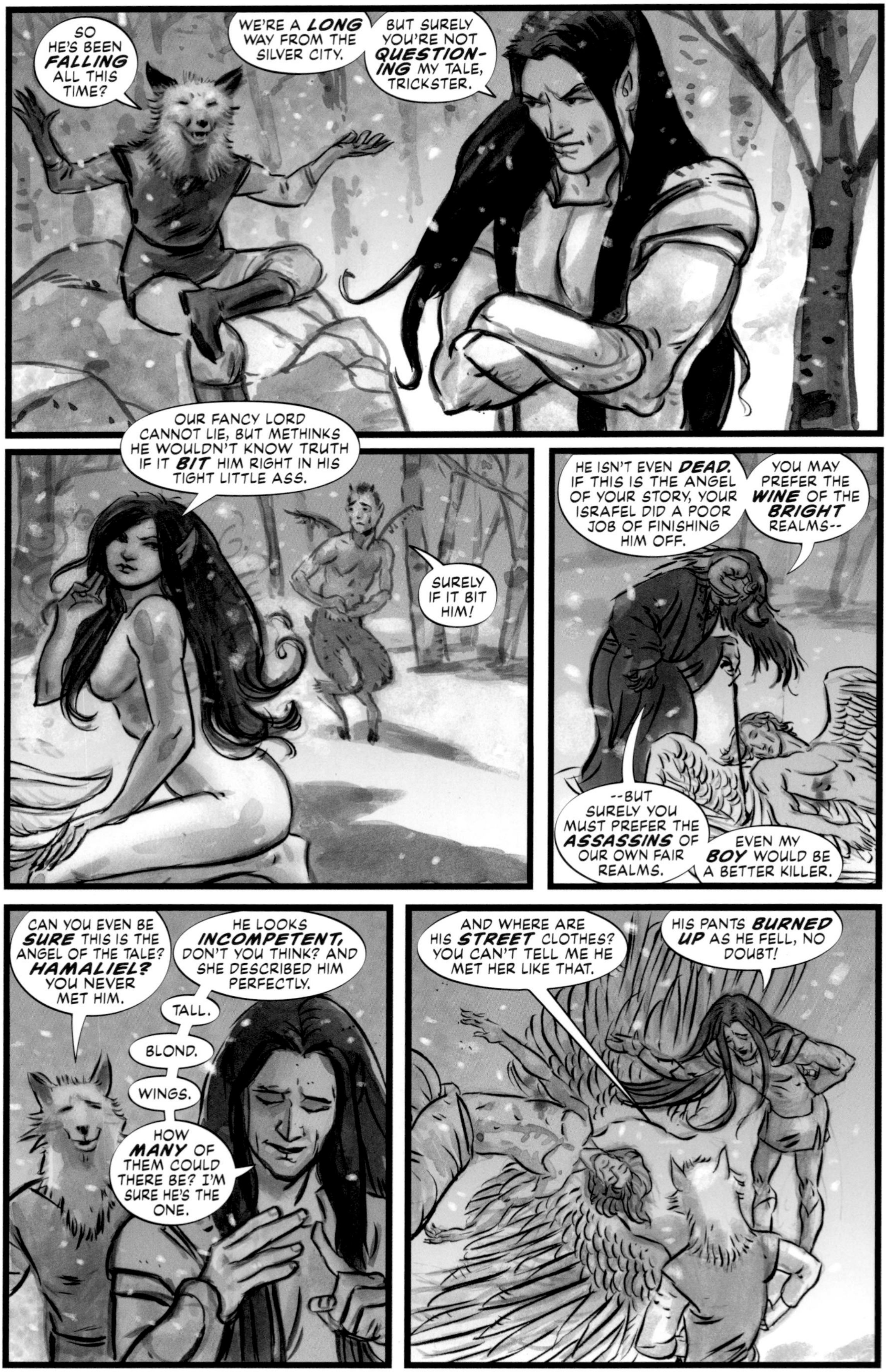
SO HE'S BEEN FALLING ALL THIS TIME?
WE'RE A LONG WAY FROM THE SILVER CITY.
BUT SURELY YOU'RE NOT QUESTION-ING MY TALE, TRICKSTER.
OUR FANCY LORD CANNOT LIE, BUT METHINKS HE WOULDN'T KNOW TRUTH IF IT BIT HIM RIGHT IN HIS TIGHT LITTLE ASS.
SURELY IF IT BIT HIM!
HE ISN'T EVEN DEAD. IF THIS IS THE ANGEL OF YOUR STORY, YOUR ISRAFEL DID A POOR JOB OF FINISHING HIM OFF.
YOU MAY PREFER THE WINE OF THE BRIGHT REALMS--
--BUT SURELY YOU MUST PREFER THE ASSASSINS OF OUR OWN FAIR REALMS.
EVEN MY BOY WOULD BE A BETTER KILLER.
CAN YOU EVEN BE SURE THIS IS THE ANGEL OF THE TALE? HAMALIEL? YOU NEVER MET HIM.
HE LOOKS INCOMPETENT, DON'T YOU THINK? AND SHE DESCRIBED HIM PERFECTLY.
TALL.
BLOND.
WINGS.
HOW MANY OF THEM COULD THERE BE? I'M SURE HE'S THE ONE.
AND WHERE ARE HIS STREET CLOTHES? YOU CAN'T TELL ME HE MET HER LIKE THAT.
HIS PANTS BURNED UP AS HE FELL, NO DOUBT!

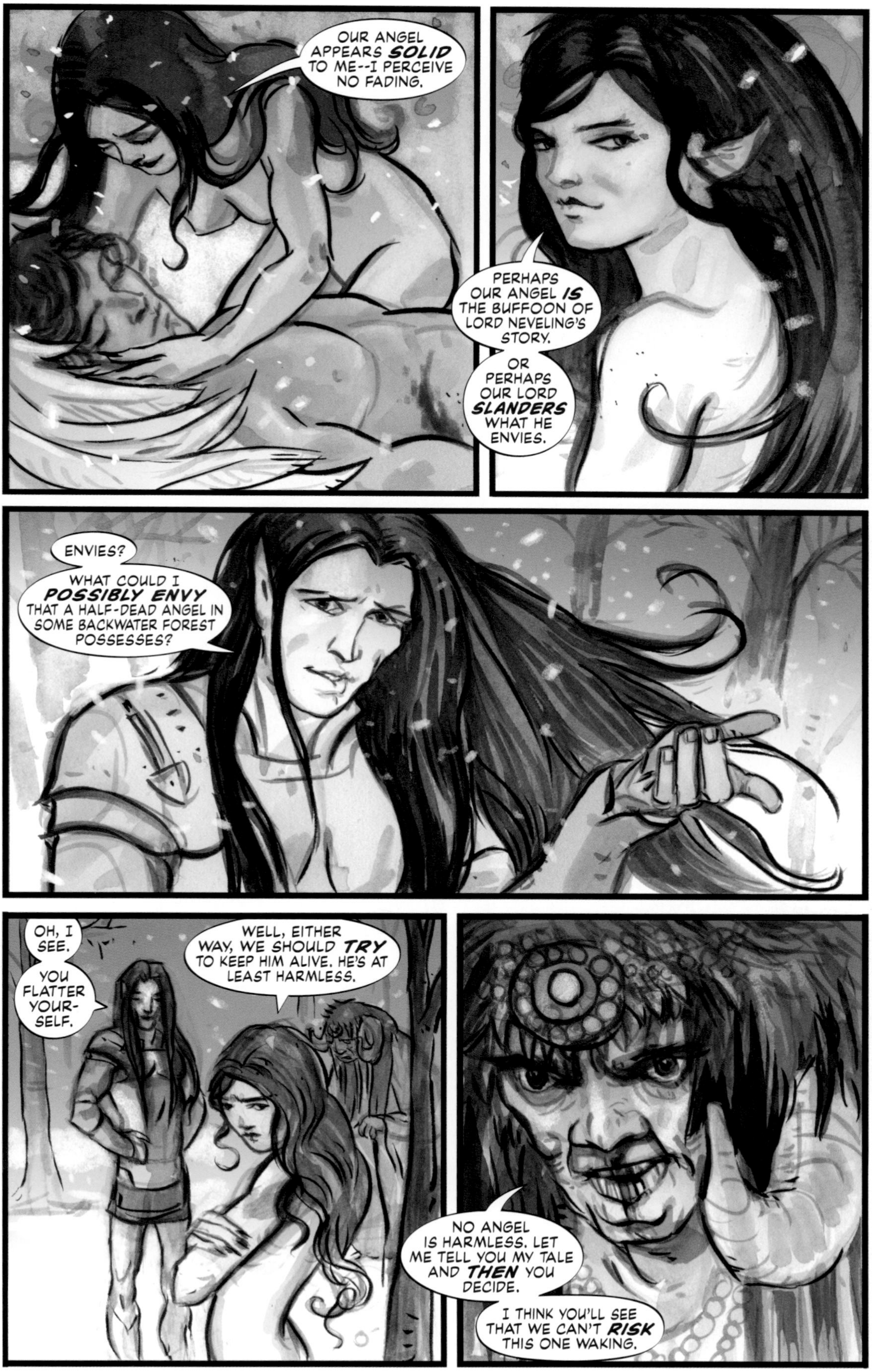
OUR ANGEL APPEARS SOLID TO ME--I PERCEIVE NO FADING.
PERHAPS OUR ANGEL IS THE BUFFOON OF LORD NEVELING'S STORY.
OR PERHAPS OUR LORD SLANDERS WHAT HE ENVIES.
ENVIES?
WHAT COULD I POSSIBLY ENVY THAT A HALF-DEAD ANGEL IN SOME BACKWATER FOREST POSSESSES?
OH, I SEE.
YOU FLATTER YOUR-SELF.
WELL, EITHER WAY, WE SHOULD TRY TO KEEP HIM ALIVE. HE'S AT LEAST HARMLESS.
NO ANGEL IS HARMLESS. LET ME TELL YOU MY TALE AND THEN YOU DECIDE.
I THINK YOU'LL SEE THAT WE CAN'T RISK THIS ONE WAKING.

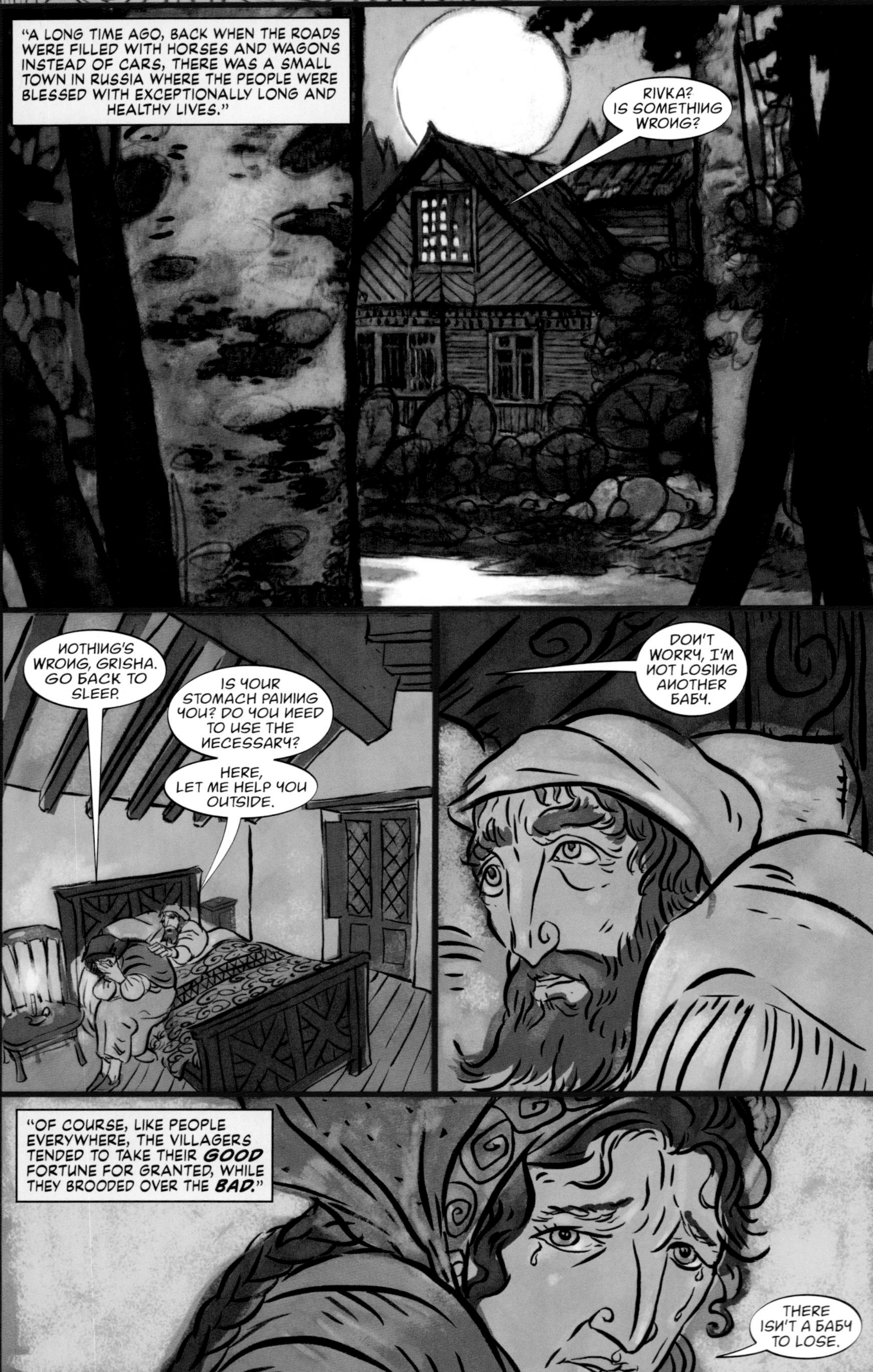
"A LONG TIME AGO, BACK WHEN THE ROADS WERE FILLED WITH HORSES AND WAGONS INSTEAD OF CARS, THERE WAS A SMALL TOWN IN RUSSIA WHERE THE PEOPLE WERE BLESSED WITH EXCEPTIONALLY LONG AND HEALTHY LIVES."
RIVKA? IS SOMETHING WRONG?
NOTHING'S WRONG, GRISHA. GO BACK TO SLEEP.
IS YOUR STOMACH PAINING YOU? DO YOU NEED TO USE THE NECESSARY?
HERE, LET ME HELP YOU OUTSIDE.
DON'T WORRY, I'M NOT LOSING ANOTHER BABY.
"OF COURSE, LIKE PEOPLE EVERYWHERE, THE VILLAGERS TENDED TO TAKE THEIR ***GOOD*** FORTUNE FOR GRANTED, WHILE THEY BROODED OVER THE ***BAD***."
THERE ISN'T A BABY TO LOSE.

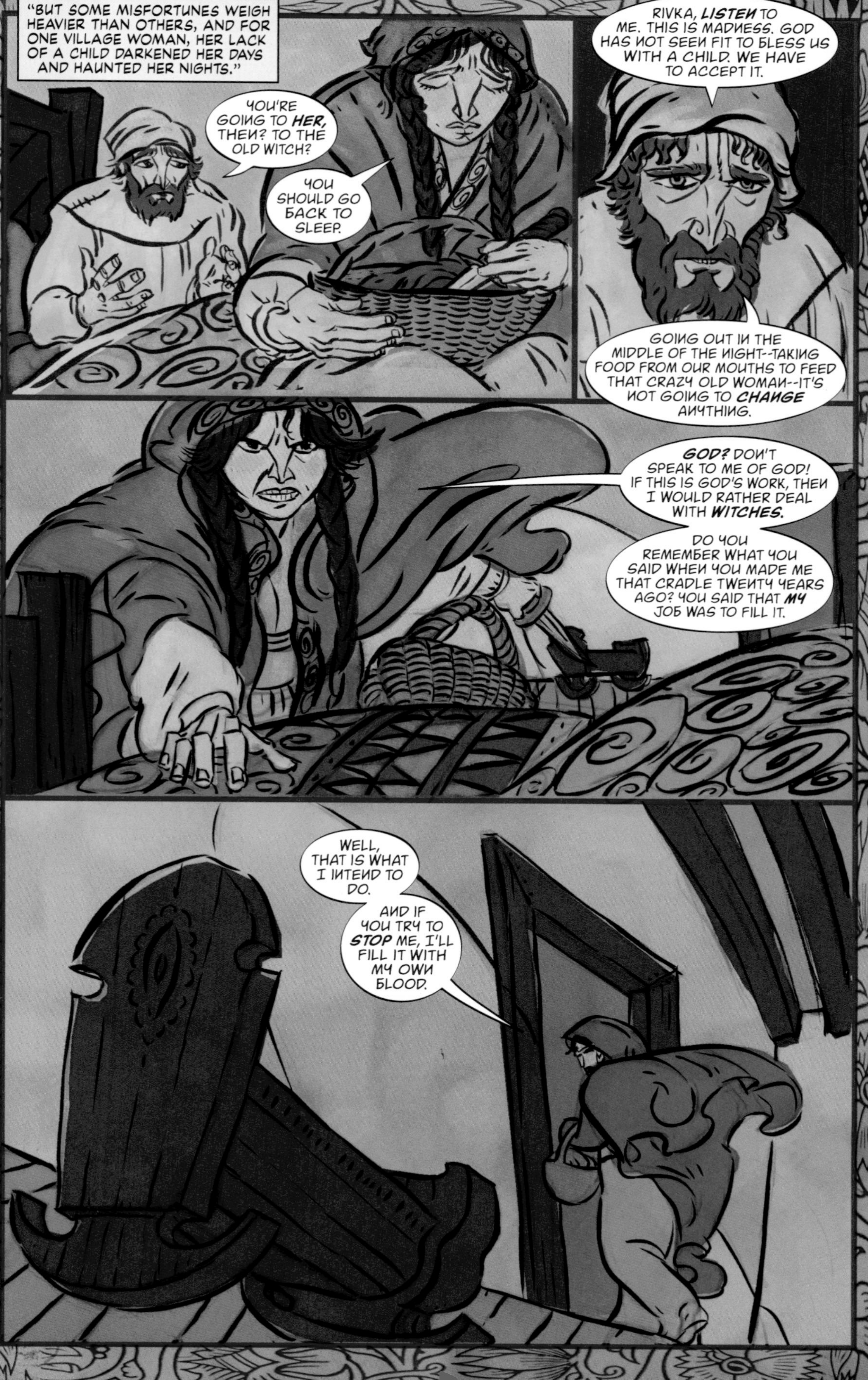
"BUT SOME MISFORTUNES WEIGH HEAVIER THAN OTHERS, AND FOR ONE VILLAGE WOMAN, HER LACK OF A CHILD DARKENED HER DAYS AND HAUNTED HER NIGHTS."
YOU'RE GOING TO *HER,* THEN? TO THE OLD WITCH?
YOU SHOULD GO BACK TO SLEEP.
RIVKA, *LISTEN* TO ME. THIS IS MADNESS. GOD HAS NOT SEEN FIT TO BLESS US WITH A CHILD. WE HAVE TO ACCEPT IT.
GOING OUT IN THE MIDDLE OF THE NIGHT--TAKING FOOD FROM OUR MOUTHS TO FEED THAT CRAZY OLD WOMAN--IT'S NOT GOING TO *CHANGE* ANYTHING.
GOD? DON'T SPEAK TO ME OF GOD! IF THIS IS GOD'S WORK, THEN I WOULD RATHER DEAL WITH *WITCHES.*
DO YOU REMEMBER WHAT YOU SAID WHEN YOU MADE ME THAT CRADLE TWENTY YEARS AGO? YOU SAID THAT *MY* JOB WAS TO FILL IT.
WELL, THAT IS WHAT I INTEND TO DO.
AND IF YOU TRY TO *STOP* ME, I'LL FILL IT WITH MY OWN BLOOD.

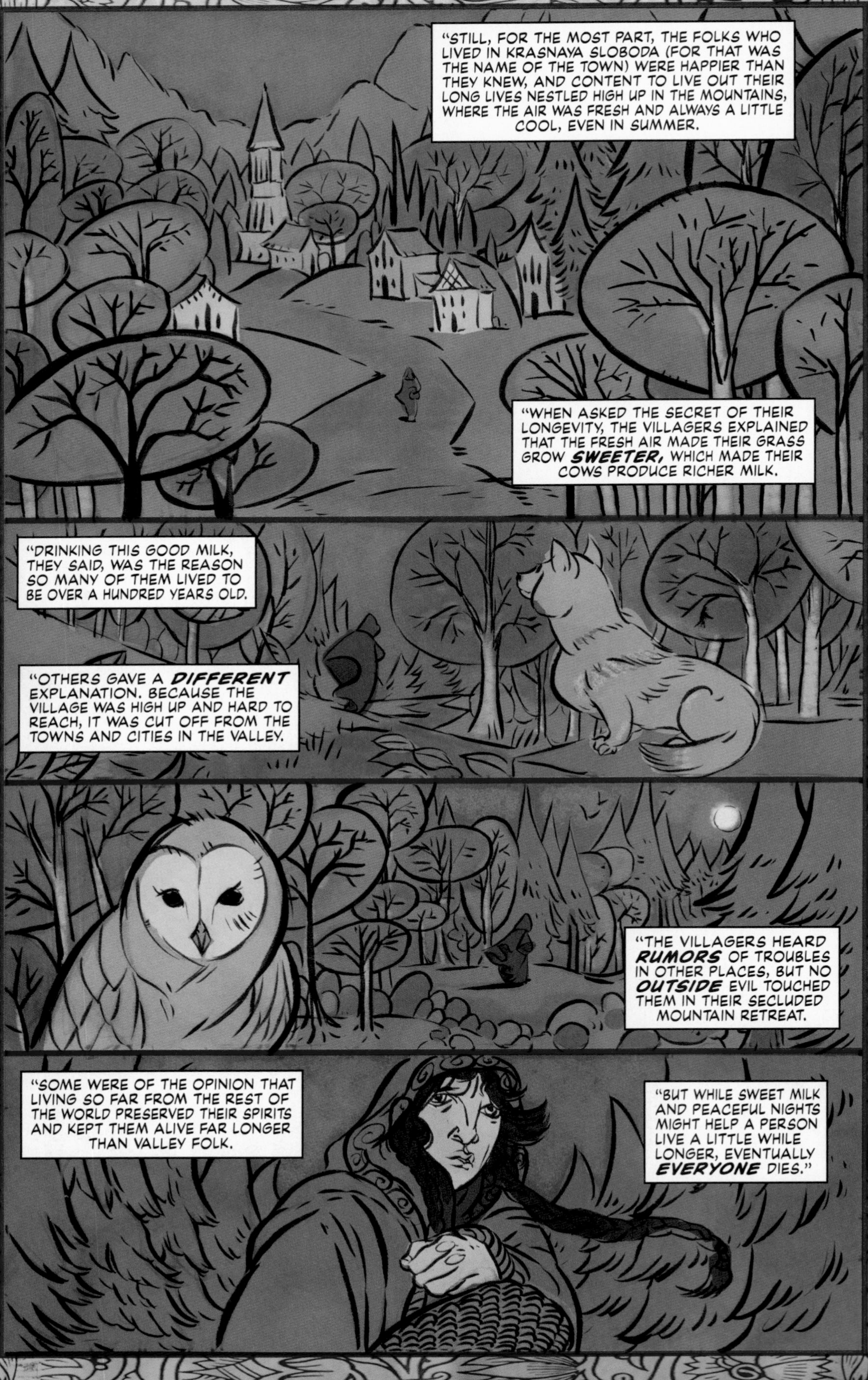
"STILL, FOR THE MOST PART, THE FOLKS WHO LIVED IN KRASNAYA SLOBODA (FOR THAT WAS THE NAME OF THE TOWN) WERE HAPPIER THAN THEY KNEW, AND CONTENT TO LIVE OUT THEIR LONG LIVES NESTLED HIGH UP IN THE MOUNTAINS, WHERE THE AIR WAS FRESH AND ALWAYS A LITTLE COOL, EVEN IN SUMMER.
"WHEN ASKED THE SECRET OF THEIR LONGEVITY, THE VILLAGERS EXPLAINED THAT THE FRESH AIR MADE THEIR GRASS GROW **SWEETER,** WHICH MADE THEIR COWS PRODUCE RICHER MILK.
"DRINKING THIS GOOD MILK, THEY SAID, WAS THE REASON SO MANY OF THEM LIVED TO BE OVER A HUNDRED YEARS OLD.
"OTHERS GAVE A **DIFFERENT** EXPLANATION. BECAUSE THE VILLAGE WAS HIGH UP AND HARD TO REACH, IT WAS CUT OFF FROM THE TOWNS AND CITIES IN THE VALLEY.
"THE VILLAGERS HEARD **RUMORS** OF TROUBLES IN OTHER PLACES, BUT NO **OUTSIDE** EVIL TOUCHED THEM IN THEIR SECLUDED MOUNTAIN RETREAT.
"SOME WERE OF THE OPINION THAT LIVING SO FAR FROM THE REST OF THE WORLD PRESERVED THEIR SPIRITS AND KEPT THEM ALIVE FAR LONGER THAN VALLEY FOLK.
"BUT WHILE SWEET MILK AND PEACEFUL NIGHTS MIGHT HELP A PERSON LIVE A LITTLE WHILE LONGER, EVENTUALLY **EVERYONE** DIES."

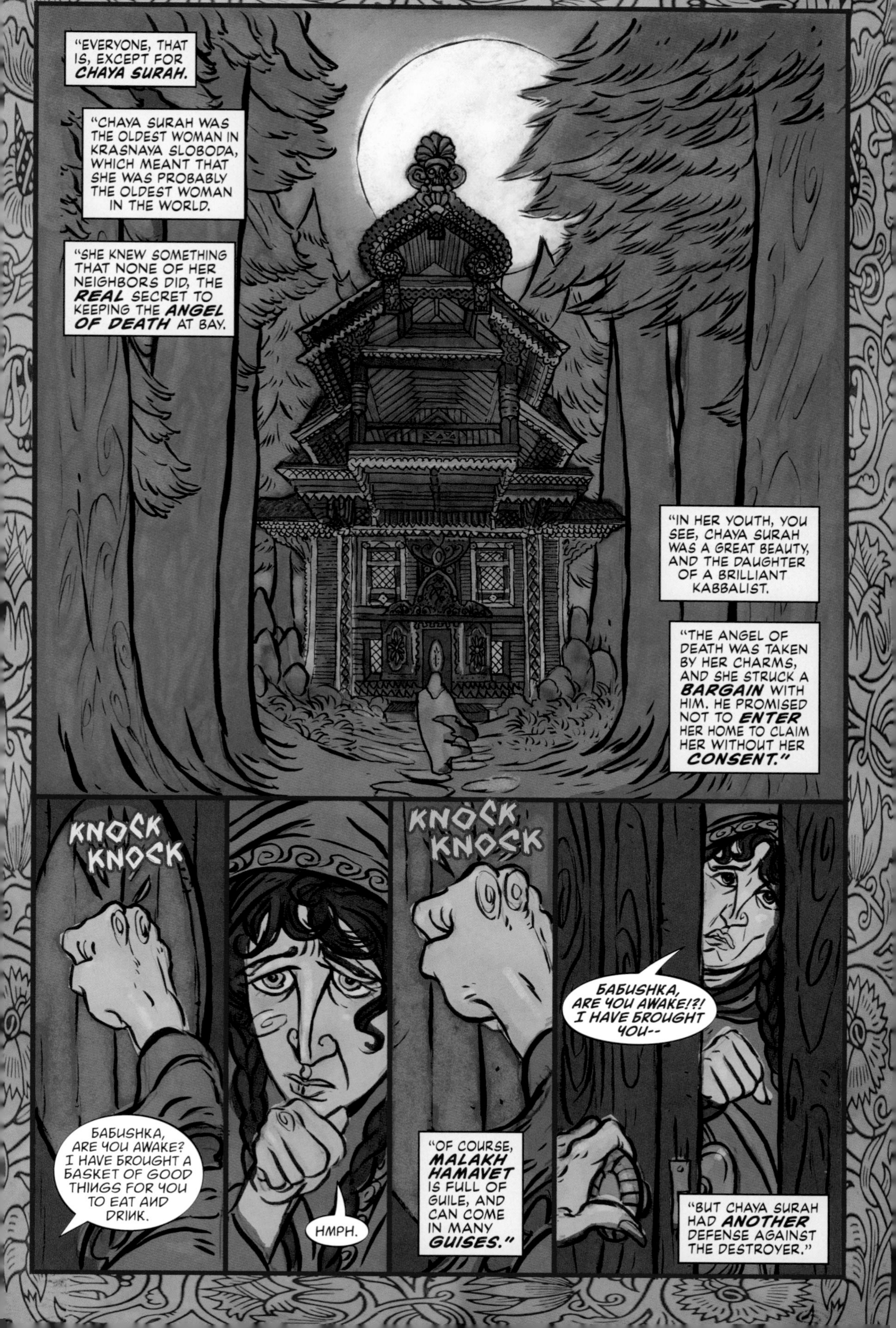
"EVERYONE, THAT IS, EXCEPT FOR CHAYA SURAH.
"CHAYA SURAH WAS THE OLDEST WOMAN IN KRASNAYA SLOBODA, WHICH MEANT THAT SHE WAS PROBABLY THE OLDEST WOMAN IN THE WORLD.
"SHE KNEW SOMETHING THAT NONE OF HER NEIGHBORS DID, THE REAL SECRET TO KEEPING THE ANGEL OF DEATH AT BAY.
"IN HER YOUTH, YOU SEE, CHAYA SURAH WAS A GREAT BEAUTY, AND THE DAUGHTER OF A BRILLIANT KABBALIST.
"THE ANGEL OF DEATH WAS TAKEN BY HER CHARMS, AND SHE STRUCK A BARGAIN WITH HIM. HE PROMISED NOT TO ENTER HER HOME TO CLAIM HER WITHOUT HER CONSENT."
KNOCK KNOCK
БАБUSHKA, ARE YOU AWAKE? I HAVE BROUGHT A BASKET OF GOOD THINGS FOR YOU TO EAT AND DRINK.
HMPH.
KNOCK KNOCK
"OF COURSE, MALAKH HAMAVET IS FULL OF GUILE, AND CAN COME IN MANY GUISES."
БАБUSHKA, ARE YOU AWAKE!?! I HAVE BROUGHT YOU--
"BUT CHAYA SURAH HAD ANOTHER DEFENSE AGAINST THE DESTROYER."

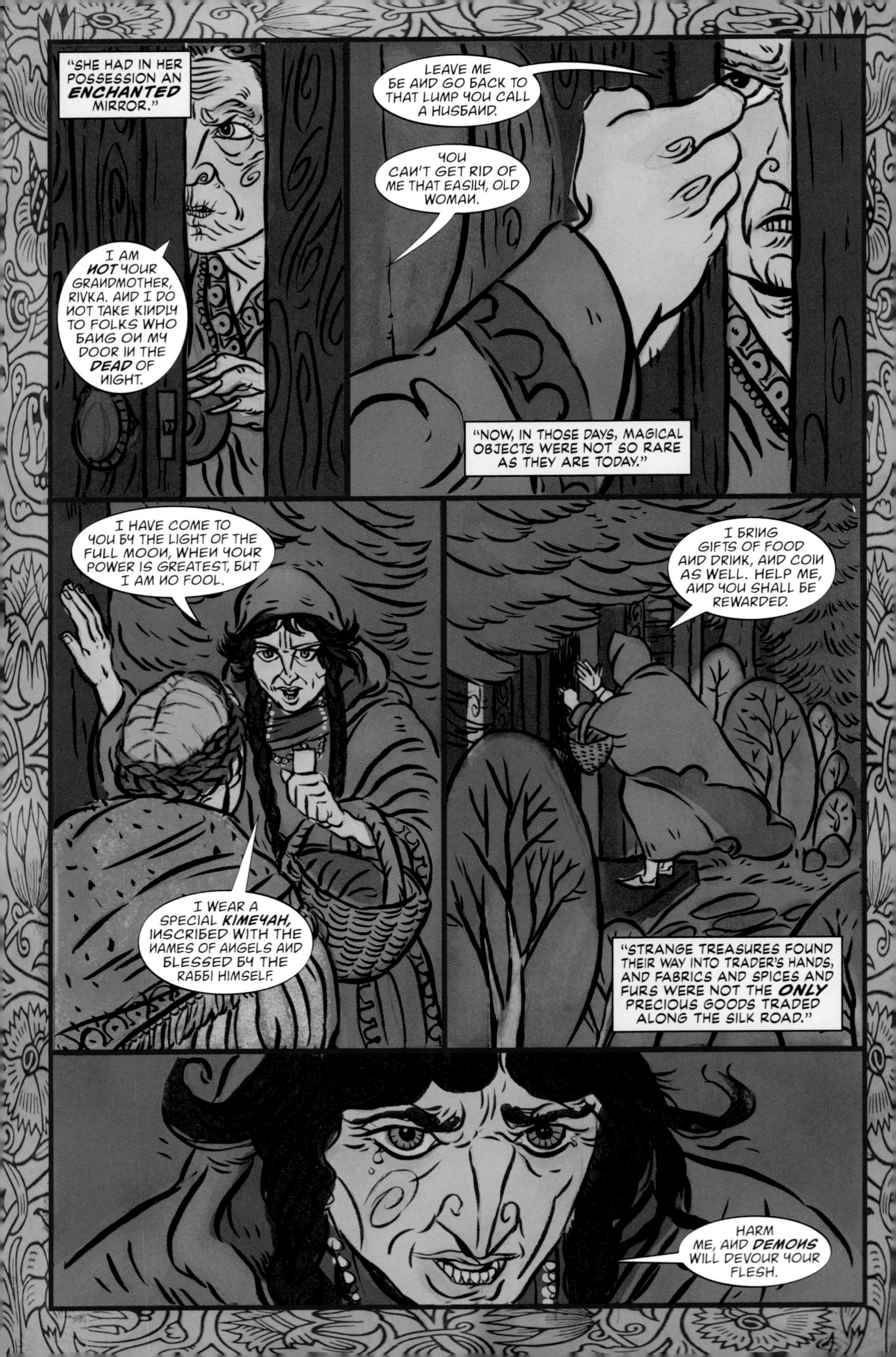
"SHE HAD IN HER POSSESSION AN ENCHANTED MIRROR."
I AM NOT YOUR GRANDMOTHER, RIVKA. AND I DO NOT TAKE KINDLY TO FOLKS WHO BANG ON MY DOOR IN THE DEAD OF NIGHT.
LEAVE ME BE AND GO BACK TO THAT LUMP YOU CALL A HUSBAND.
YOU CAN'T GET RID OF ME THAT EASILY, OLD WOMAN.
"NOW, IN THOSE DAYS, MAGICAL OBJECTS WERE NOT SO RARE AS THEY ARE TODAY."
I HAVE COME TO YOU BY THE LIGHT OF THE FULL MOON, WHEN YOUR POWER IS GREATEST, BUT I AM NO FOOL.
I WEAR A SPECIAL KIMEYAH, INSCRIBED WITH THE NAMES OF ANGELS AND BLESSED BY THE RABBI HIMSELF.
I BRING GIFTS OF FOOD AND DRINK, AND COIN AS WELL. HELP ME, AND YOU SHALL BE REWARDED.
"STRANGE TREASURES FOUND THEIR WAY INTO TRADER'S HANDS, AND FABRICS AND SPICES AND FURS WERE NOT THE ONLY PRECIOUS GOODS TRADED ALONG THE SILK ROAD."
HARM ME, AND DEMONS WILL DEVOUR YOUR FLESH.

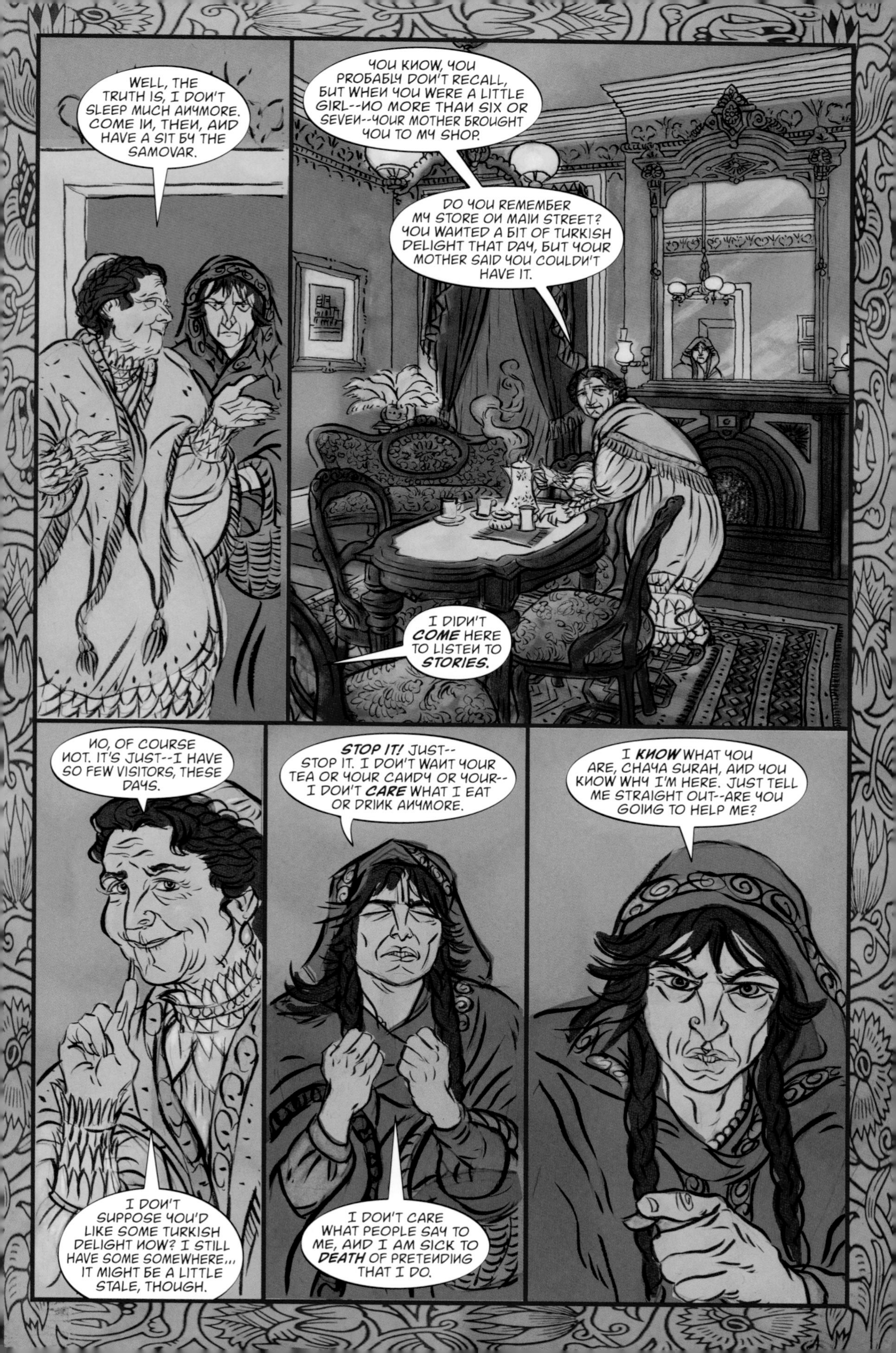
WELL, THE TRUTH IS, I DON'T SLEEP MUCH ANYMORE. COME IN, THEN, AND HAVE A SIT BY THE SAMOVAR.
YOU KNOW, YOU PROBABLY DON'T RECALL, BUT WHEN YOU WERE A LITTLE GIRL--NO MORE THAN SIX OR SEVEN--YOUR MOTHER BROUGHT YOU TO MY SHOP.
DO YOU REMEMBER MY STORE ON MAIN STREET? YOU WANTED A BIT OF TURKISH DELIGHT THAT DAY, BUT YOUR MOTHER SAID YOU COULDN'T HAVE IT.
I DIDN'T **COME** HERE TO LISTEN TO **STORIES.**
NO, OF COURSE NOT. IT'S JUST--I HAVE SO FEW VISITORS, THESE DAYS.
I DON'T SUPPOSE YOU'D LIKE SOME TURKISH DELIGHT NOW? I STILL HAVE SOME SOMEWHERE... IT MIGHT BE A LITTLE STALE, THOUGH.
STOP IT! JUST--STOP IT. I DON'T WANT YOUR TEA OR YOUR CANDY OR YOUR--I DON'T **CARE** WHAT I EAT OR DRINK ANYMORE.
I DON'T CARE WHAT PEOPLE SAY TO ME, AND I AM SICK TO **DEATH** OF PRETENDING THAT I DO.
I **KNOW** WHAT YOU ARE, CHAYA SURAH, AND YOU KNOW WHY I'M HERE. JUST TELL ME STRAIGHT OUT--ARE YOU GOING TO HELP ME?

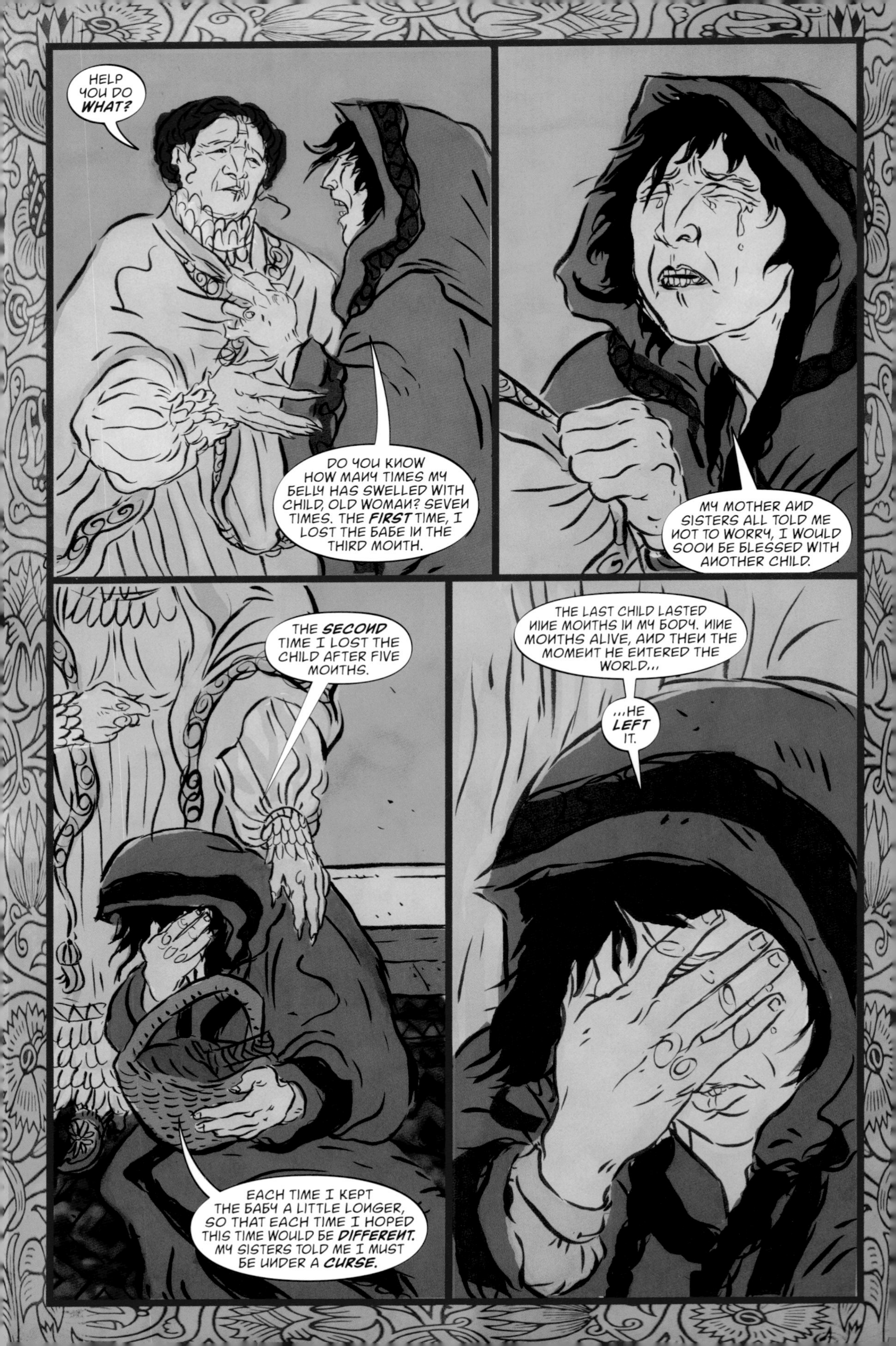
HELP YOU DO *WHAT?*
DO YOU KNOW HOW MANY TIMES MY BELLY HAS SWELLED WITH CHILD, OLD WOMAN? SEVEN TIMES. THE *FIRST* TIME, I LOST THE BABE IN THE THIRD MONTH.
MY MOTHER AND SISTERS ALL TOLD ME NOT TO WORRY, I WOULD SOON BE BLESSED WITH ANOTHER CHILD.
THE *SECOND* TIME I LOST THE CHILD AFTER FIVE MONTHS.
EACH TIME I KEPT THE BABY A LITTLE LONGER, SO THAT EACH TIME I HOPED THIS TIME WOULD BE *DIFFERENT.* MY SISTERS TOLD ME I MUST BE UNDER A *CURSE.*
THE LAST CHILD LASTED NINE MONTHS IN MY BODY. NINE MONTHS ALIVE, AND THEN THE MOMENT HE ENTERED THE WORLD...
...HE *LEFT* IT.

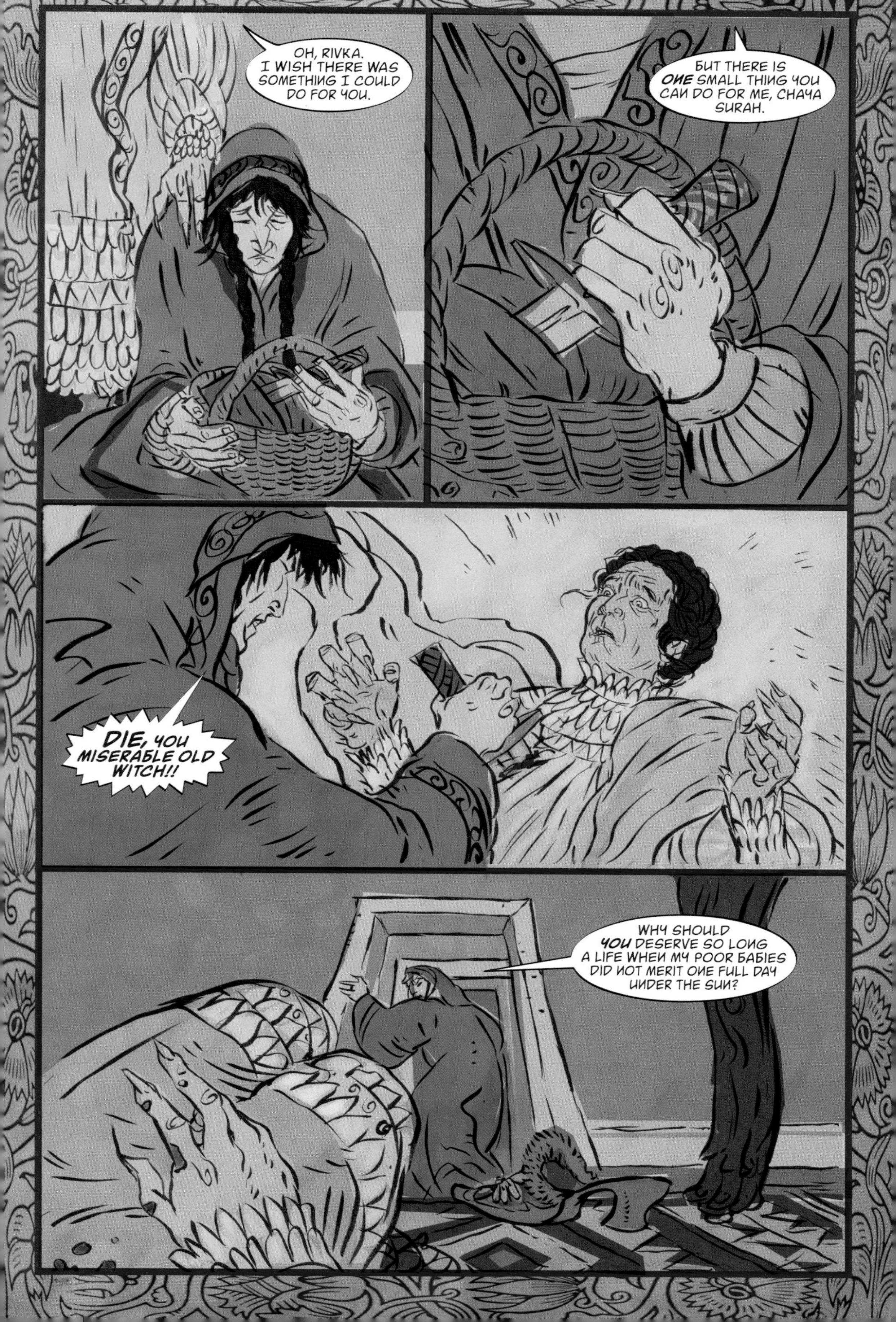
OH, RIVKA. I WISH THERE WAS SOMETHING I COULD DO FOR YOU.
BUT THERE IS ONE SMALL THING YOU CAN DO FOR ME, CHAYA SURAH.
DIE, YOU MISERABLE OLD WITCH!!
WHY SHOULD YOU DESERVE SO LONG A LIFE WHEN MY POOR BABIES DID NOT MERIT ONE FULL DAY UNDER THE SUN?

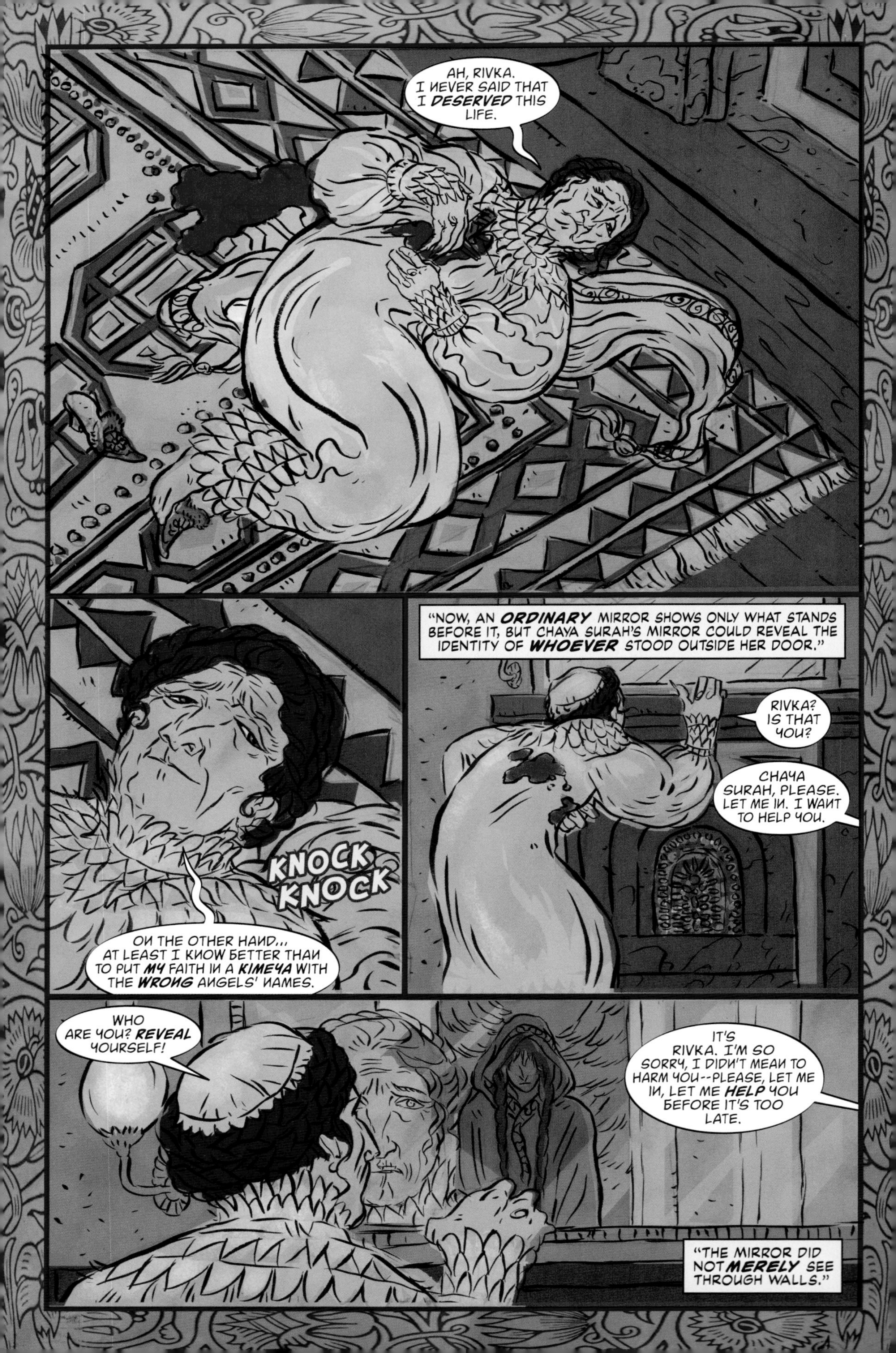
AH, RIVKA. I NEVER SAID THAT I DESERVED THIS LIFE.
KNOCK KNOCK
ON THE OTHER HAND... AT LEAST I KNOW BETTER THAN TO PUT MY FAITH IN A KIMEYA WITH THE WRONG ANGELS' NAMES.
"NOW, AN ORDINARY MIRROR SHOWS ONLY WHAT STANDS BEFORE IT, BUT CHAYA SURAH'S MIRROR COULD REVEAL THE IDENTITY OF WHOEVER STOOD OUTSIDE HER DOOR."
RIVKA? IS THAT YOU?
CHAYA SURAH, PLEASE. LET ME IN. I WANT TO HELP YOU.
WHO ARE YOU? REVEAL YOURSELF!
IT'S RIVKA. I'M SO SORRY, I DIDN'T MEAN TO HARM YOU--PLEASE, LET ME IN, LET ME HELP YOU BEFORE IT'S TOO LATE.
"THE MIRROR DID NOT MERELY SEE THROUGH WALLS."

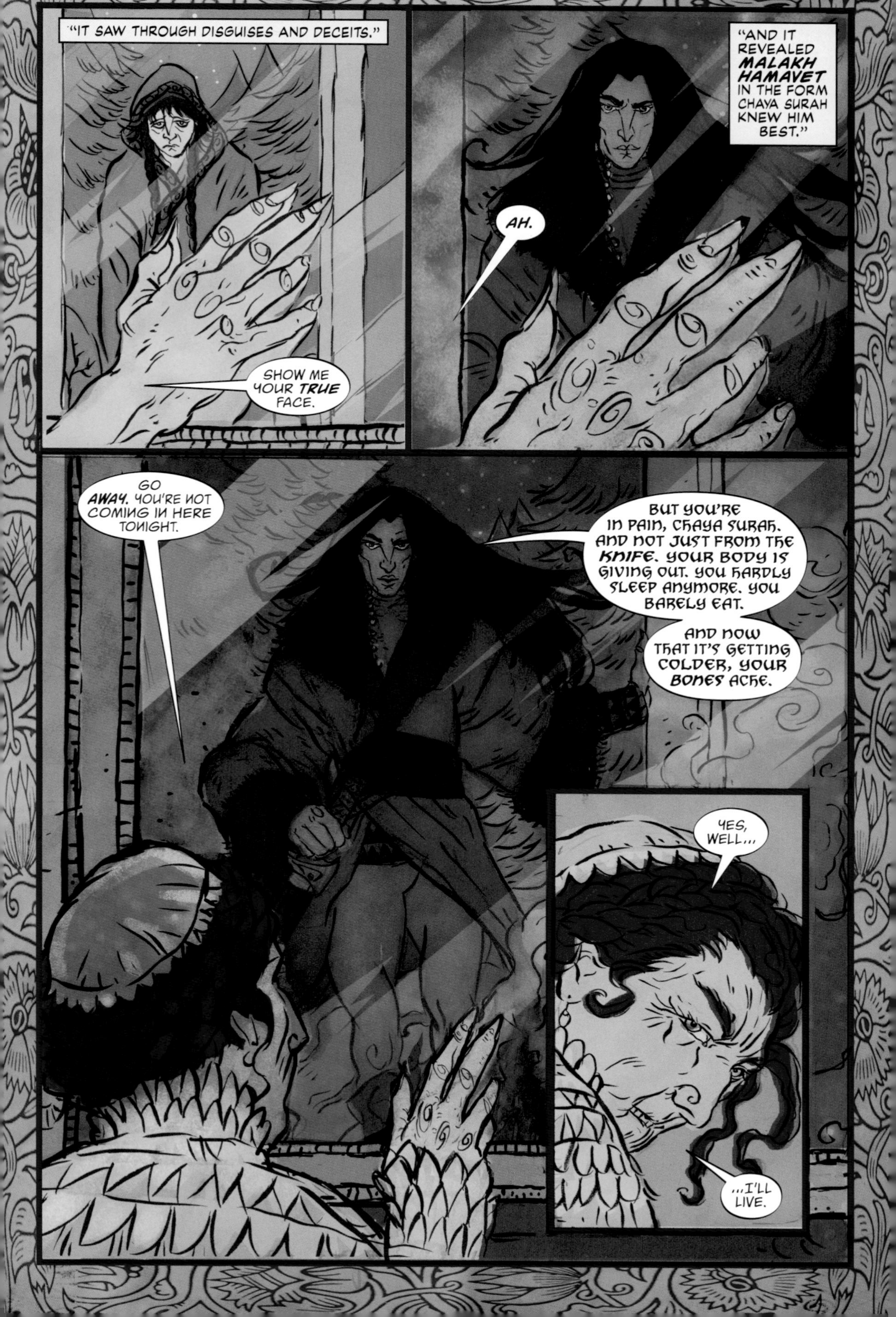

"IT SAW THROUGH DISGUISES AND DECEITS."
SHOW ME YOUR TRUE FACE.
"AND IT REVEALED MALAKH HAMAVET IN THE FORM CHAYA SURAH KNEW HIM BEST."
AH.
GO AWAY. YOU'RE NOT COMING IN HERE TONIGHT.
BUT YOU'RE IN PAIN, CHAYA SURAH. AND NOT JUST FROM THE KNIFE. YOUR BODY IS GIVING OUT. YOU HARDLY SLEEP ANYMORE. YOU BARELY EAT.
AND NOW THAT IT'S GETTING COLDER, YOUR BONES ACHE.
YES, WELL...
...I'LL LIVE.

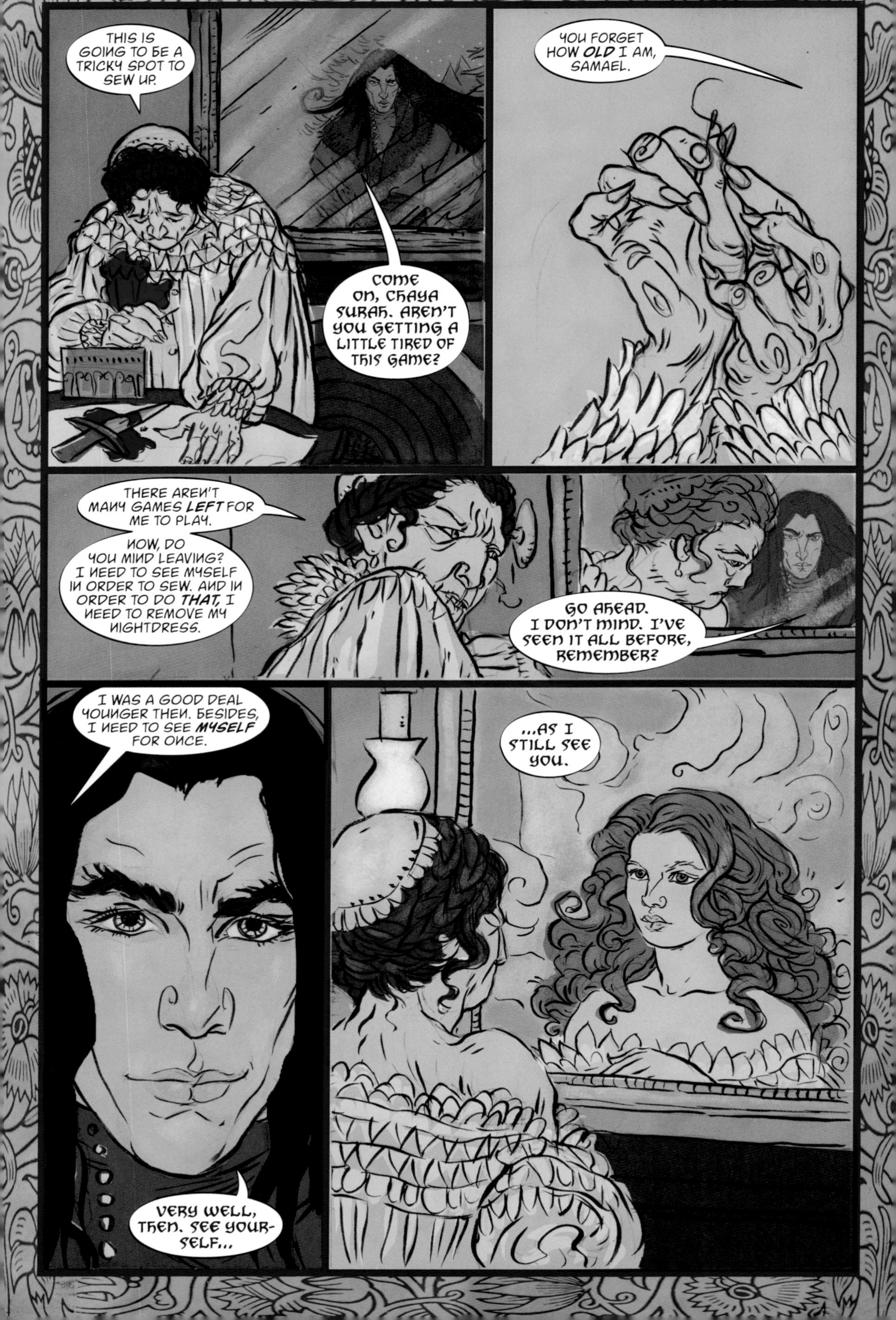
THIS IS GOING TO BE A TRICKY SPOT TO SEW UP.
COME ON, CHAYA SURAH. AREN'T YOU GETTING A LITTLE TIRED OF THIS GAME?
YOU FORGET HOW **OLD** I AM, SAMAEL.
THERE AREN'T MANY GAMES **LEFT** FOR ME TO PLAY.
NOW, DO YOU MIND LEAVING? I NEED TO SEE MYSELF IN ORDER TO SEW. AND IN ORDER TO DO **THAT,** I NEED TO REMOVE MY NIGHTDRESS.
GO AHEAD. I DON'T MIND. I'VE SEEN IT ALL BEFORE, REMEMBER?
I WAS A GOOD DEAL YOUNGER THEN. BESIDES, I NEED TO SEE **MYSELF** FOR ONCE.
VERY WELL, THEN. SEE YOURSELF...
...AS I STILL SEE YOU.

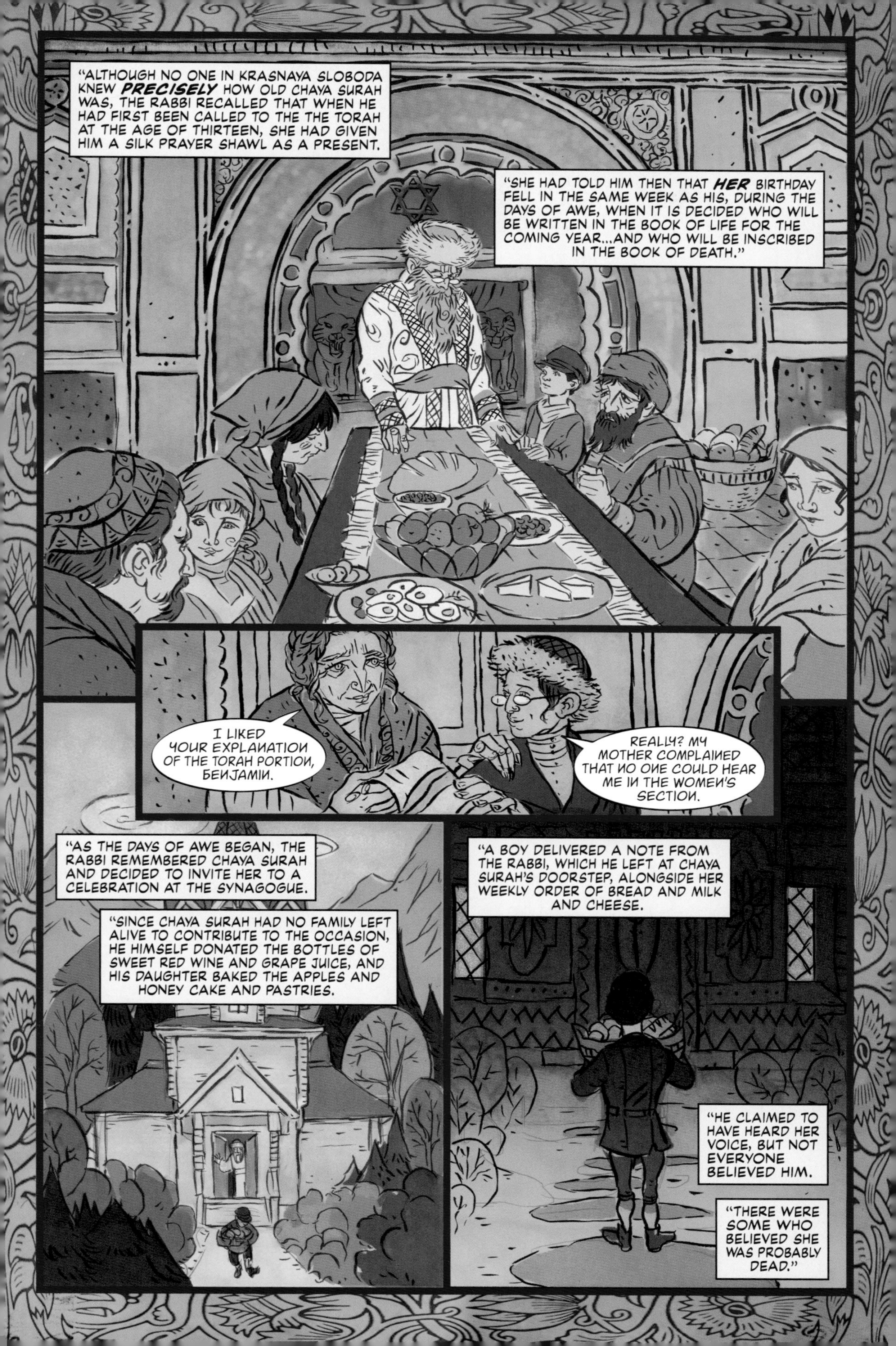
"ALTHOUGH NO ONE IN KRASNAYA SLOBODA KNEW **PRECISELY** HOW OLD CHAYA SURAH WAS, THE RABBI RECALLED THAT WHEN HE HAD FIRST BEEN CALLED TO THE THE TORAH AT THE AGE OF THIRTEEN, SHE HAD GIVEN HIM A SILK PRAYER SHAWL AS A PRESENT.
"SHE HAD TOLD HIM THEN THAT **HER** BIRTHDAY FELL IN THE SAME WEEK AS HIS, DURING THE DAYS OF AWE, WHEN IT IS DECIDED WHO WILL BE WRITTEN IN THE BOOK OF LIFE FOR THE COMING YEAR...AND WHO WILL BE INSCRIBED IN THE BOOK OF DEATH."
I LIKED YOUR EXPLANATION OF THE TORAH PORTION, BENJAMIN.
REALLY? MY MOTHER COMPLAINED THAT NO ONE COULD HEAR ME IN THE WOMEN'S SECTION.
"AS THE DAYS OF AWE BEGAN, THE RABBI REMEMBERED CHAYA SURAH AND DECIDED TO INVITE HER TO A CELEBRATION AT THE SYNAGOGUE.
"SINCE CHAYA SURAH HAD NO FAMILY LEFT ALIVE TO CONTRIBUTE TO THE OCCASION, HE HIMSELF DONATED THE BOTTLES OF SWEET RED WINE AND GRAPE JUICE, AND HIS DAUGHTER BAKED THE APPLES AND HONEY CAKE AND PASTRIES.
"A BOY DELIVERED A NOTE FROM THE RABBI, WHICH HE LEFT AT CHAYA SURAH'S DOORSTEP, ALONGSIDE HER WEEKLY ORDER OF BREAD AND MILK AND CHEESE.
"HE CLAIMED TO HAVE HEARD HER VOICE, BUT NOT EVERYONE BELIEVED HIM.
"THERE WERE SOME WHO BELIEVED SHE WAS PROBABLY DEAD."

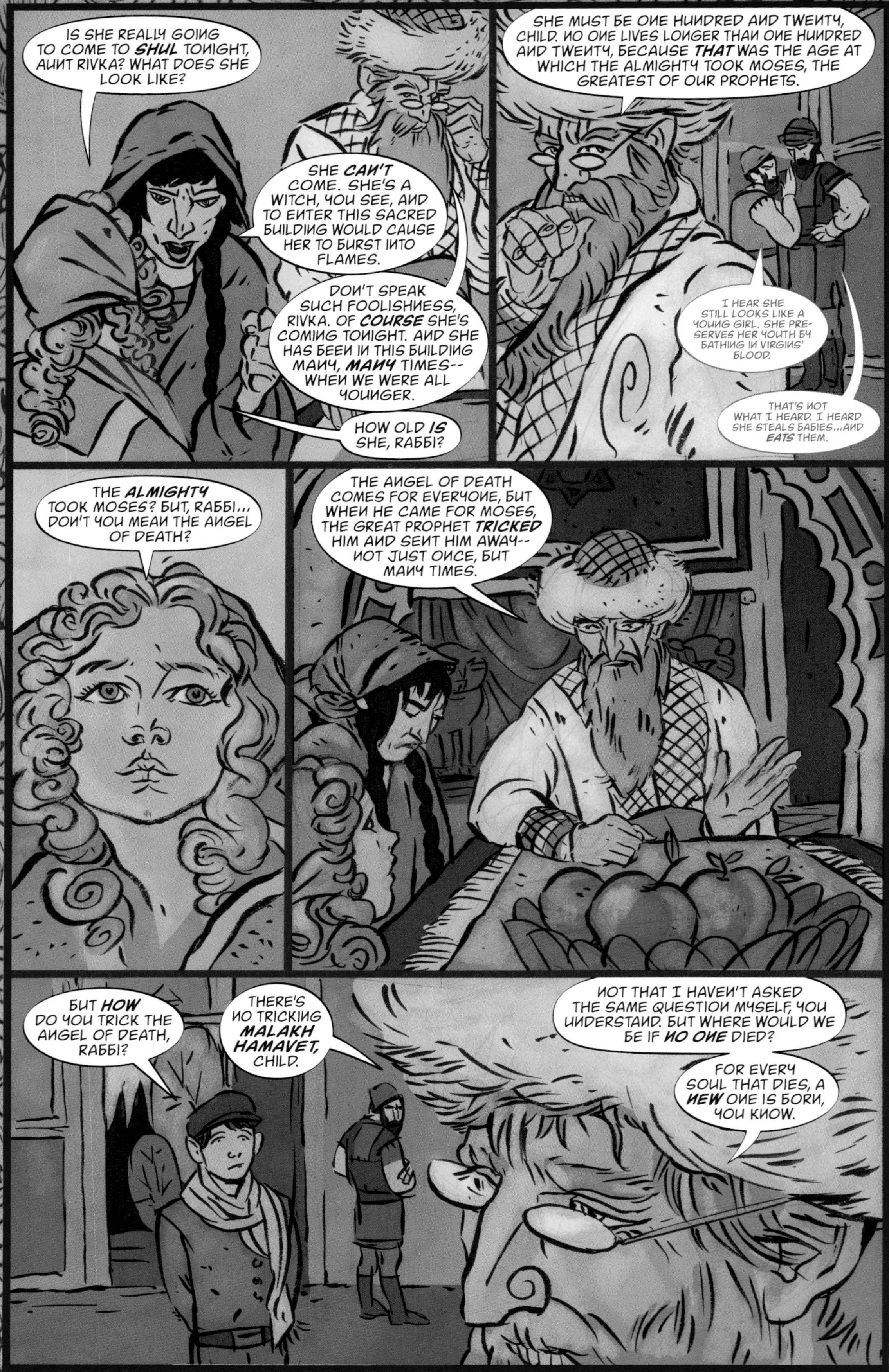
IS SHE REALLY GOING TO COME TO SHUL TONIGHT, AUNT RIVKA? WHAT DOES SHE LOOK LIKE?
SHE CAN'T COME. SHE'S A WITCH, YOU SEE, AND TO ENTER THIS SACRED BUILDING WOULD CAUSE HER TO BURST INTO FLAMES.
DON'T SPEAK SUCH FOOLISHNESS, RIVKA. OF COURSE SHE'S COMING TONIGHT. AND SHE HAS BEEN IN THIS BUILDING MANY, MANY TIMES-- WHEN WE WERE ALL YOUNGER.
HOW OLD IS SHE, RABBI?
SHE MUST BE ONE HUNDRED AND TWENTY, CHILD. NO ONE LIVES LONGER THAN ONE HUNDRED AND TWENTY, BECAUSE THAT WAS THE AGE AT WHICH THE ALMIGHTY TOOK MOSES, THE GREATEST OF OUR PROPHETS.
I HEAR SHE STILL LOOKS LIKE A YOUNG GIRL. SHE PRESERVES HER YOUTH BY BATHING IN VIRGINS' BLOOD.
THAT'S NOT WHAT I HEARD. I HEARD SHE STEALS BABIES...AND EATS THEM.
THE ALMIGHTY TOOK MOSES? BUT, RABBI... DON'T YOU MEAN THE ANGEL OF DEATH?
THE ANGEL OF DEATH COMES FOR EVERYONE, BUT WHEN HE CAME FOR MOSES, THE GREAT PROPHET TRICKED HIM AND SENT HIM AWAY-- NOT JUST ONCE, BUT MANY TIMES.
BUT HOW DO YOU TRICK THE ANGEL OF DEATH, RABBI?
THERE'S NO TRICKING MALAKH HAMAVET, CHILD.
NOT THAT I HAVEN'T ASKED THE SAME QUESTION MYSELF, YOU UNDERSTAND. BUT WHERE WOULD WE BE IF NO ONE DIED?
FOR EVERY SOUL THAT DIES, A NEW ONE IS BORN, YOU KNOW.

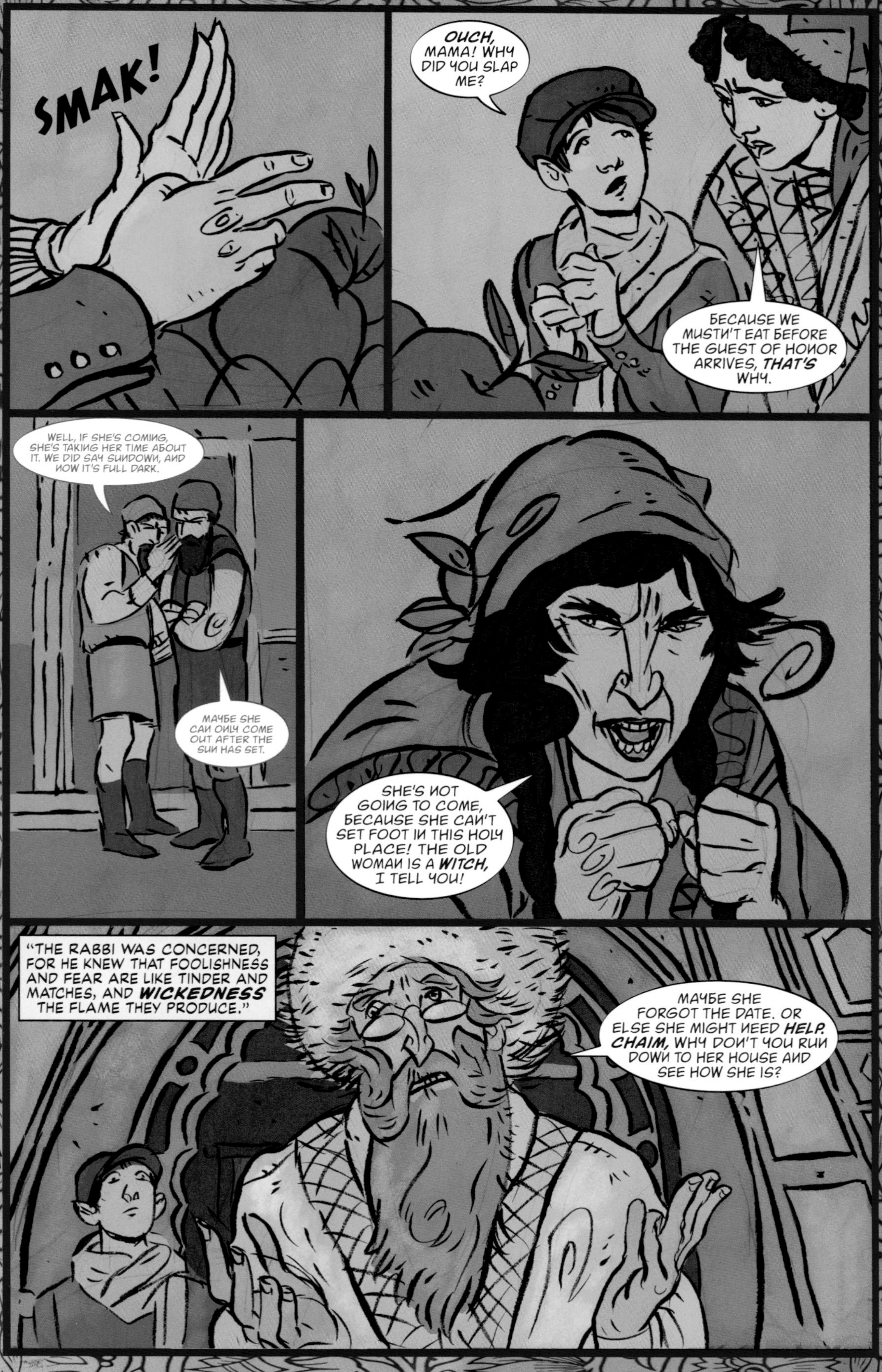
SMAK!
OUCH, MAMA! WHY DID YOU SLAP ME?
BECAUSE WE MUSTN'T EAT BEFORE THE GUEST OF HONOR ARRIVES, THAT'S WHY.
WELL, IF SHE'S COMING, SHE'S TAKING HER TIME ABOUT IT. WE DID SAY SUNDOWN, AND NOW IT'S FULL DARK.
MAYBE SHE CAN ONLY COME OUT AFTER THE SUN HAS SET.
SHE'S NOT GOING TO COME, BECAUSE SHE CAN'T SET FOOT IN THIS HOLY PLACE! THE OLD WOMAN IS A WITCH, I TELL YOU!
"THE RABBI WAS CONCERNED, FOR HE KNEW THAT FOOLISHNESS AND FEAR ARE LIKE TINDER AND MATCHES, AND WICKEDNESS THE FLAME THEY PRODUCE."
MAYBE SHE FORGOT THE DATE. OR ELSE SHE MIGHT NEED HELP. CHAIM, WHY DON'T YOU RUN DOWN TO HER HOUSE AND SEE HOW SHE IS?

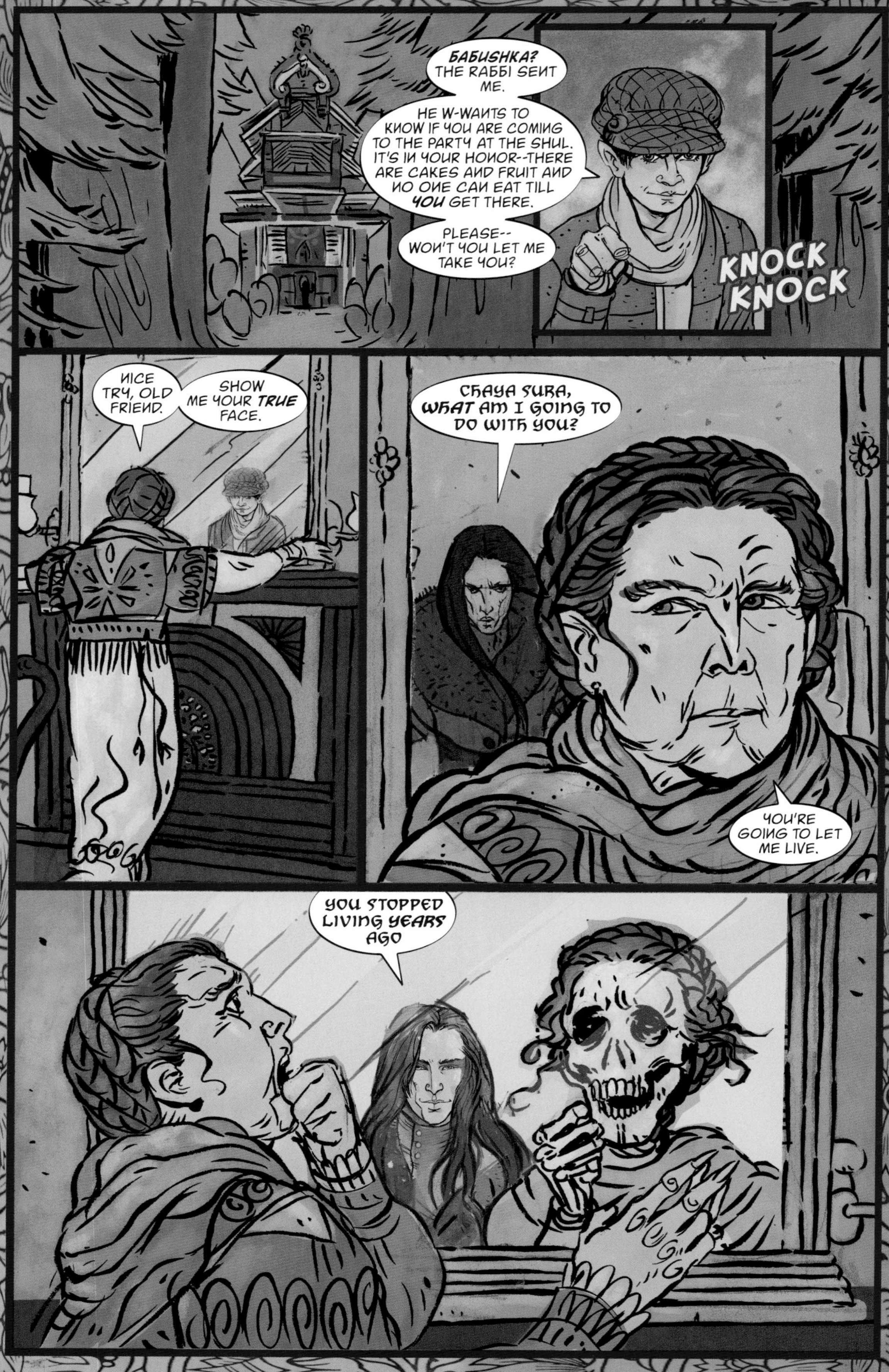

БАБUSHKA? THE RABBI SENT ME.
HE W-WANTS TO KNOW IF YOU ARE COMING TO THE PARTY AT THE SHUL. IT'S IN YOUR HONOR--THERE ARE CAKES AND FRUIT AND NO ONE CAN EAT TILL YOU GET THERE.
PLEASE-- WON'T YOU LET ME TAKE YOU?
KNOCK KNOCK
NICE TRY, OLD FRIEND.
SHOW ME YOUR TRUE FACE.
CHAYA SURA, WHAT AM I GOING TO DO WITH YOU?
YOU'RE GOING TO LET ME LIVE.
YOU STOPPED LIVING YEARS AGO

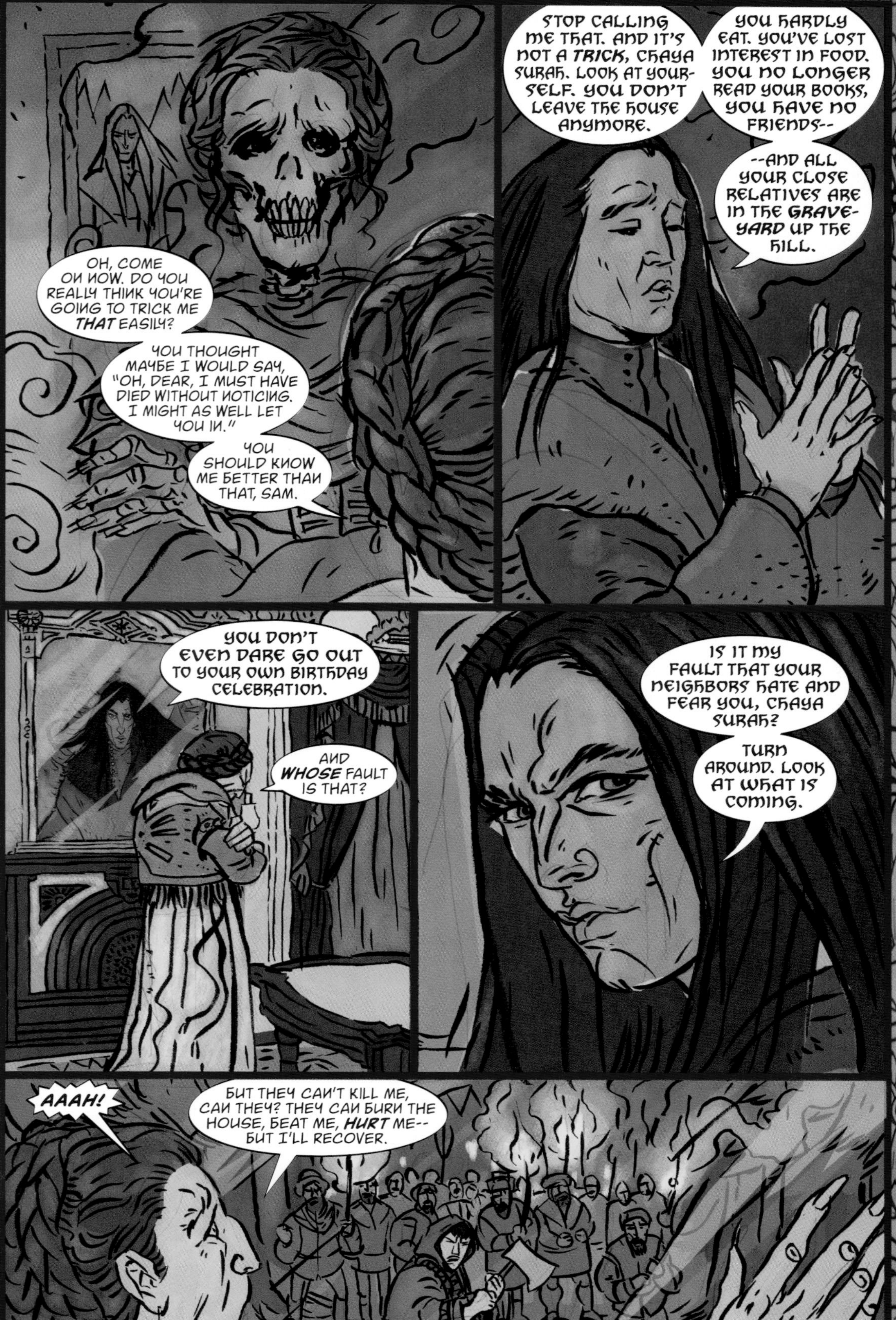
OH, COME ON NOW. DO YOU REALLY THINK YOU'RE GOING TO TRICK ME THAT EASILY?
YOU THOUGHT MAYBE I WOULD SAY, "OH, DEAR, I MUST HAVE DIED WITHOUT NOTICING. I MIGHT AS WELL LET YOU IN."
YOU SHOULD KNOW ME BETTER THAN THAT, SAM.
STOP CALLING ME THAT. AND IT'S NOT A TRICK, CHAYA SURAH. LOOK AT YOURSELF. YOU DON'T LEAVE THE HOUSE ANYMORE.
YOU HARDLY EAT. YOU'VE LOST INTEREST IN FOOD. YOU NO LONGER READ YOUR BOOKS, YOU HAVE NO FRIENDS--
--AND ALL YOUR CLOSE RELATIVES ARE IN THE GRAVEYARD UP THE HILL.
YOU DON'T EVEN DARE GO OUT TO YOUR OWN BIRTHDAY CELEBRATION.
AND WHOSE FAULT IS THAT?
IS IT MY FAULT THAT YOUR NEIGHBORS HATE AND FEAR YOU, CHAYA SURAH?
TURN AROUND. LOOK AT WHAT IS COMING.
AAAH!
BUT THEY CAN'T KILL ME, CAN THEY? THEY CAN BURN THE HOUSE, BEAT ME, HURT ME-- BUT I'LL RECOVER.

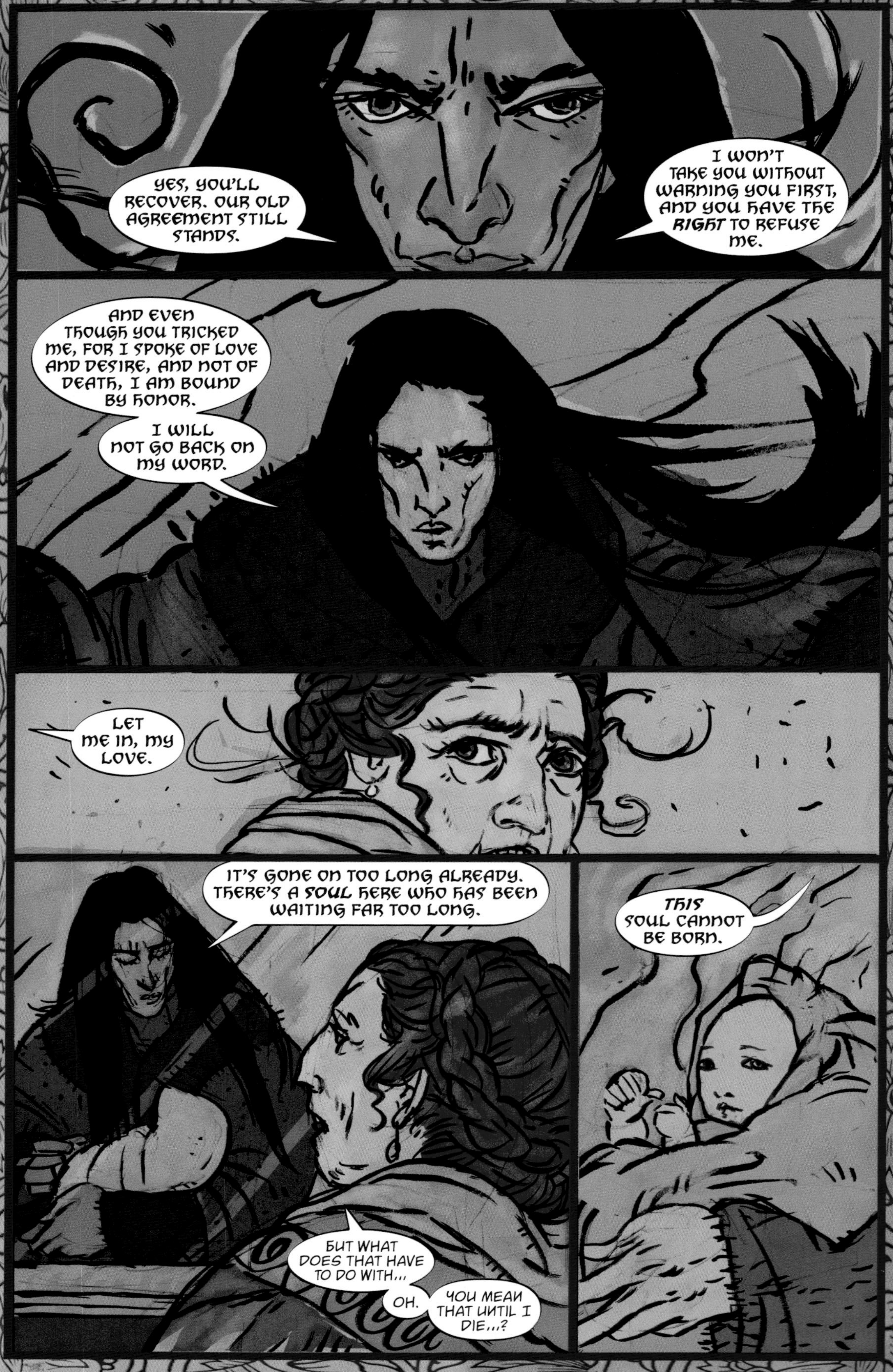
YES, YOU'LL RECOVER. OUR OLD AGREEMENT STILL STANDS.
I WON'T TAKE YOU WITHOUT WARNING YOU FIRST, AND YOU HAVE THE *RIGHT* TO REFUSE ME.
AND EVEN THOUGH YOU TRICKED ME, FOR I SPOKE OF LOVE AND DESIRE, AND NOT OF DEATH, I AM BOUND BY HONOR.
I WILL NOT GO BACK ON MY WORD.
LET ME IN, MY LOVE.
IT'S GONE ON TOO LONG ALREADY. THERE'S A *SOUL* HERE WHO HAS BEEN WAITING FAR TOO LONG.
BUT WHAT DOES THAT HAVE TO DO WITH...
OH.
YOU MEAN THAT UNTIL I DIE...?
THIS SOUL CANNOT BE BORN.

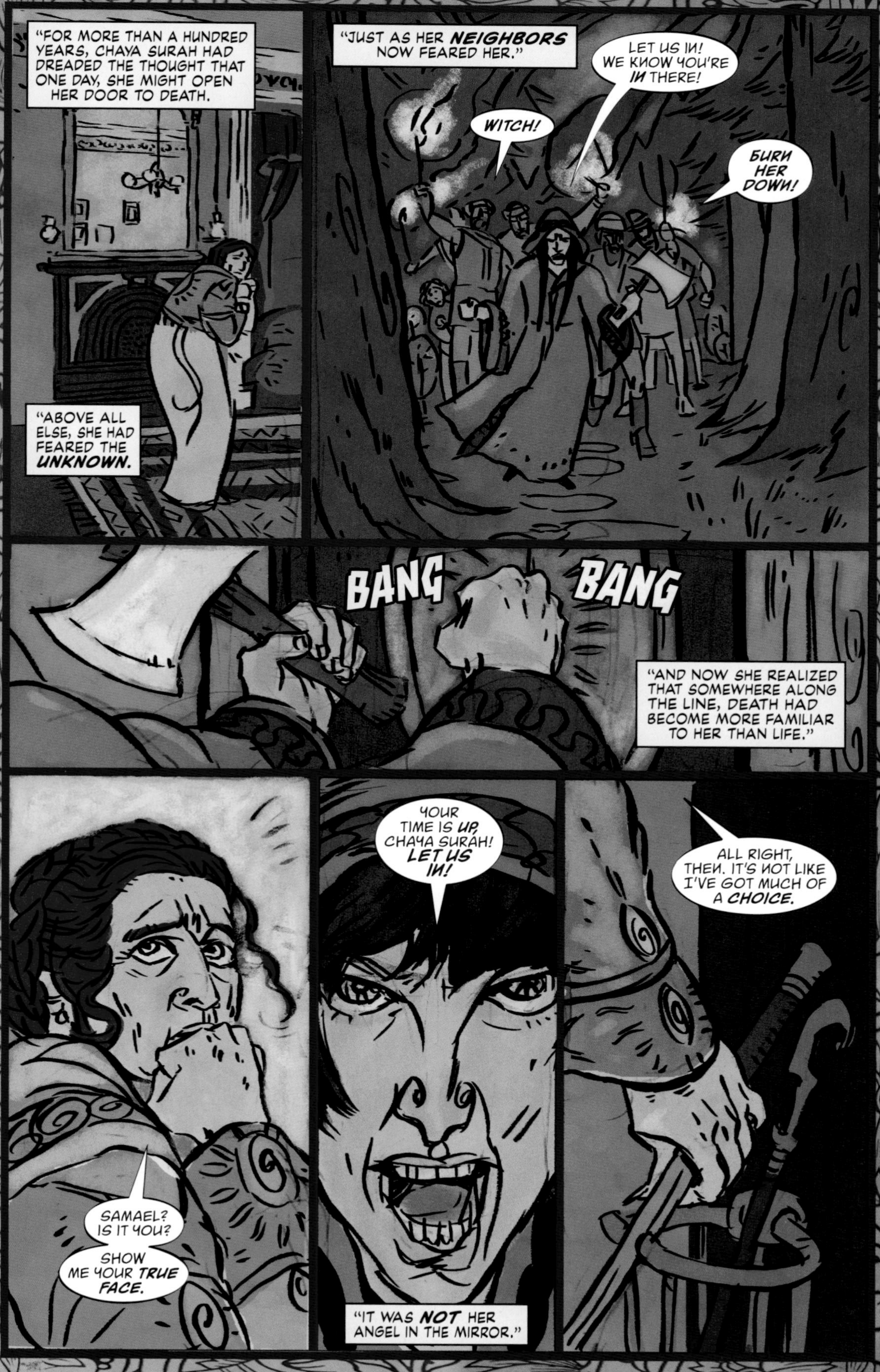
"FOR MORE THAN A HUNDRED YEARS, CHAYA SURAH HAD DREADED THE THOUGHT THAT ONE DAY, SHE MIGHT OPEN HER DOOR TO DEATH.
"ABOVE ALL ELSE, SHE HAD FEARED THE UNKNOWN.
"JUST AS HER NEIGHBORS NOW FEARED HER."
LET US IN! WE KNOW YOU'RE IN THERE!
WITCH!
BURN HER DOWN!
BANG
BANG
"AND NOW SHE REALIZED THAT SOMEWHERE ALONG THE LINE, DEATH HAD BECOME MORE FAMILIAR TO HER THAN LIFE."
SAMAEL? IS IT YOU?
SHOW ME YOUR TRUE FACE.
YOUR TIME IS UP, CHAYA SURAH! LET US IN!
"IT WAS NOT HER ANGEL IN THE MIRROR."
ALL RIGHT, THEN. IT'S NOT LIKE I'VE GOT MUCH OF A CHOICE.

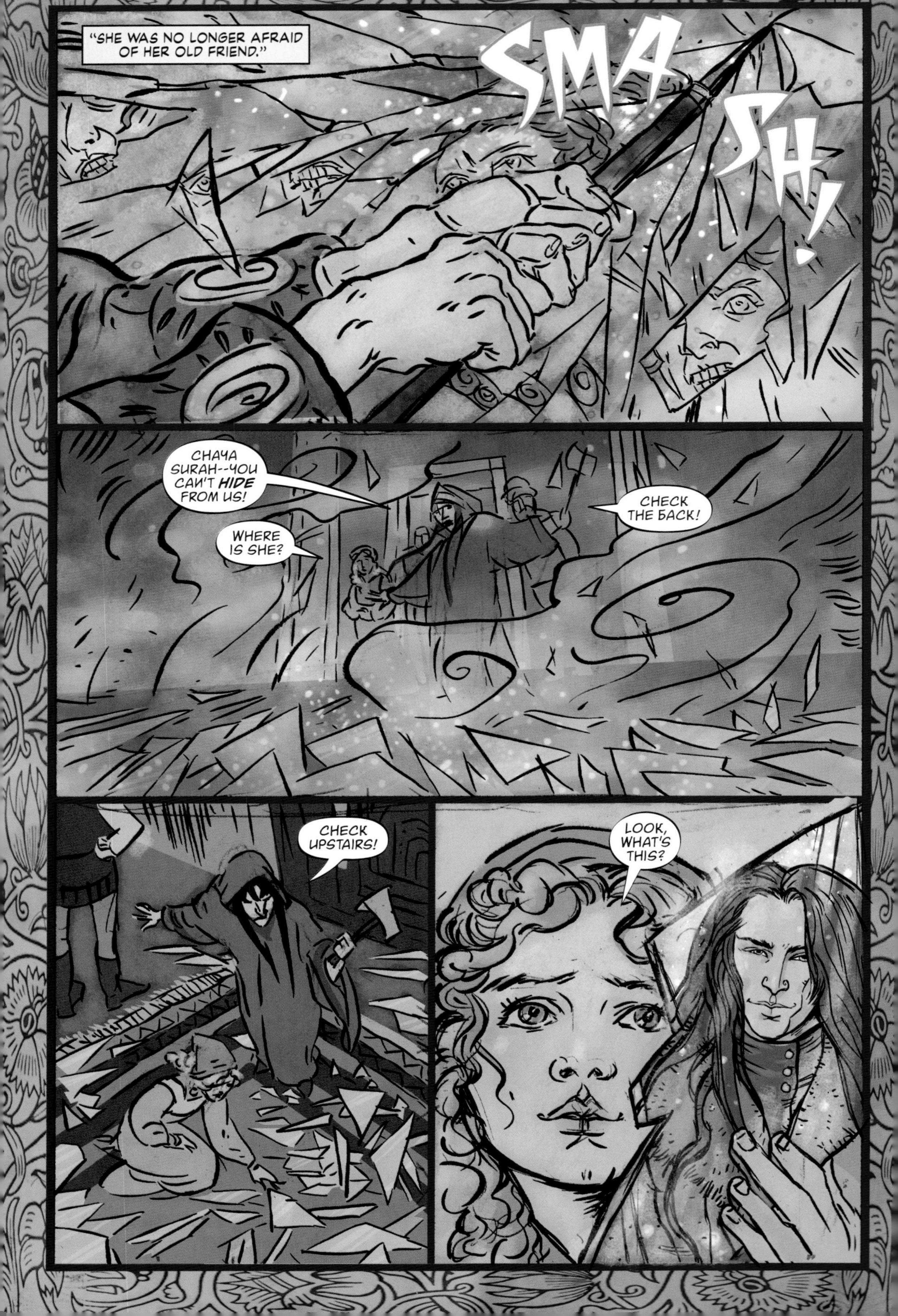
"SHE WAS NO LONGER AFRAID OF HER OLD FRIEND."
SMASH!
CHAYA SURAH--YOU CAN'T HIDE FROM US!
CHECK THE BACK!
WHERE IS SHE?
CHECK UPSTAIRS!
LOOK, WHAT'S THIS?

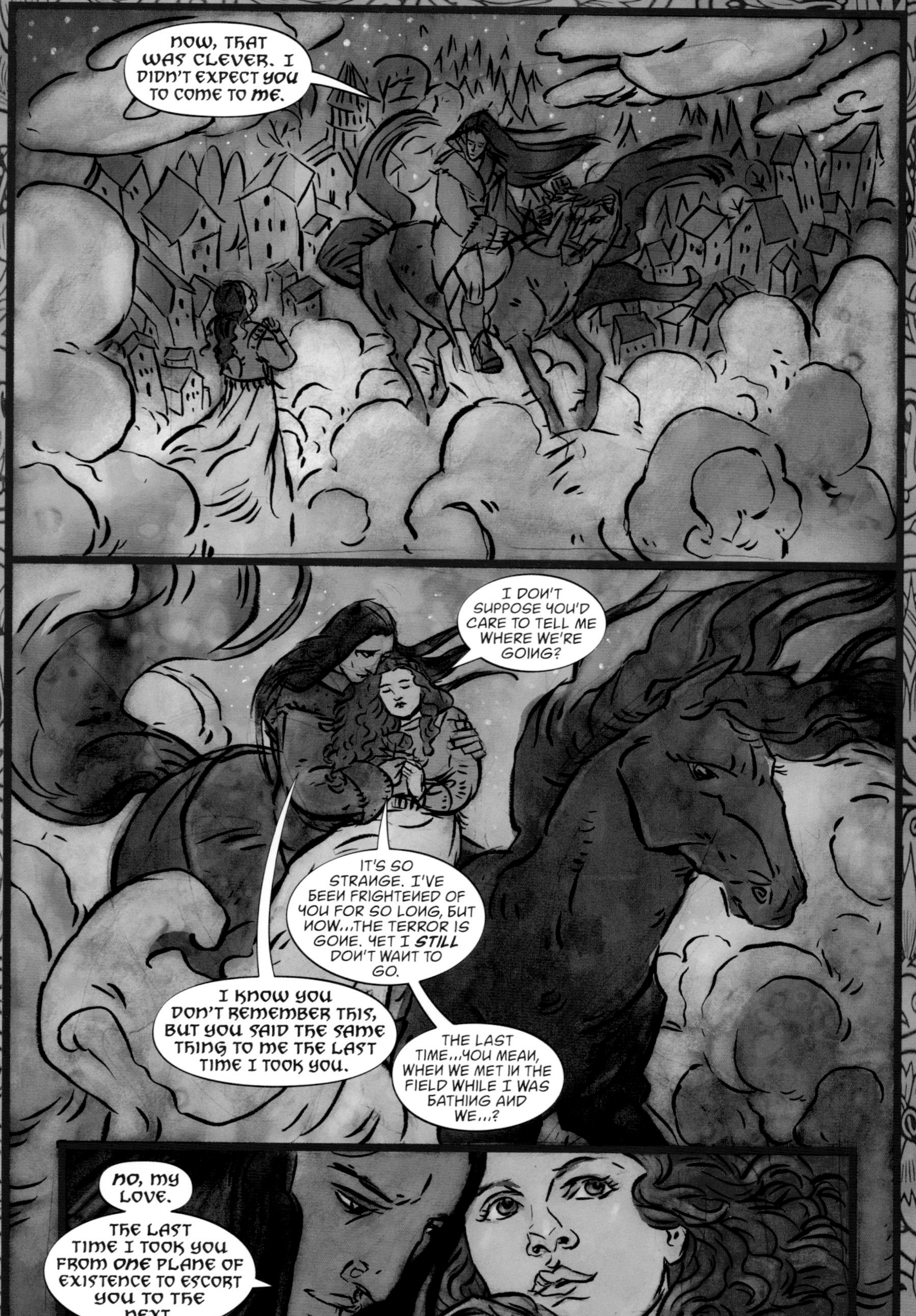
NOW, THAT WAS CLEVER. I DIDN'T EXPECT YOU TO COME TO ME.
I DON'T SUPPOSE YOU'D CARE TO TELL ME WHERE WE'RE GOING?
IT'S SO STRANGE. I'VE BEEN FRIGHTENED OF YOU FOR SO LONG, BUT NOW...THE TERROR IS GONE. YET I STILL DON'T WANT TO GO.
I KNOW YOU DON'T REMEMBER THIS, BUT YOU SAID THE SAME THING TO ME THE LAST TIME I TOOK YOU.
THE LAST TIME...YOU MEAN, WHEN WE MET IN THE FIELD WHILE I WAS BATHING AND WE...?
NO, MY LOVE.
THE LAST TIME I TOOK YOU FROM ONE PLANE OF EXISTENCE TO ESCORT YOU TO THE NEXT.

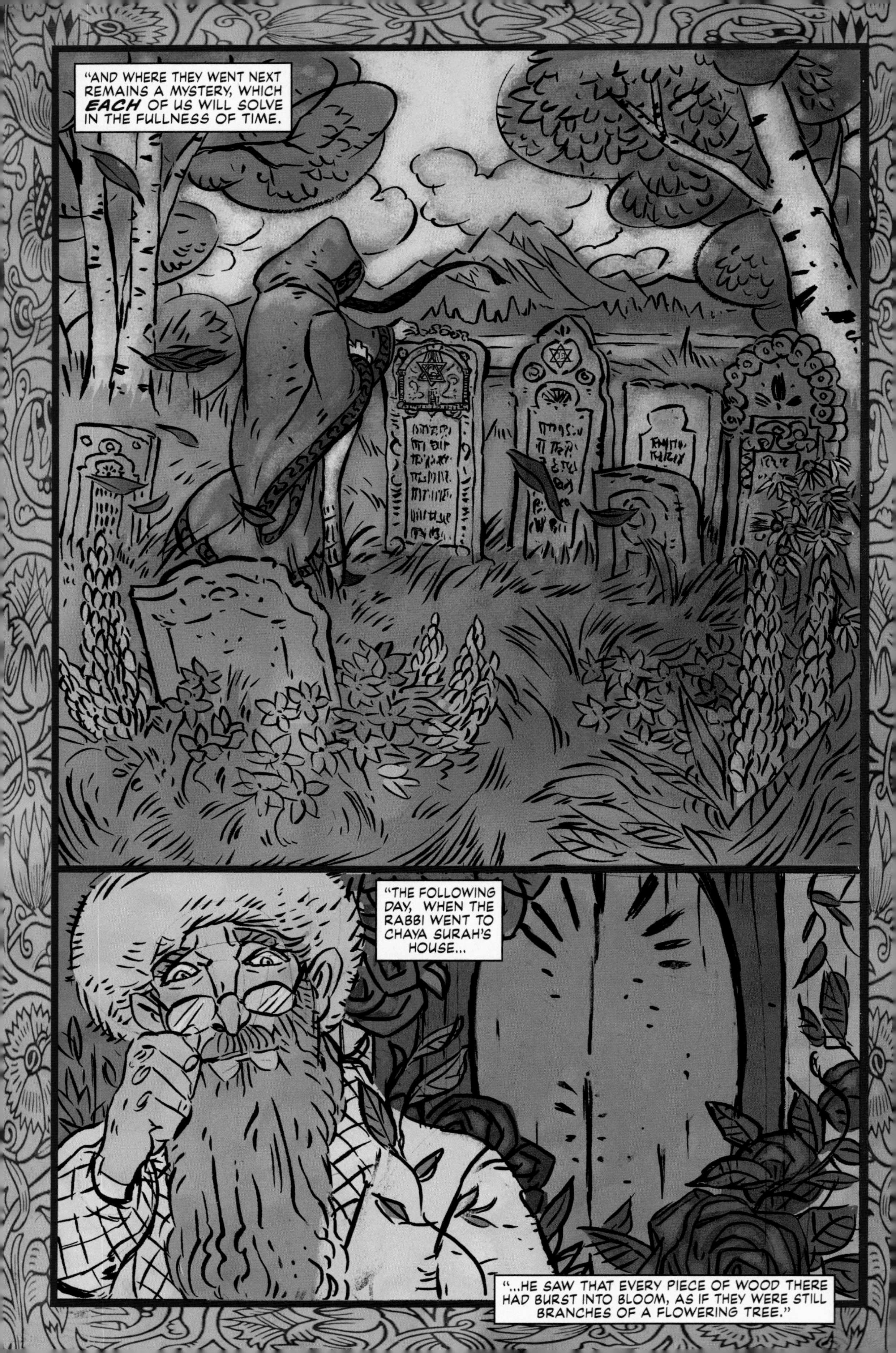
"AND WHERE THEY WENT NEXT REMAINS A MYSTERY, WHICH **EACH** OF US WILL SOLVE IN THE FULLNESS OF TIME.
"THE FOLLOWING DAY, WHEN THE RABBI WENT TO CHAYA SURAH'S HOUSE...
"...HE SAW THAT EVERY PIECE OF WOOD THERE HAD BURST INTO BLOOM, AS IF THEY WERE STILL BRANCHES OF A FLOWERING TREE."

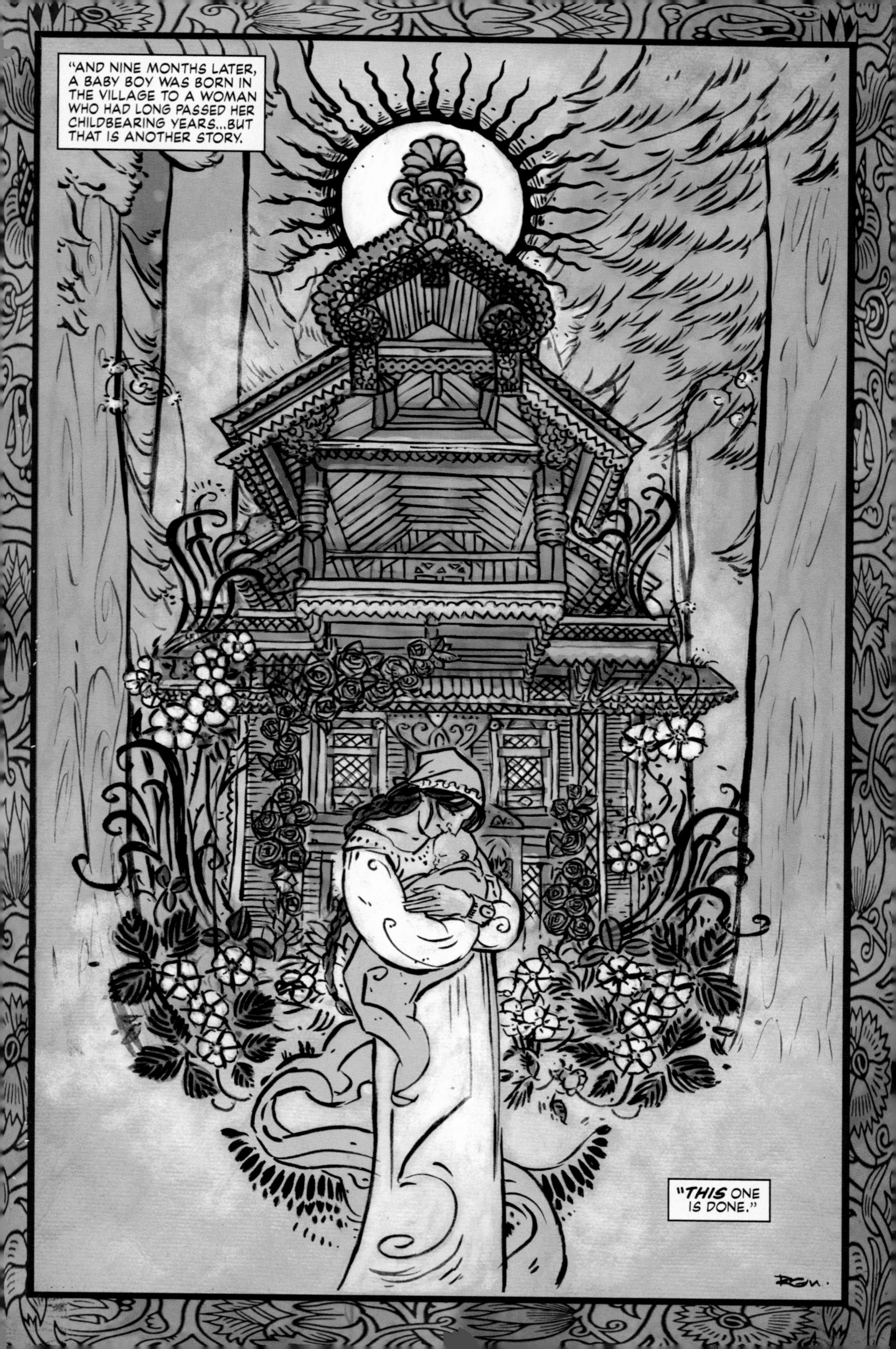
"AND NINE MONTHS LATER, A BABY BOY WAS BORN IN THE VILLAGE TO A WOMAN WHO HAD LONG PASSED HER CHILDBEARING YEARS...BUT THAT IS ANOTHER STORY.
"THIS ONE IS DONE."

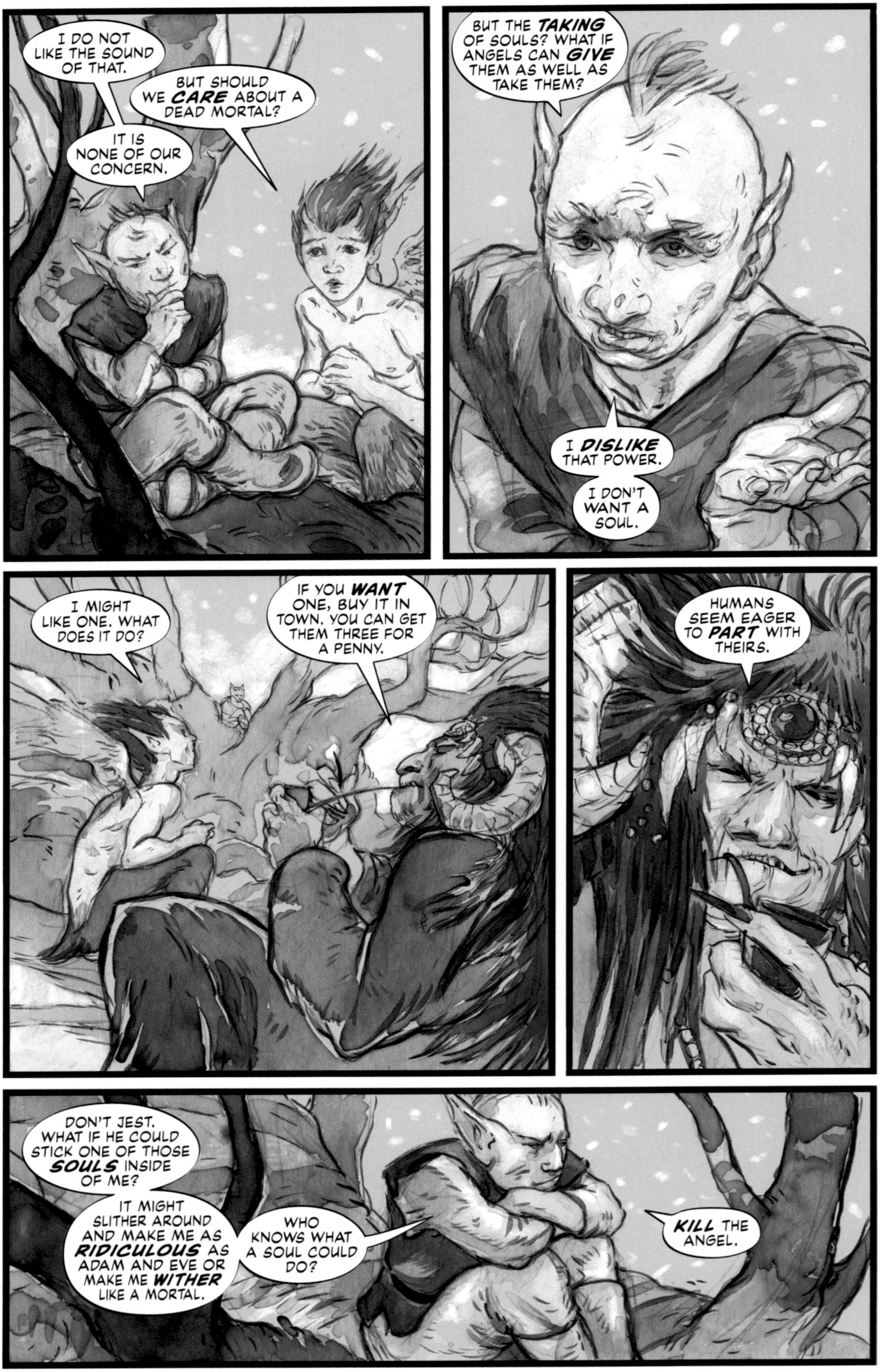

I DO NOT LIKE THE SOUND OF THAT.
IT IS NONE OF OUR CONCERN.
BUT SHOULD WE CARE ABOUT A DEAD MORTAL?
BUT THE TAKING OF SOULS? WHAT IF ANGELS CAN GIVE THEM AS WELL AS TAKE THEM?
I DISLIKE THAT POWER.
I DON'T WANT A SOUL.
I MIGHT LIKE ONE. WHAT DOES IT DO?
IF YOU WANT ONE, BUY IT IN TOWN. YOU CAN GET THEM THREE FOR A PENNY.
HUMANS SEEM EAGER TO PART WITH THEIRS.
DON'T JEST. WHAT IF HE COULD STICK ONE OF THOSE SOULS INSIDE OF ME?
IT MIGHT SLITHER AROUND AND MAKE ME AS RIDICULOUS AS ADAM AND EVE OR MAKE ME WITHER LIKE A MORTAL.
WHO KNOWS WHAT A SOUL COULD DO?
KILL THE ANGEL.

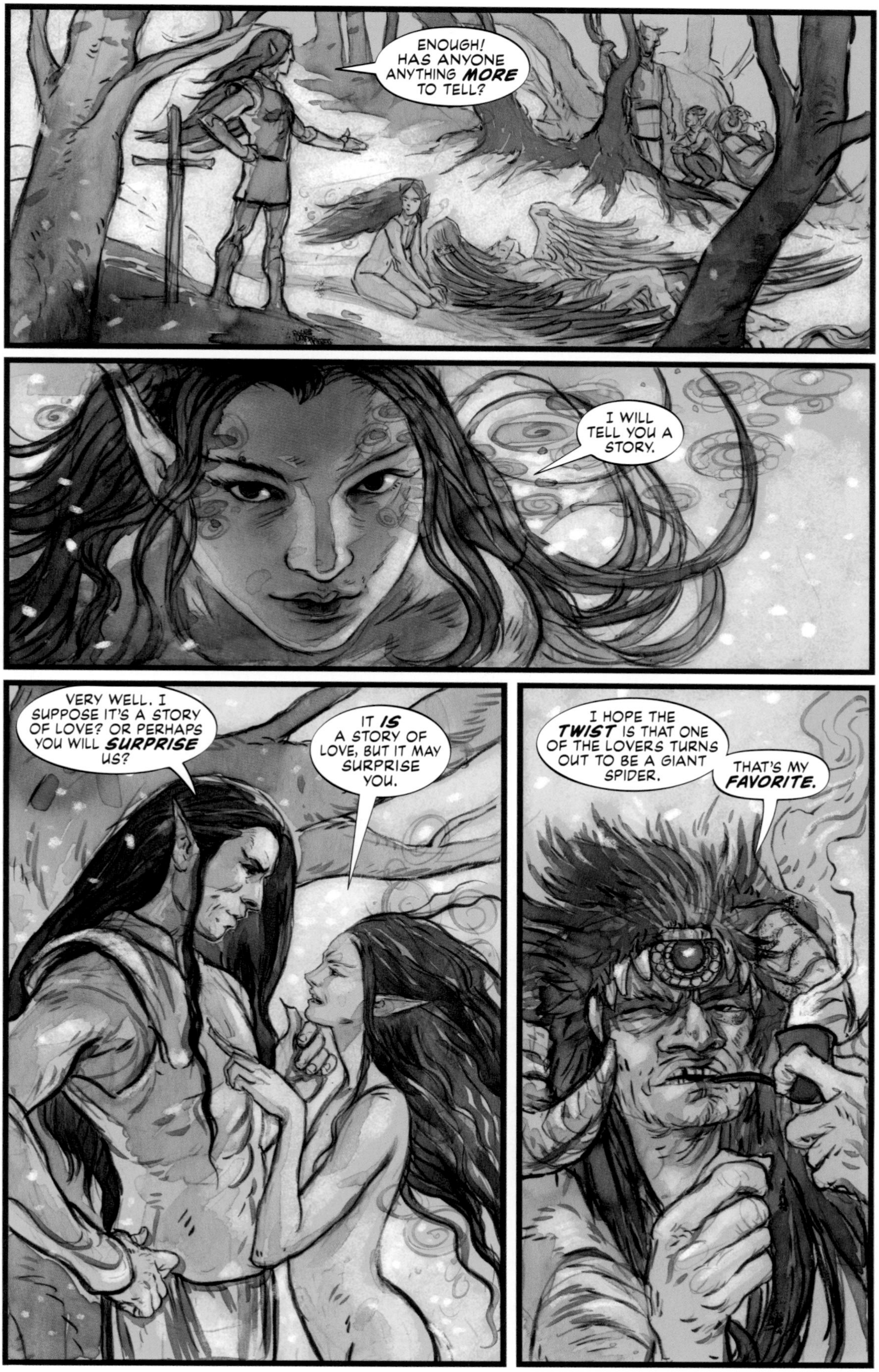
ENOUGH! HAS ANYONE ANYTHING **MORE** TO TELL?
I WILL TELL YOU A STORY.
VERY WELL. I SUPPOSE IT'S A STORY OF LOVE? OR PERHAPS YOU WILL **SURPRISE** US?
IT **IS** A STORY OF LOVE, BUT IT MAY SURPRISE YOU.
I HOPE THE **TWIST** IS THAT ONE OF THE LOVERS TURNS OUT TO BE A GIANT SPIDER.
THAT'S MY **FAVORITE.**

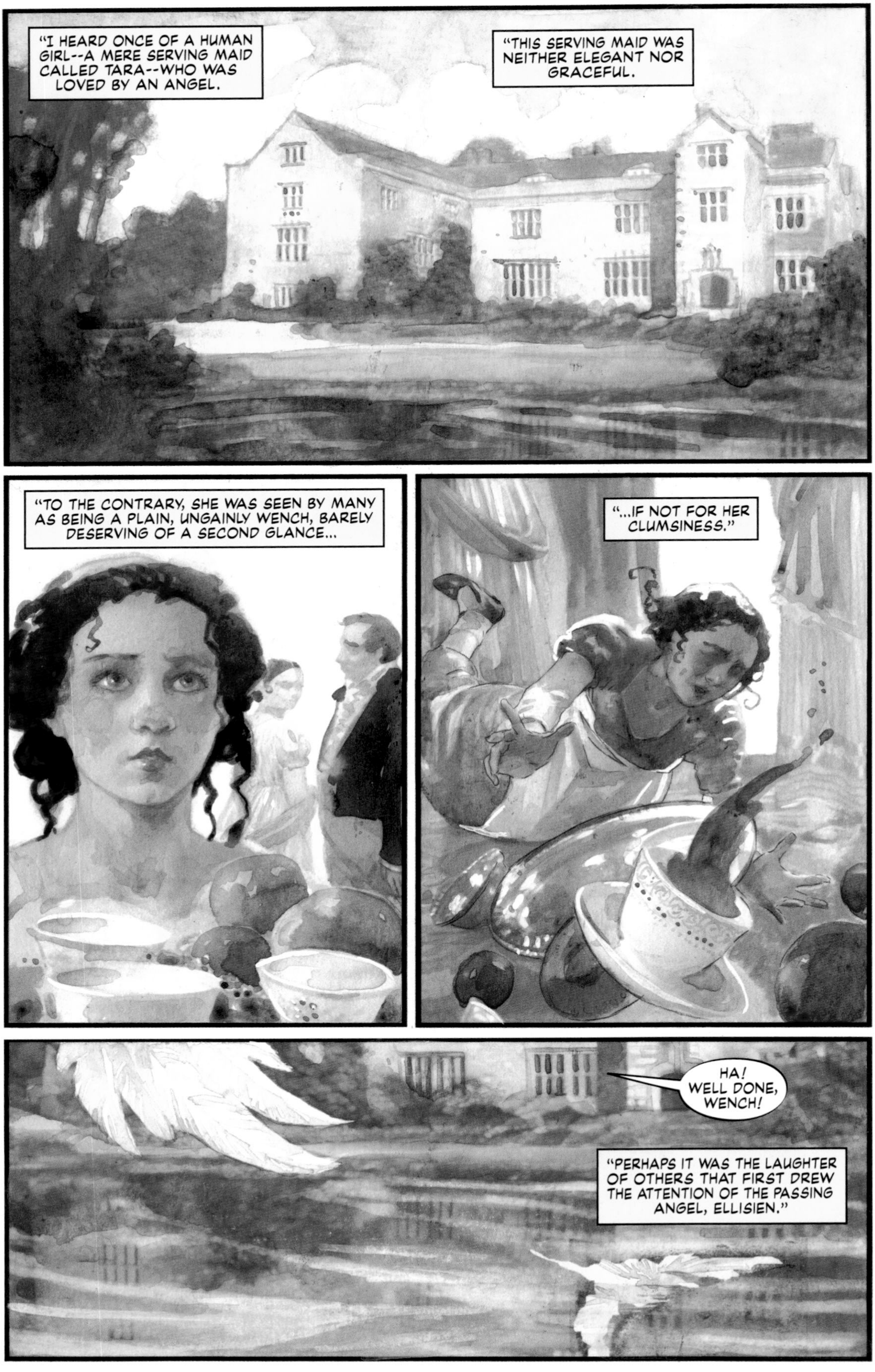
"I HEARD ONCE OF A HUMAN GIRL--A MERE SERVING MAID CALLED TARA--WHO WAS LOVED BY AN ANGEL.
"THIS SERVING MAID WAS NEITHER ELEGANT NOR GRACEFUL.
"TO THE CONTRARY, SHE WAS SEEN BY MANY AS BEING A PLAIN, UNGAINLY WENCH, BARELY DESERVING OF A SECOND GLANCE...
"...IF NOT FOR HER CLUMSINESS."
HA! WELL DONE, WENCH!
"PERHAPS IT WAS THE LAUGHTER OF OTHERS THAT FIRST DREW THE ATTENTION OF THE PASSING ANGEL, ELLISIEN."

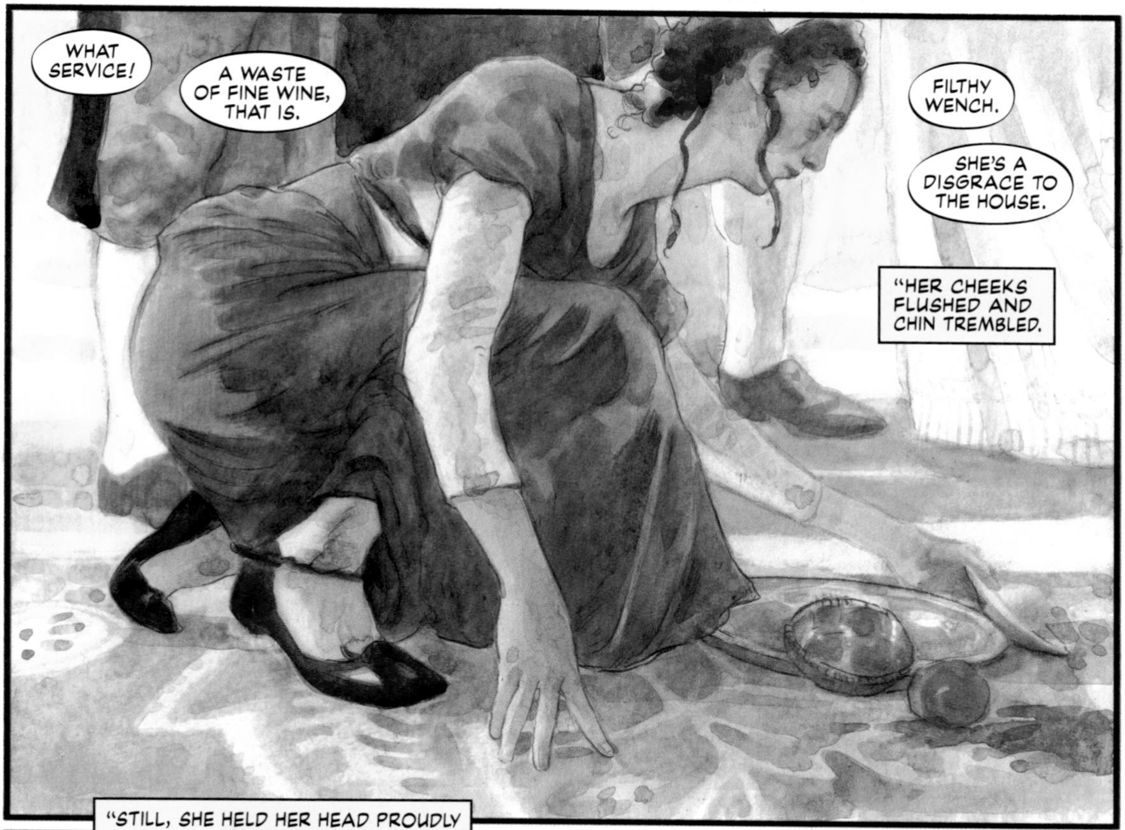
WHAT SERVICE!
A WASTE OF FINE WINE, THAT IS.
FILTHY WENCH.
SHE'S A DISGRACE TO THE HOUSE.
"HER CHEEKS FLUSHED AND CHIN TREMBLED.

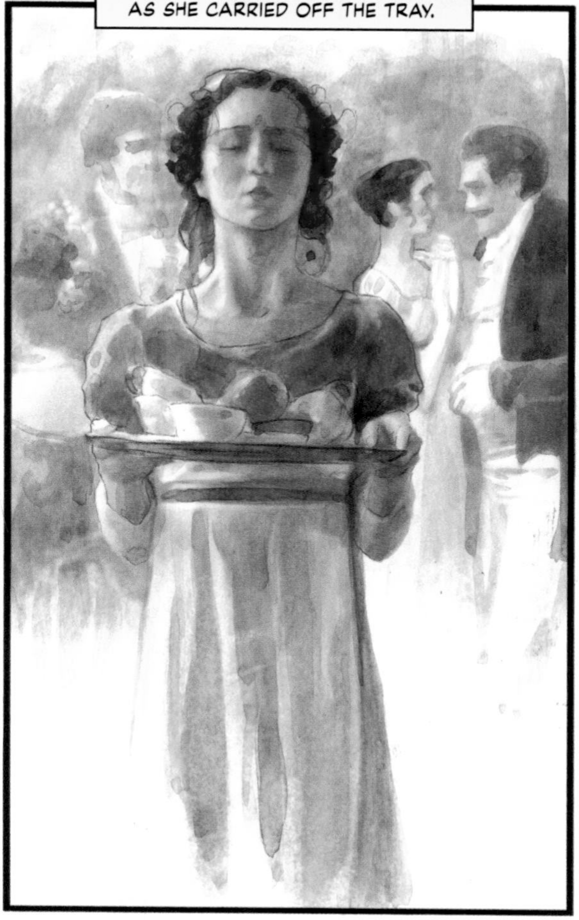
"STILL, SHE HELD HER HEAD PROUDLY AS SHE CARRIED OFF THE TRAY.

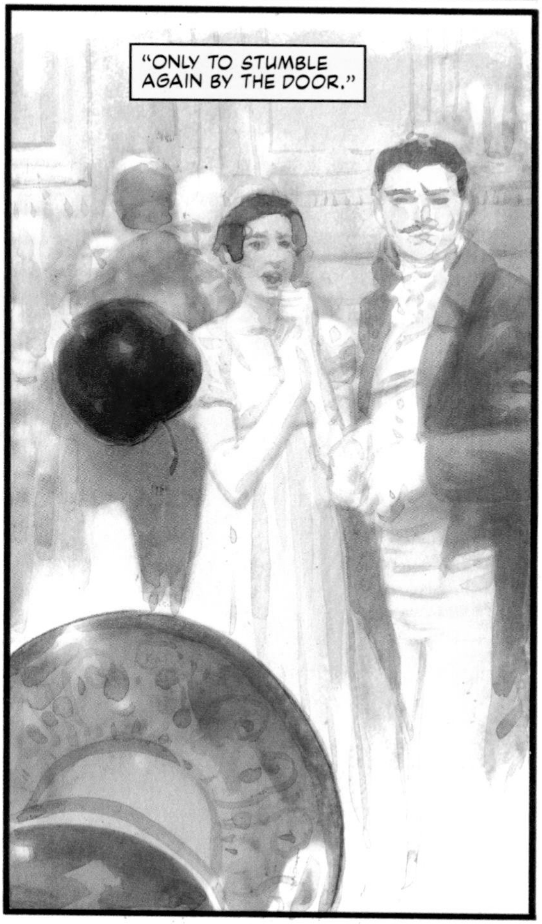
"ONLY TO STUMBLE AGAIN BY THE DOOR."

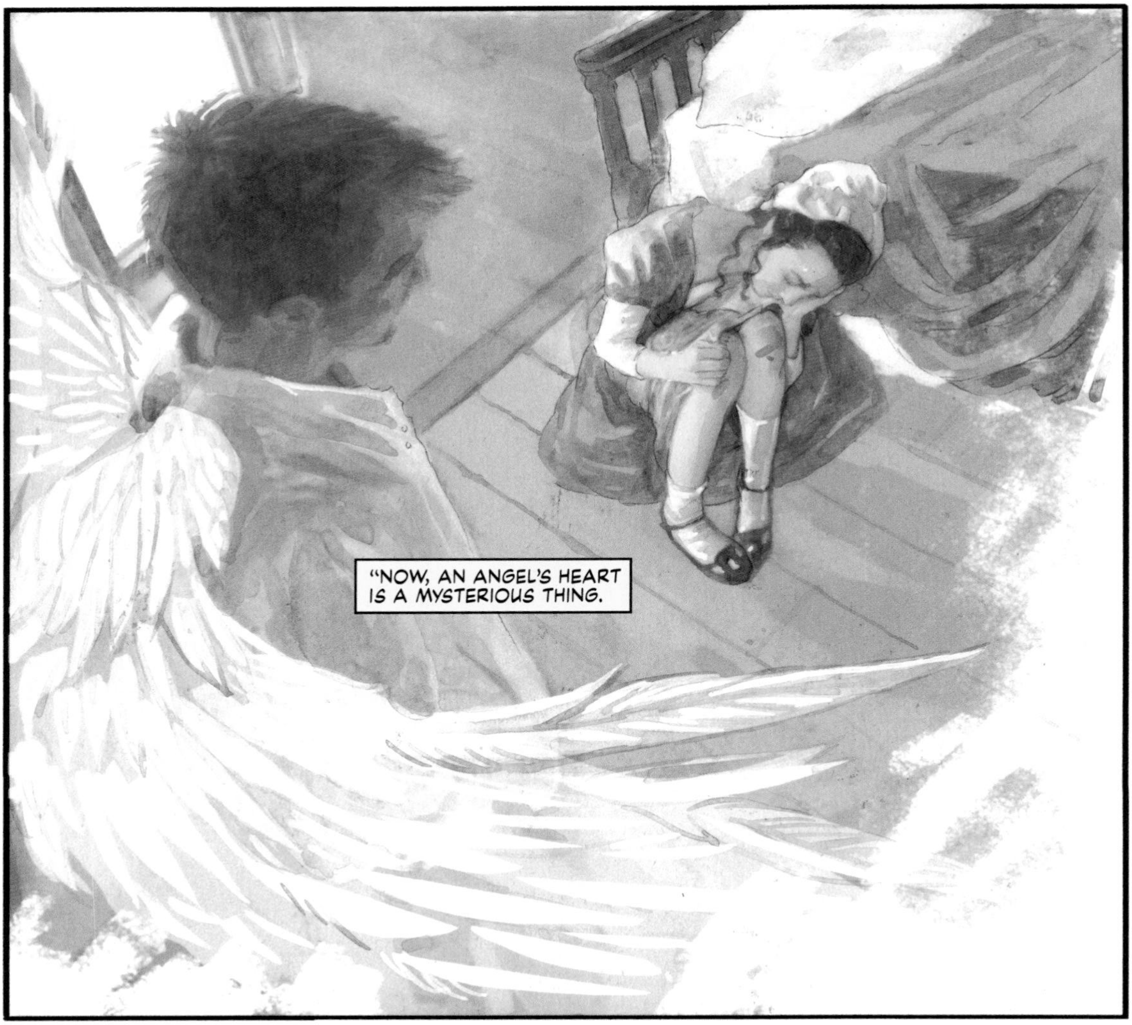
"NOW, AN ANGEL'S HEART
IS A MYSTERIOUS THING.

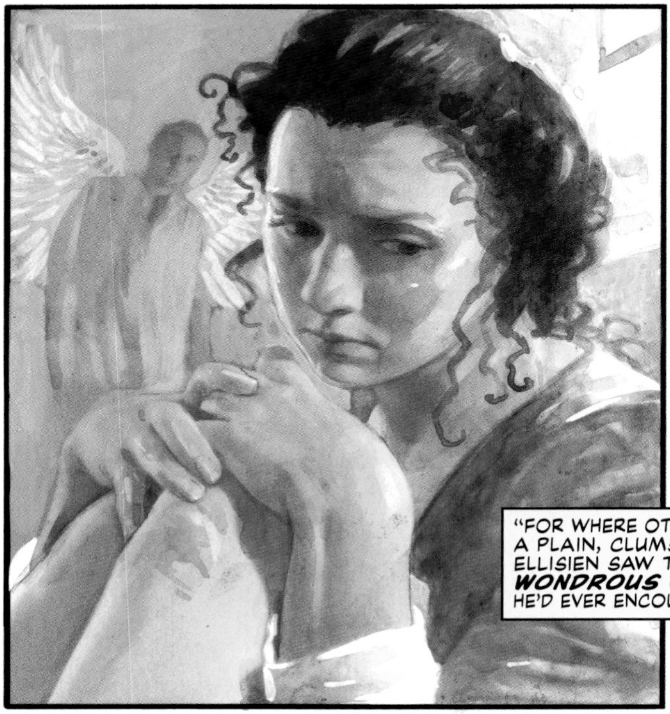

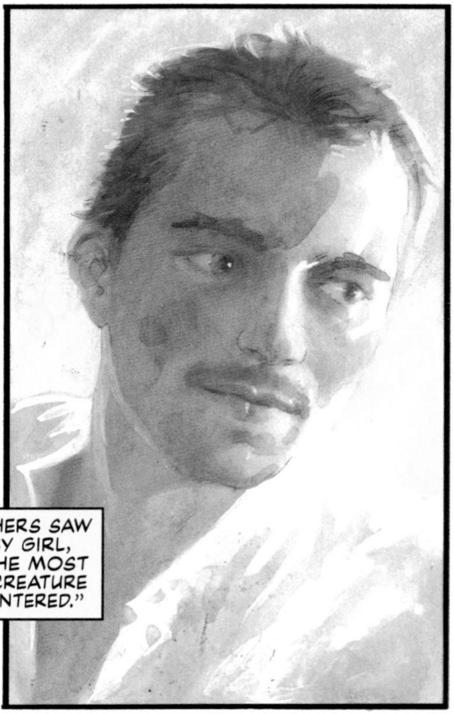
"FOR WHERE OTHERS SAW A PLAIN, CLUMSY GIRL, ELLISIEN SAW THE MOST WONDROUS CREATURE HE'D EVER ENCOUNTERED."

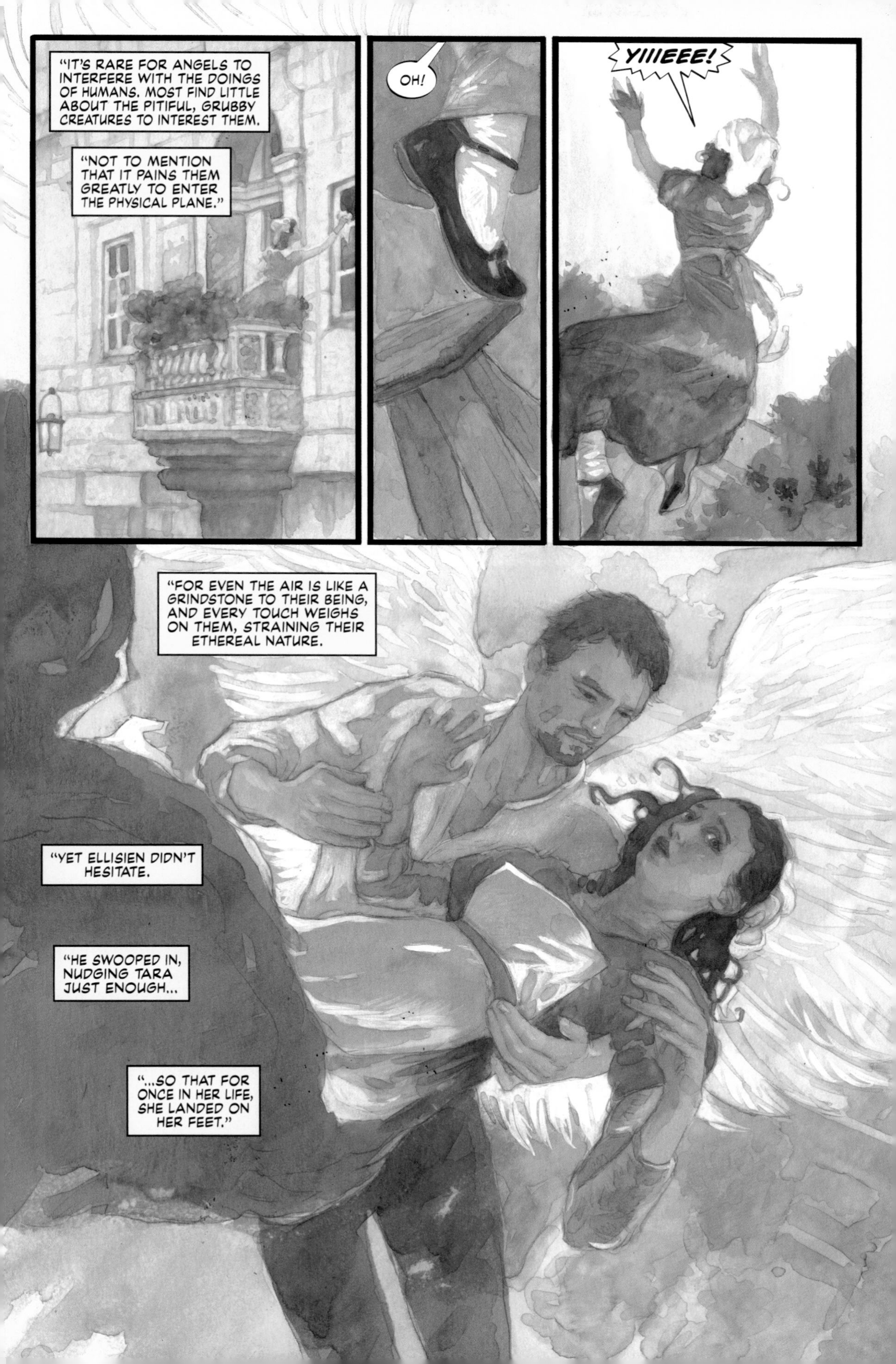
"IT'S RARE FOR ANGELS TO INTERFERE WITH THE DOINGS OF HUMANS. MOST FIND LITTLE ABOUT THE PITIFUL, GRUBBY CREATURES TO INTEREST THEM.
"NOT TO MENTION THAT IT PAINS THEM GREATLY TO ENTER THE PHYSICAL PLANE."
OH!
YIIIEEE!
"FOR EVEN THE AIR IS LIKE A GRINDSTONE TO THEIR BEING, AND EVERY TOUCH WEIGHS ON THEM, STRAINING THEIR ETHEREAL NATURE.
"YET ELLISIEN DIDN'T HESITATE.
"HE SWOOPED IN, NUDGING TARA JUST ENOUGH...
"...SO THAT FOR ONCE IN HER LIFE, SHE LANDED ON HER FEET."

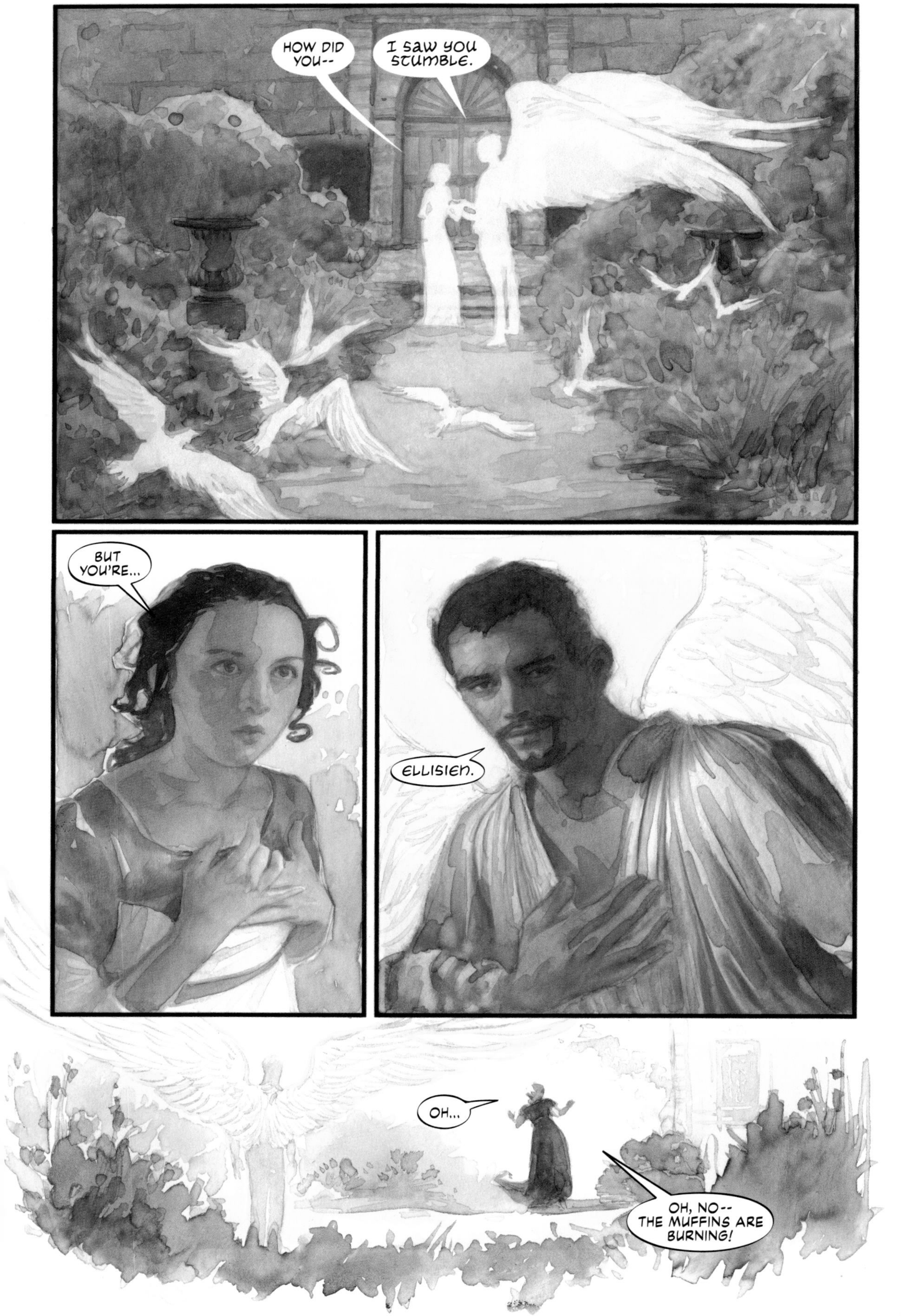
HOW DID YOU--
I SAW YOU STUMBLE.
BUT YOU'RE...
ELLISIEN.
OH...
OH, NO-- THE MUFFINS ARE BURNING!

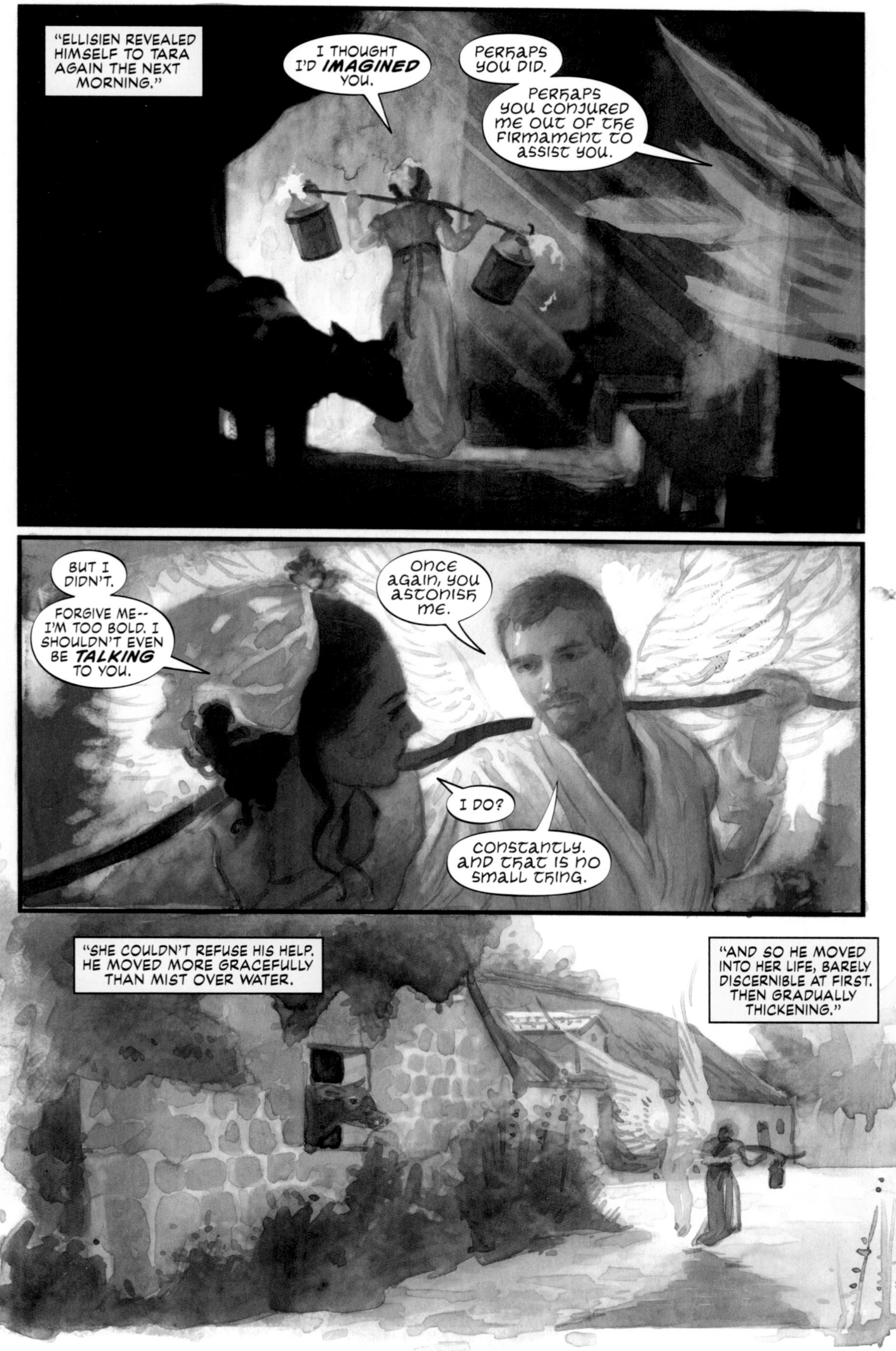
"ELLISIEN REVEALED HIMSELF TO TARA AGAIN THE NEXT MORNING."
I THOUGHT I'D IMAGINED YOU.
PERHAPS YOU DID.
PERHAPS YOU CONJURED ME OUT OF THE FIRMAMENT TO ASSIST YOU.
BUT I DIDN'T.
FORGIVE ME-- I'M TOO BOLD. I SHOULDN'T EVEN BE TALKING TO YOU.
ONCE AGAIN, YOU ASTONISH ME.
I DO?
CONSTANTLY. AND THAT IS NO SMALL THING.
"SHE COULDN'T REFUSE HIS HELP. HE MOVED MORE GRACEFULLY THAN MIST OVER WATER.
"AND SO HE MOVED INTO HER LIFE, BARELY DISCERNIBLE AT FIRST. THEN GRADUALLY THICKENING."

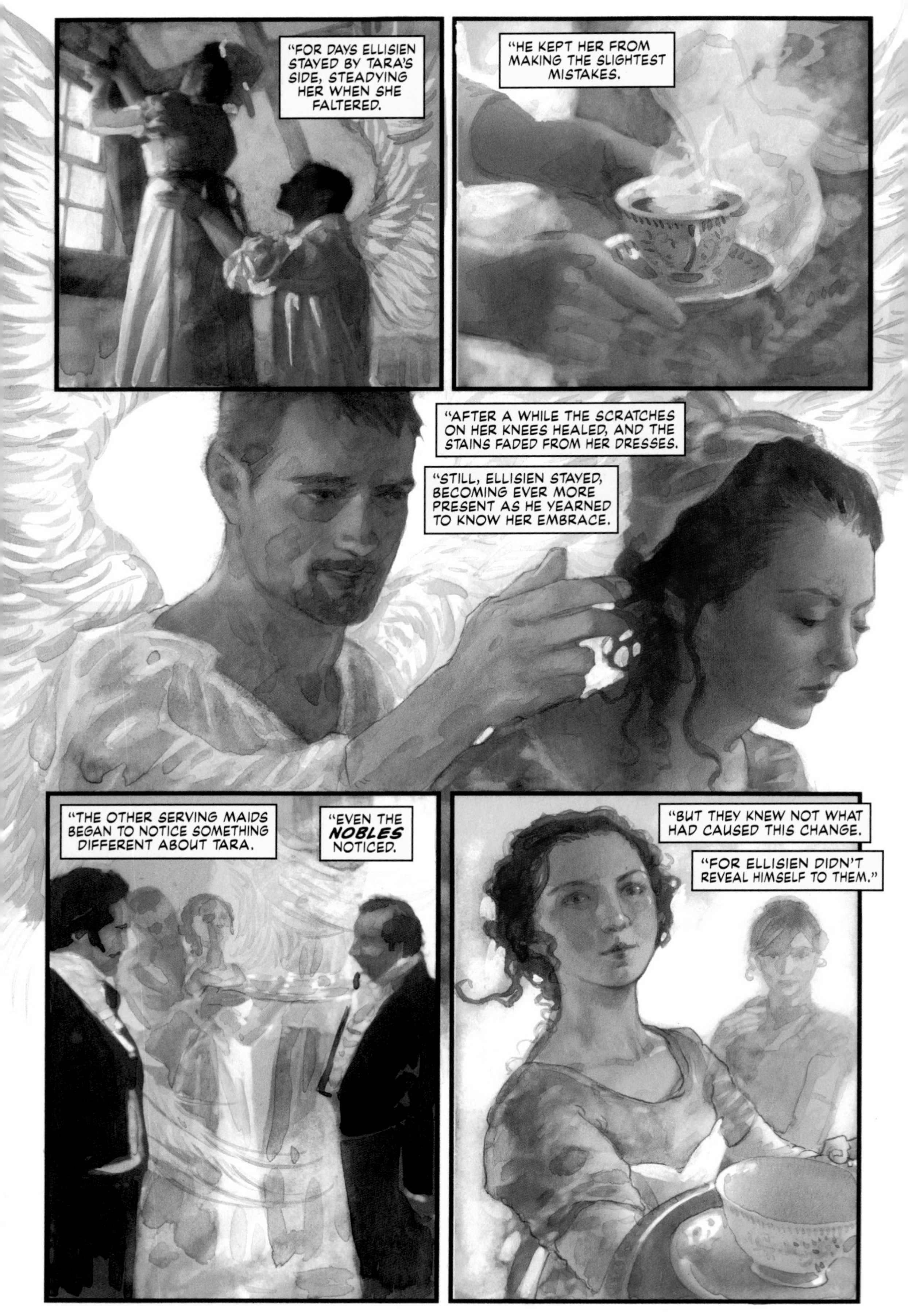
"FOR DAYS ELLISIEN STAYED BY TARA'S SIDE, STEADYING HER WHEN SHE FALTERED.
"HE KEPT HER FROM MAKING THE SLIGHTEST MISTAKES.
"AFTER A WHILE THE SCRATCHES ON HER KNEES HEALED, AND THE STAINS FADED FROM HER DRESSES.
"STILL, ELLISIEN STAYED, BECOMING EVER MORE PRESENT AS HE YEARNED TO KNOW HER EMBRACE.
"THE OTHER SERVING MAIDS BEGAN TO NOTICE SOMETHING DIFFERENT ABOUT TARA.
"EVEN THE ***NOBLES*** NOTICED.
"BUT THEY KNEW NOT WHAT HAD CAUSED THIS CHANGE.
"FOR ELLISIEN DIDN'T REVEAL HIMSELF TO THEM."

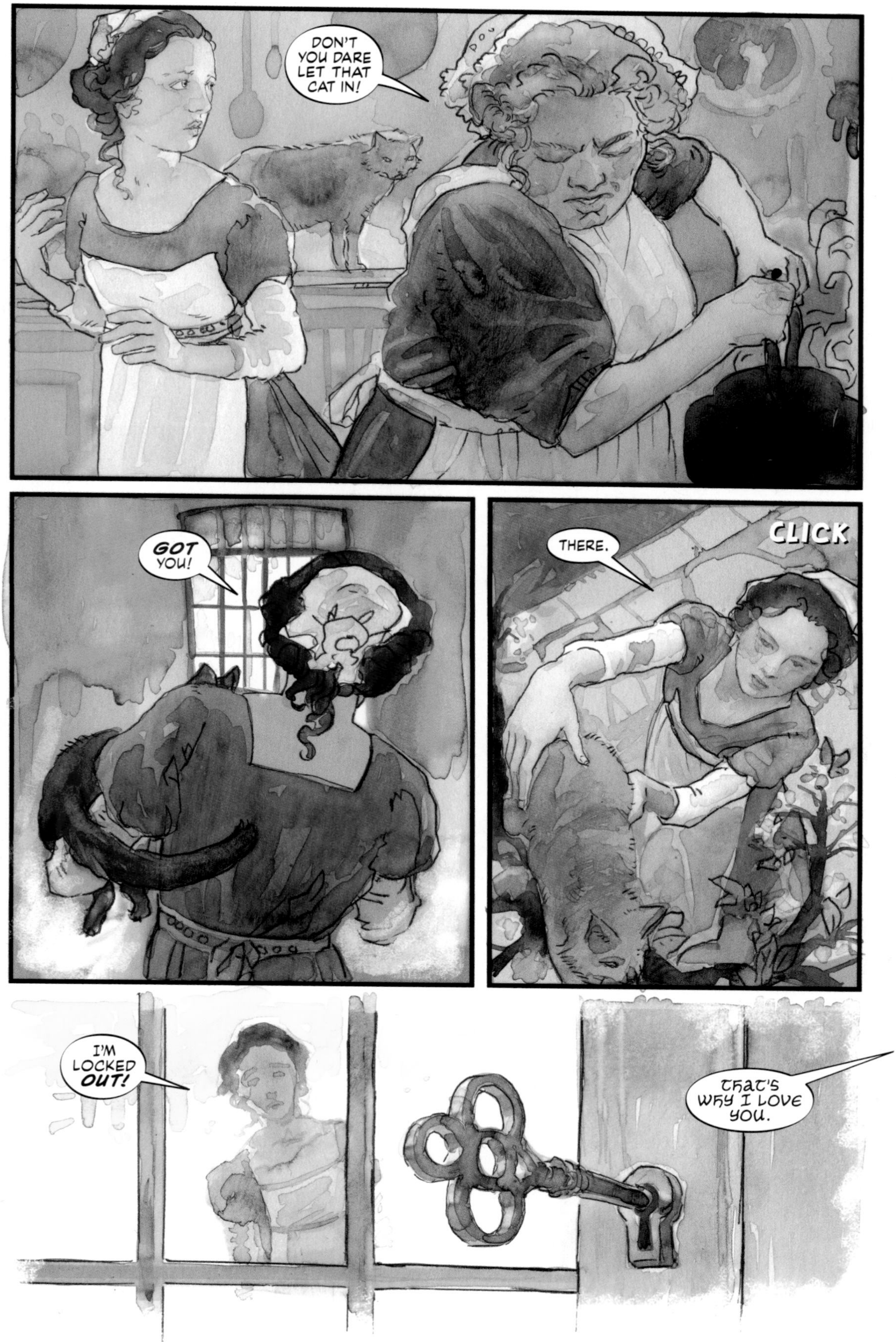
DON'T YOU DARE LET THAT CAT IN!
GOT YOU!
THERE.
CLICK
I'M LOCKED OUT!
THAT'S WHY I LOVE YOU.

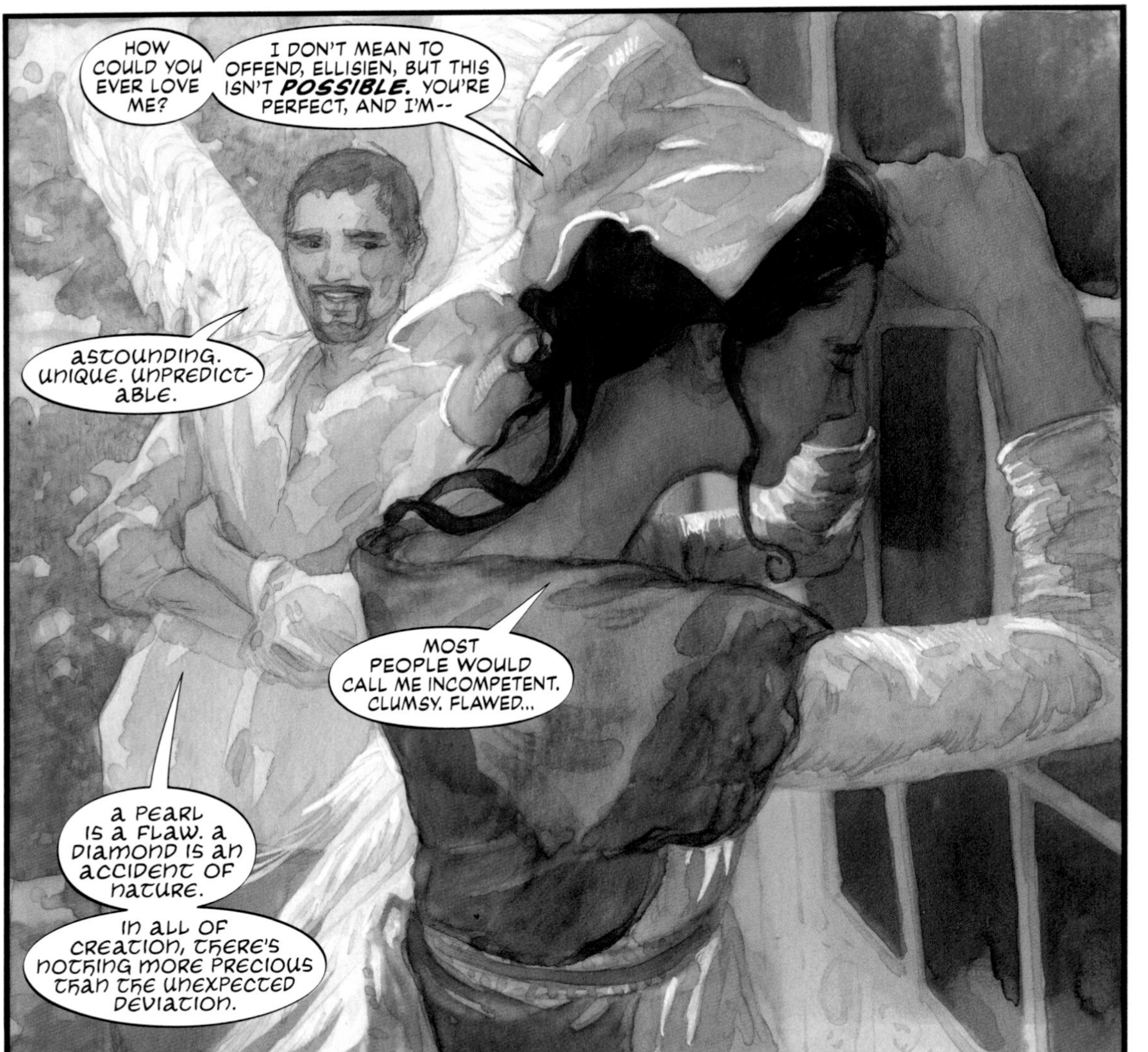
HOW COULD YOU EVER LOVE ME?
I DON'T MEAN TO OFFEND, ELLISIEN, BUT THIS ISN'T **POSSIBLE.** YOU'RE PERFECT, AND I'M--
ASTOUNDING. UNIQUE. UNPREDICTABLE.
MOST PEOPLE WOULD CALL ME INCOMPETENT. CLUMSY. FLAWED...
A PEARL IS A FLAW. A DIAMOND IS AN ACCIDENT OF NATURE.
IN ALL OF CREATION, THERE'S NOTHING MORE PRECIOUS THAN THE UNEXPECTED DEVIATION.

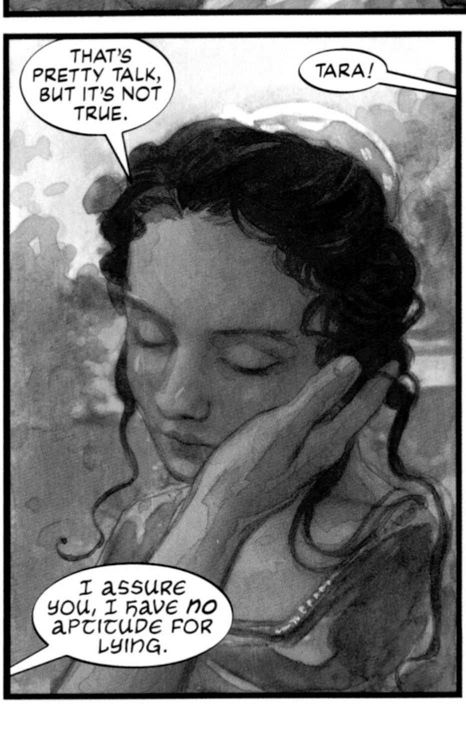
THAT'S PRETTY TALK, BUT IT'S NOT TRUE.
TARA!
I ASSURE YOU, I HAVE ***NO*** APTITUDE FOR LYING.

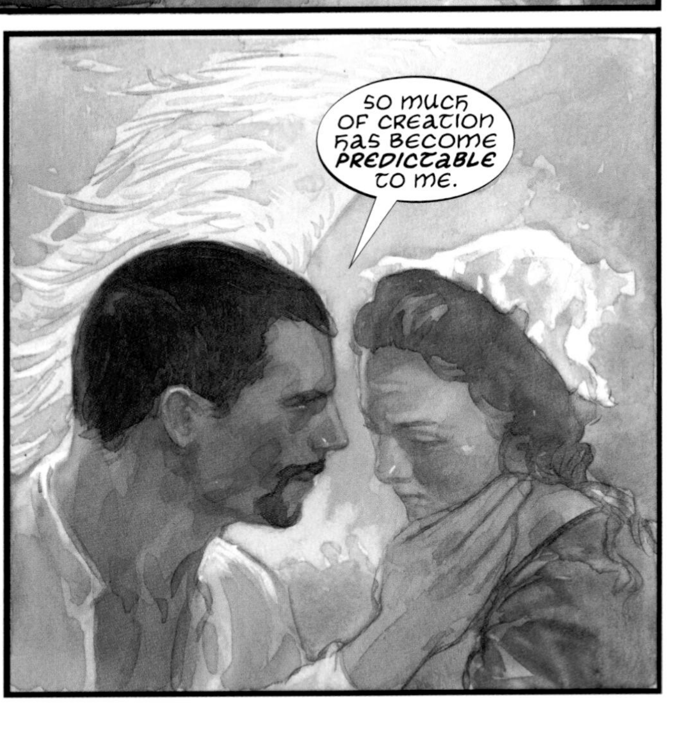
SO MUCH OF CREATION HAS BECOME ***PREDICTABLE*** TO ME.

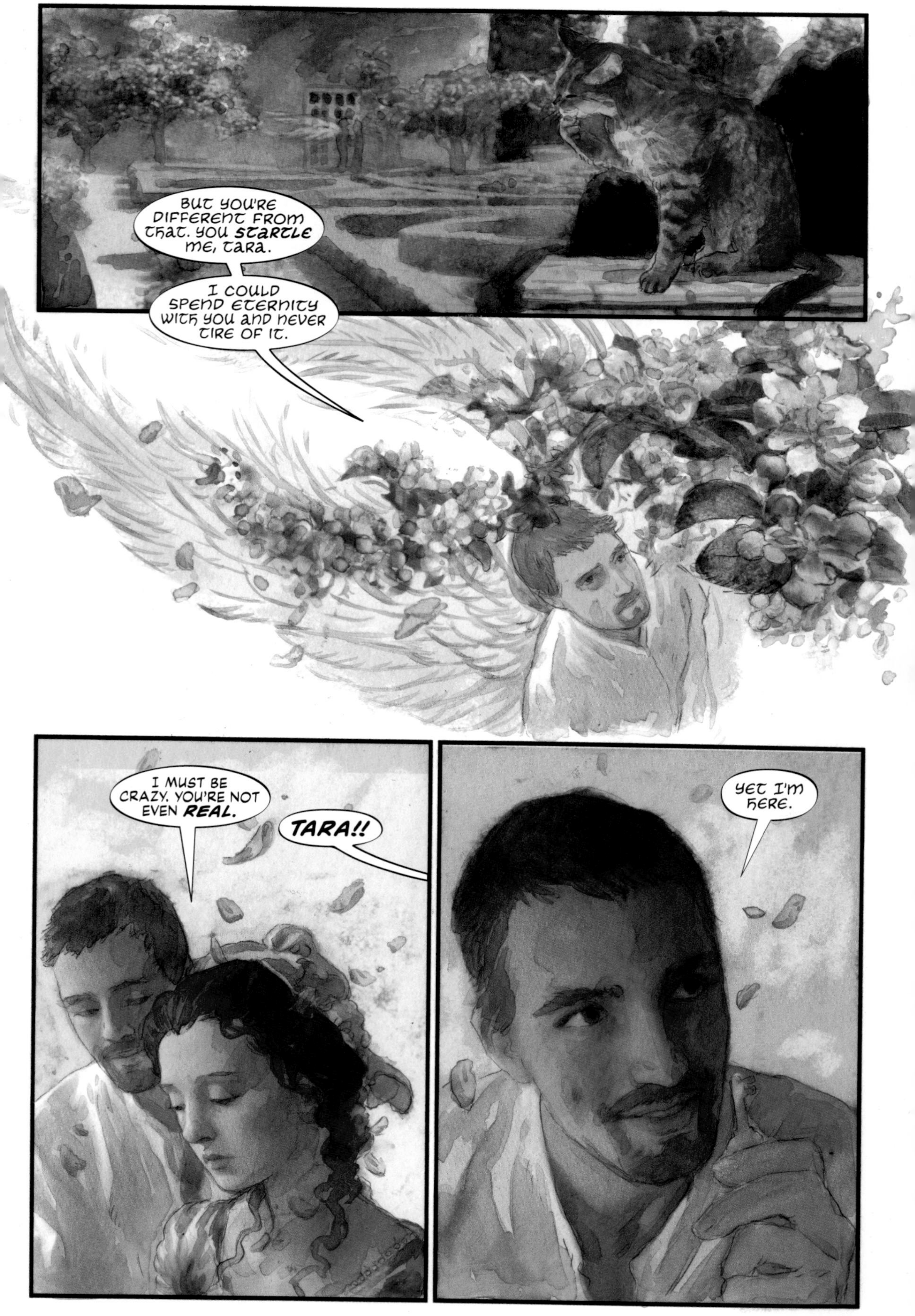
BUT YOU'RE DIFFERENT FROM THAT. YOU STARTLE ME, TARA.
I COULD SPEND ETERNITY WITH YOU AND NEVER TIRE OF IT.
I MUST BE CRAZY. YOU'RE NOT EVEN REAL.
TARA!!
YET I'M HERE.

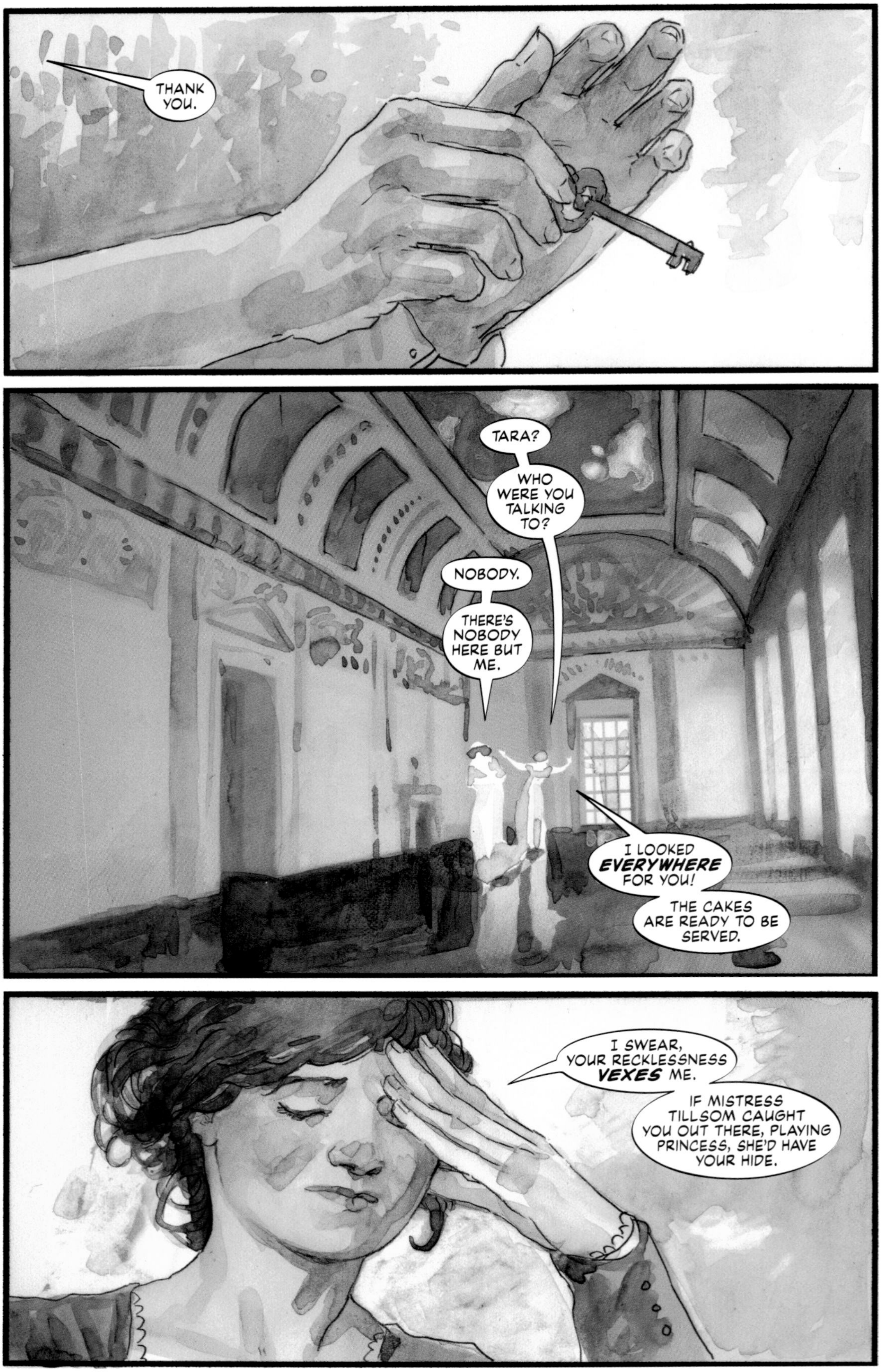
THANK YOU.
TARA?
WHO WERE YOU TALKING TO?
NOBODY.
THERE'S NOBODY HERE BUT ME.
I LOOKED EVERYWHERE FOR YOU!
THE CAKES ARE READY TO BE SERVED.
I SWEAR, YOUR RECKLESSNESS VEXES ME.
IF MISTRESS TILLSOM CAUGHT YOU OUT THERE, PLAYING PRINCESS, SHE'D HAVE YOUR HIDE.

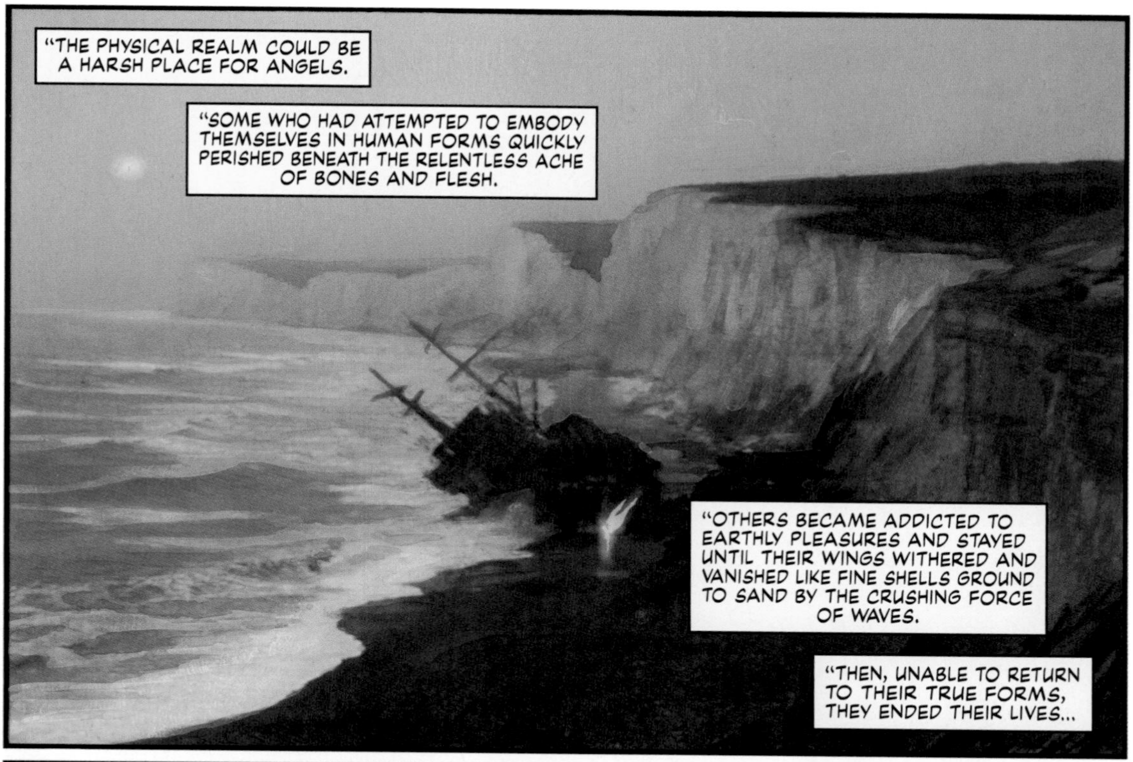
"THE PHYSICAL REALM COULD BE A HARSH PLACE FOR ANGELS.
"SOME WHO HAD ATTEMPTED TO EMBODY THEMSELVES IN HUMAN FORMS QUICKLY PERISHED BENEATH THE RELENTLESS ACHE OF BONES AND FLESH.
"OTHERS BECAME ADDICTED TO EARTHLY PLEASURES AND STAYED UNTIL THEIR WINGS WITHERED AND VANISHED LIKE FINE SHELLS GROUND TO SAND BY THE CRUSHING FORCE OF WAVES.
"THEN, UNABLE TO RETURN TO THEIR TRUE FORMS, THEY ENDED THEIR LIVES...

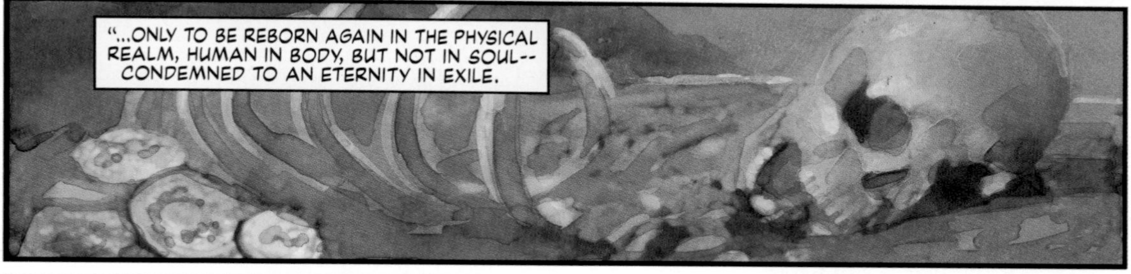
"...ONLY TO BE REBORN AGAIN IN THE PHYSICAL REALM, HUMAN IN BODY, BUT NOT IN SOUL--CONDEMNED TO AN ETERNITY IN EXILE.

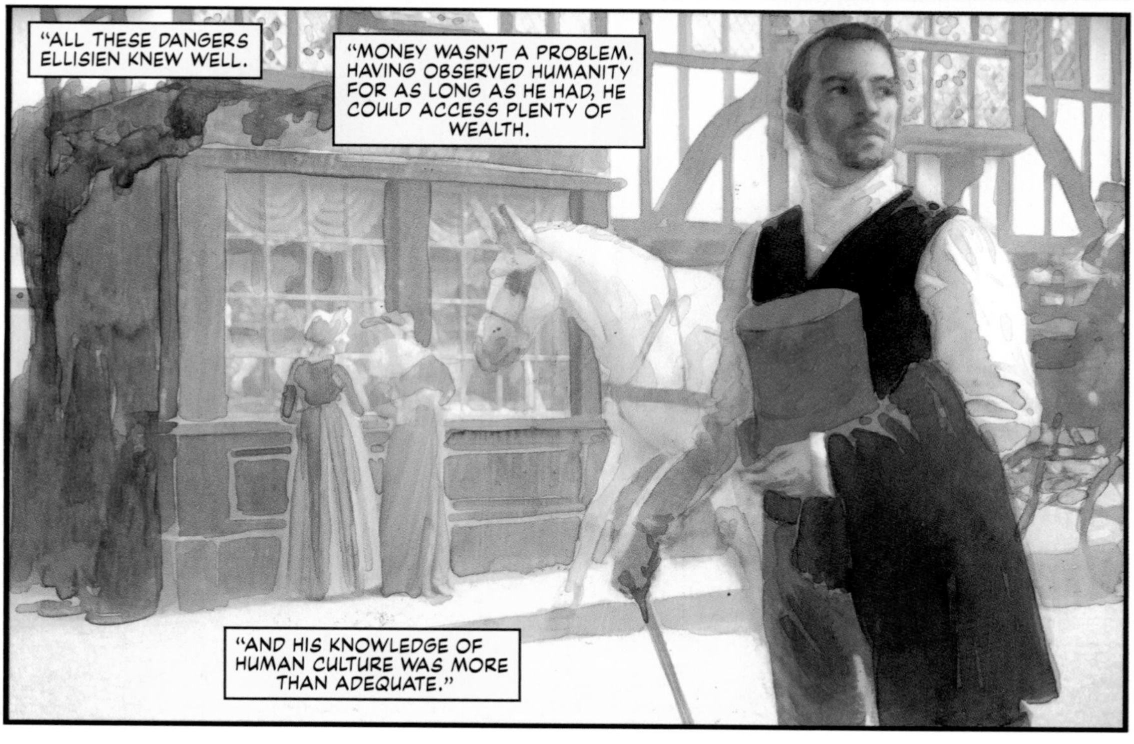
"ALL THESE DANGERS ELLISIEN KNEW WELL.
"MONEY WASN'T A PROBLEM. HAVING OBSERVED HUMANITY FOR AS LONG AS HE HAD, HE COULD ACCESS PLENTY OF WEALTH.
"AND HIS KNOWLEDGE OF HUMAN CULTURE WAS MORE THAN ADEQUATE."

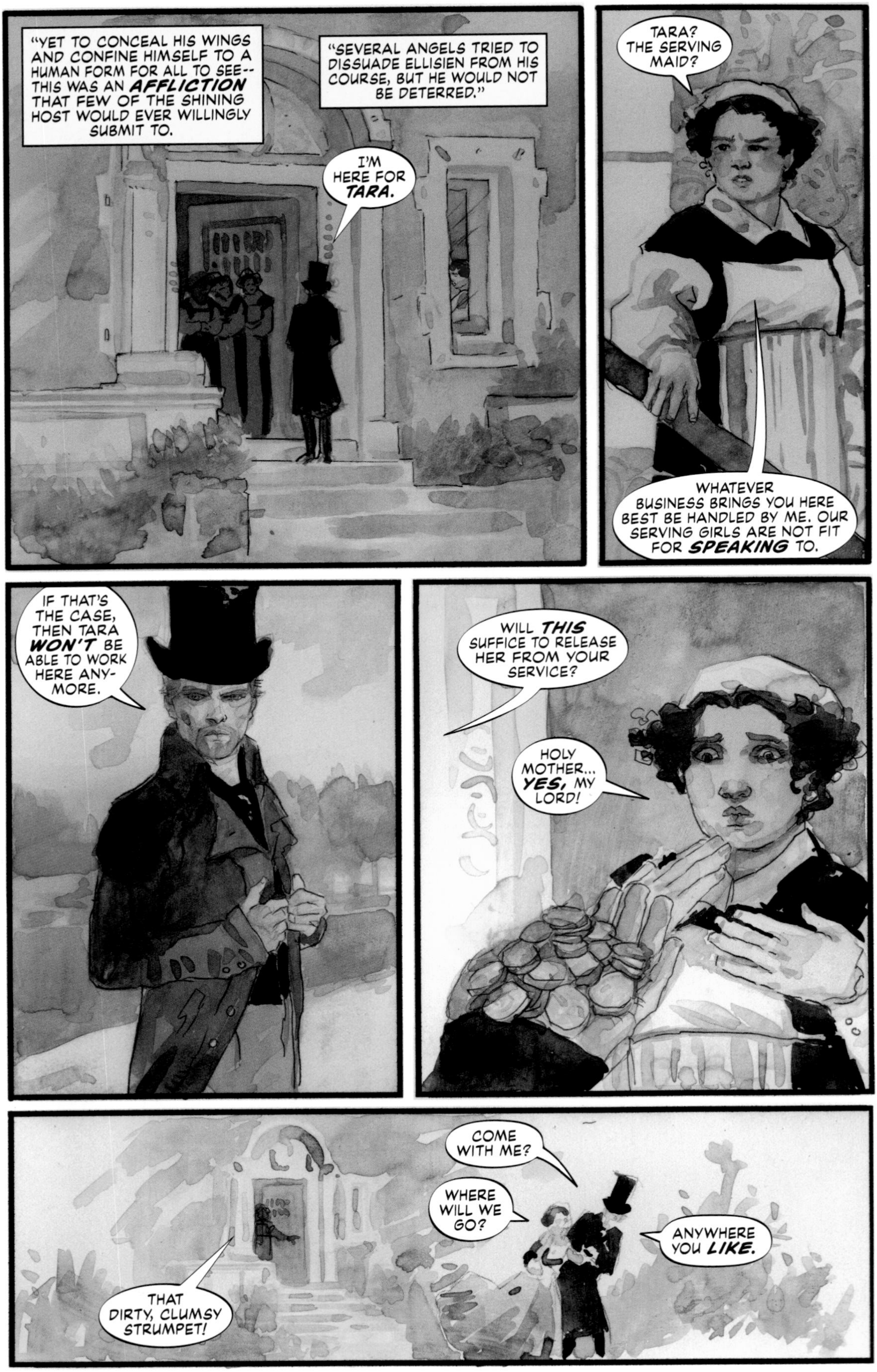
"YET TO CONCEAL HIS WINGS AND CONFINE HIMSELF TO A HUMAN FORM FOR ALL TO SEE-- THIS WAS AN AFFLICTION THAT FEW OF THE SHINING HOST WOULD EVER WILLINGLY SUBMIT TO.
"SEVERAL ANGELS TRIED TO DISSUADE ELLISIEN FROM HIS COURSE, BUT HE WOULD NOT BE DETERRED."
I'M HERE FOR TARA.
TARA? THE SERVING MAID?
WHATEVER BUSINESS BRINGS YOU HERE BEST BE HANDLED BY ME. OUR SERVING GIRLS ARE NOT FIT FOR SPEAKING TO.
IF THAT'S THE CASE, THEN TARA WON'T BE ABLE TO WORK HERE ANYMORE.
WILL THIS SUFFICE TO RELEASE HER FROM YOUR SERVICE?
HOLY MOTHER... YES, MY LORD!
COME WITH ME?
WHERE WILL WE GO?
ANYWHERE YOU LIKE.
THAT DIRTY, CLUMSY STRUMPET!

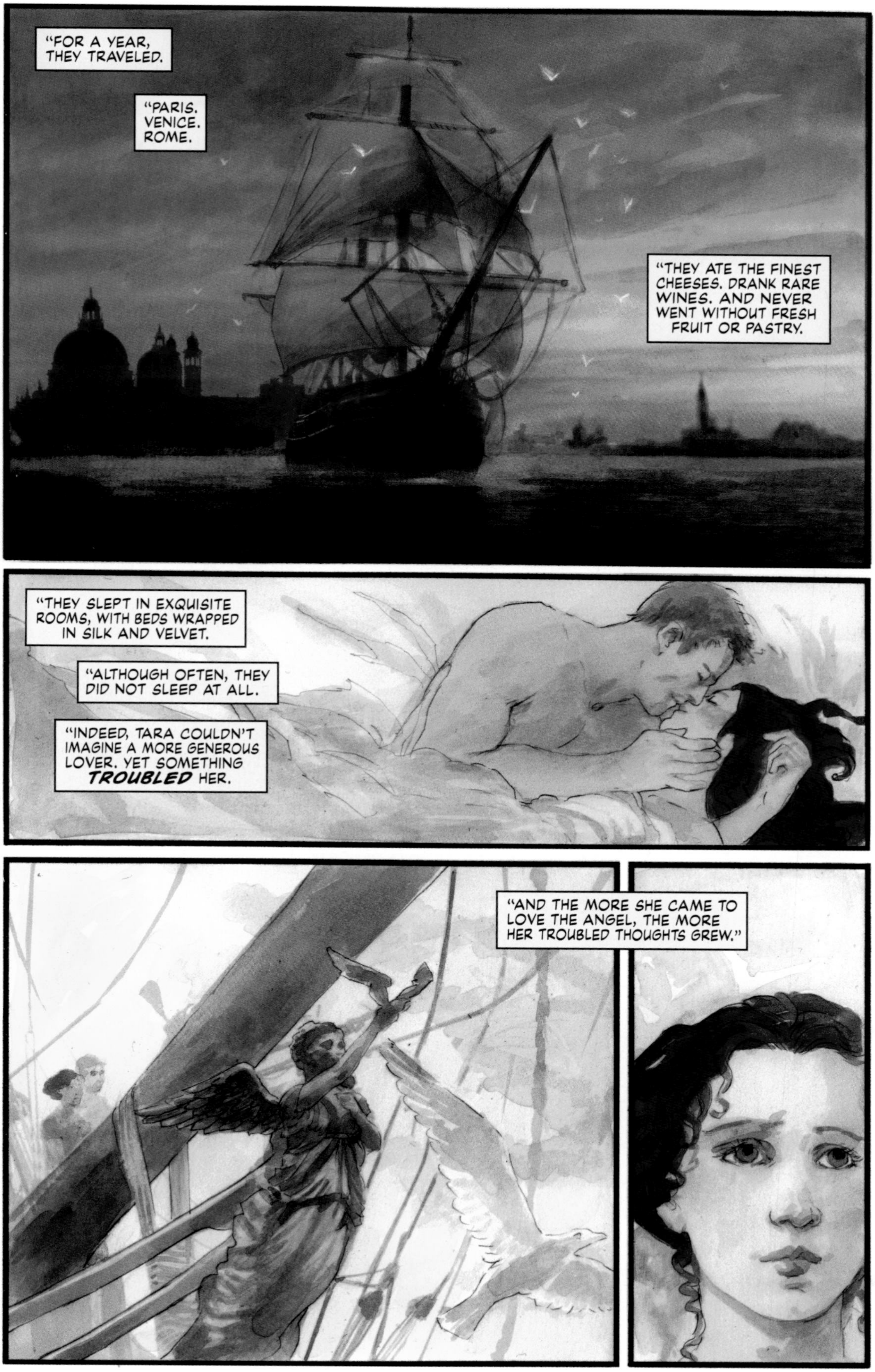
"FOR A YEAR, THEY TRAVELED.
"PARIS. VENICE. ROME.
"THEY ATE THE FINEST CHEESES. DRANK RARE WINES. AND NEVER WENT WITHOUT FRESH FRUIT OR PASTRY.
"THEY SLEPT IN EXQUISITE ROOMS, WITH BEDS WRAPPED IN SILK AND VELVET.
"ALTHOUGH OFTEN, THEY DID NOT SLEEP AT ALL.
"INDEED, TARA COULDN'T IMAGINE A MORE GENEROUS LOVER. YET SOMETHING ***TROUBLED*** HER.
"AND THE MORE SHE CAME TO LOVE THE ANGEL, THE MORE HER TROUBLED THOUGHTS GREW."

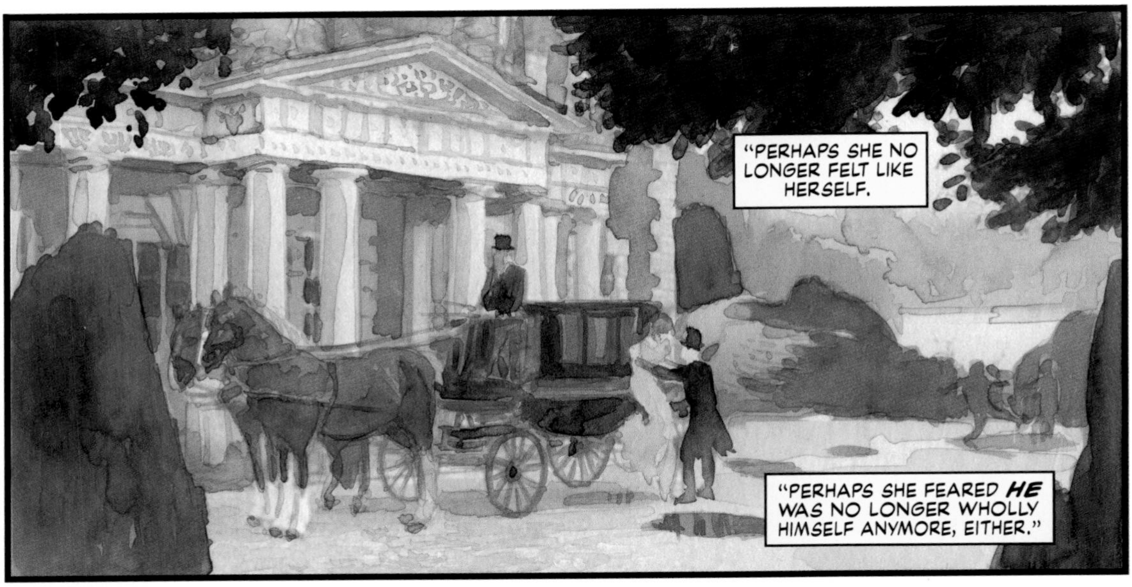
"PERHAPS SHE NO LONGER FELT LIKE HERSELF.
"PERHAPS SHE FEARED HE WAS NO LONGER WHOLLY HIMSELF ANYMORE, EITHER."

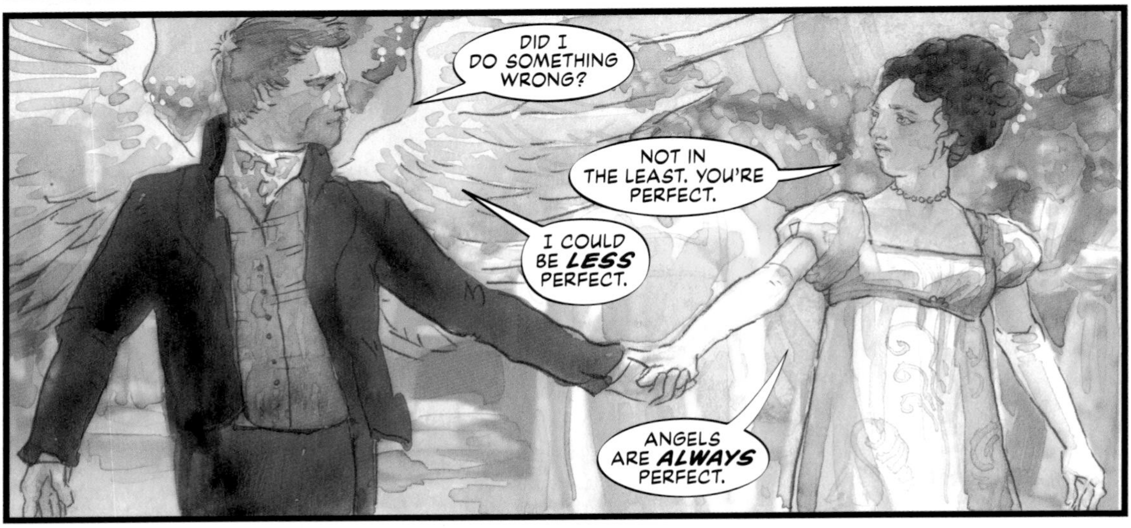
DID I DO SOMETHING WRONG?
NOT IN THE LEAST. YOU'RE PERFECT.
I COULD BE LESS PERFECT.
ANGELS ARE ALWAYS PERFECT.

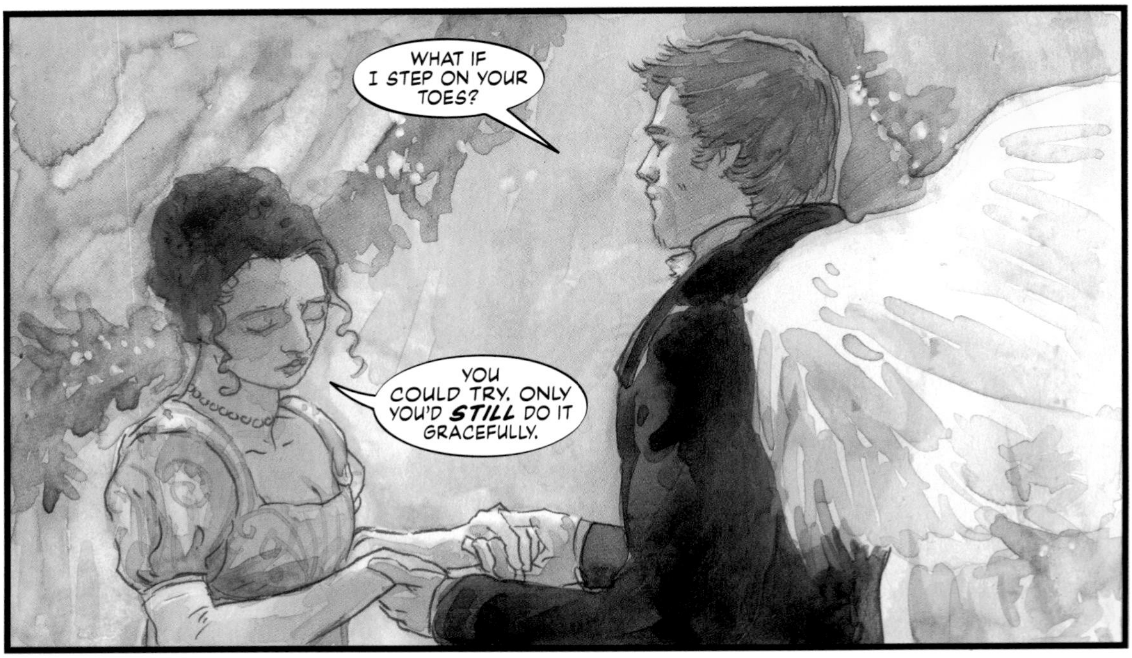
WHAT IF I STEP ON YOUR TOES?
YOU COULD TRY. ONLY YOU'D STILL DO IT GRACEFULLY.

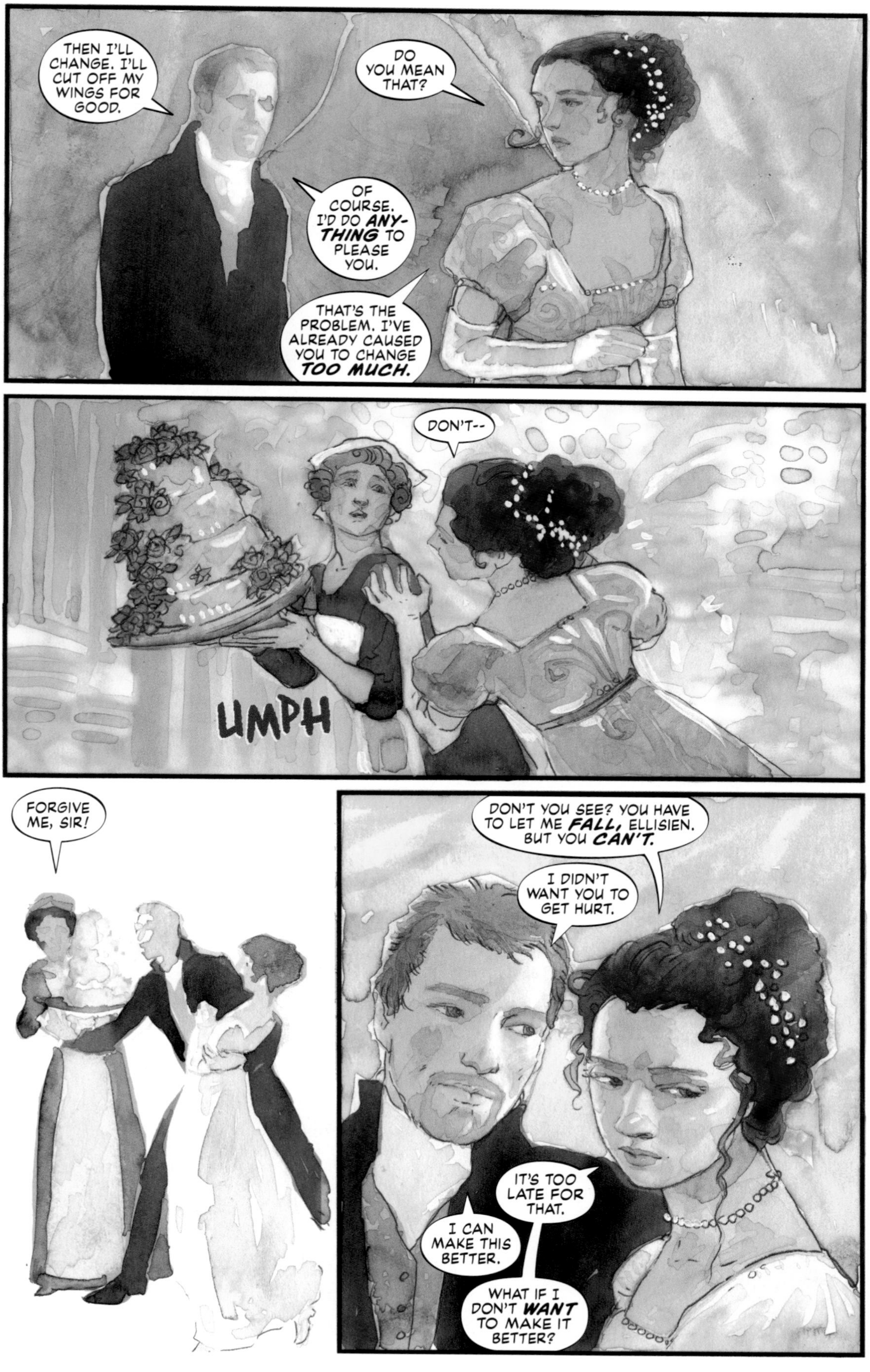
THEN I'LL CHANGE. I'LL CUT OFF MY WINGS FOR GOOD.
DO YOU MEAN THAT?
OF COURSE. I'D DO ANYTHING TO PLEASE YOU.
THAT'S THE PROBLEM. I'VE ALREADY CAUSED YOU TO CHANGE TOO MUCH.
DON'T--
UMPH
FORGIVE ME, SIR!
DON'T YOU SEE? YOU HAVE TO LET ME FALL, ELLISIEN. BUT YOU CAN'T.
I DIDN'T WANT YOU TO GET HURT.
IT'S TOO LATE FOR THAT.
I CAN MAKE THIS BETTER.
WHAT IF I DON'T WANT TO MAKE IT BETTER?

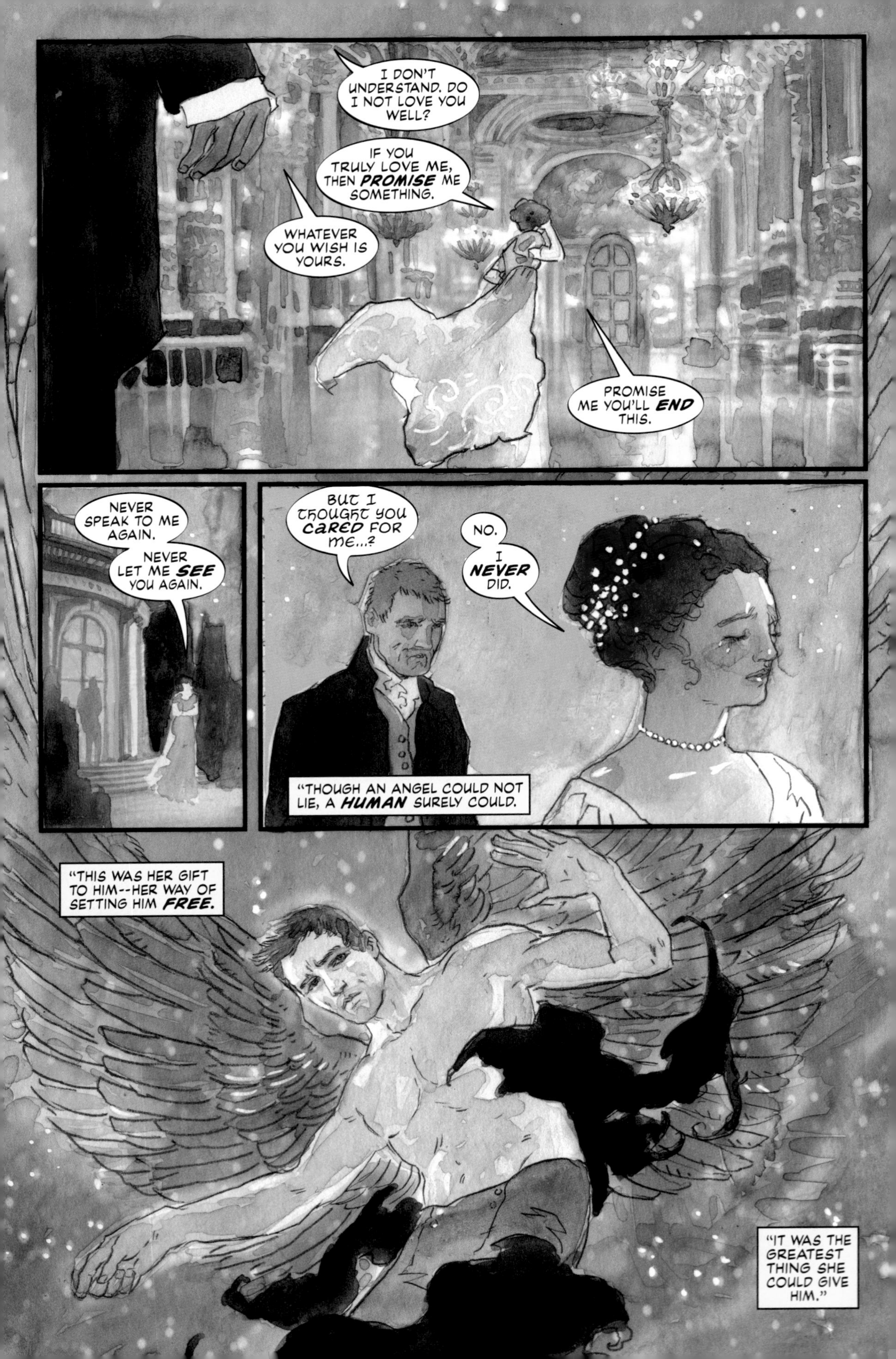
I DON'T UNDERSTAND. DO I NOT LOVE YOU WELL?
IF YOU TRULY LOVE ME, THEN PROMISE ME SOMETHING.
WHATEVER YOU WISH IS YOURS.
PROMISE ME YOU'LL END THIS.
NEVER SPEAK TO ME AGAIN.
NEVER LET ME SEE YOU AGAIN.
BUT I THOUGHT YOU CARED FOR ME...?
NO.
I NEVER DID.
"THOUGH AN ANGEL COULD NOT LIE, A HUMAN SURELY COULD.
"THIS WAS HER GIFT TO HIM--HER WAY OF SETTING HIM FREE.
"IT WAS THE GREATEST THING SHE COULD GIVE HIM."

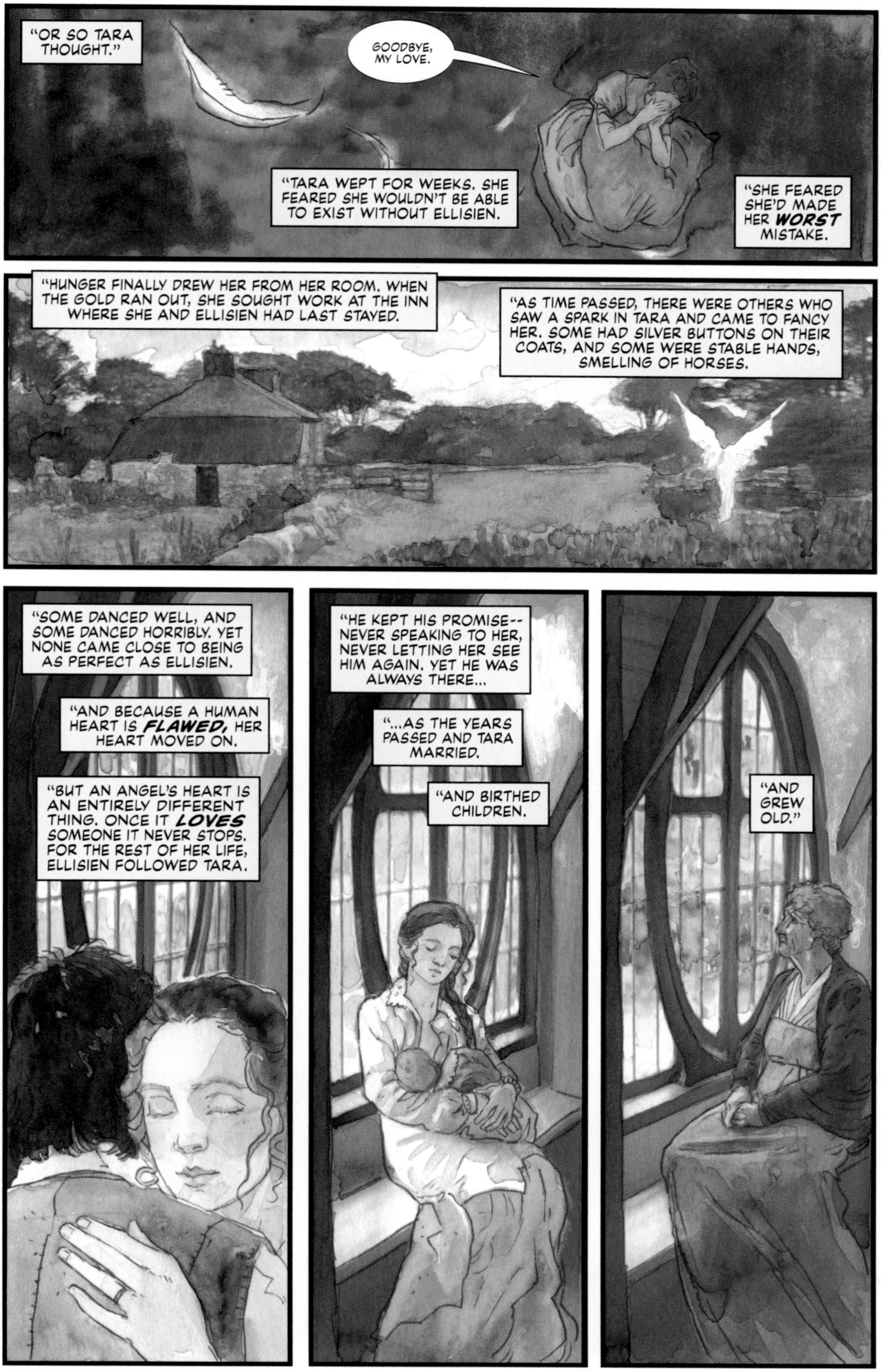
"OR SO TARA THOUGHT."
GOODBYE, MY LOVE.
"TARA WEPT FOR WEEKS. SHE FEARED SHE WOULDN'T BE ABLE TO EXIST WITHOUT ELLISIEN.
"SHE FEARED SHE'D MADE HER WORST MISTAKE.
"HUNGER FINALLY DREW HER FROM HER ROOM. WHEN THE GOLD RAN OUT, SHE SOUGHT WORK AT THE INN WHERE SHE AND ELLISIEN HAD LAST STAYED.
"AS TIME PASSED, THERE WERE OTHERS WHO SAW A SPARK IN TARA AND CAME TO FANCY HER. SOME HAD SILVER BUTTONS ON THEIR COATS, AND SOME WERE STABLE HANDS, SMELLING OF HORSES.
"SOME DANCED WELL, AND SOME DANCED HORRIBLY. YET NONE CAME CLOSE TO BEING AS PERFECT AS ELLISIEN.
"AND BECAUSE A HUMAN HEART IS FLAWED, HER HEART MOVED ON.
"BUT AN ANGEL'S HEART IS AN ENTIRELY DIFFERENT THING. ONCE IT LOVES SOMEONE IT NEVER STOPS. FOR THE REST OF HER LIFE, ELLISIEN FOLLOWED TARA.
"HE KEPT HIS PROMISE--NEVER SPEAKING TO HER, NEVER LETTING HER SEE HIM AGAIN. YET HE WAS ALWAYS THERE...
"...AS THE YEARS PASSED AND TARA MARRIED.
"AND BIRTHED CHILDREN.
"AND GREW OLD."

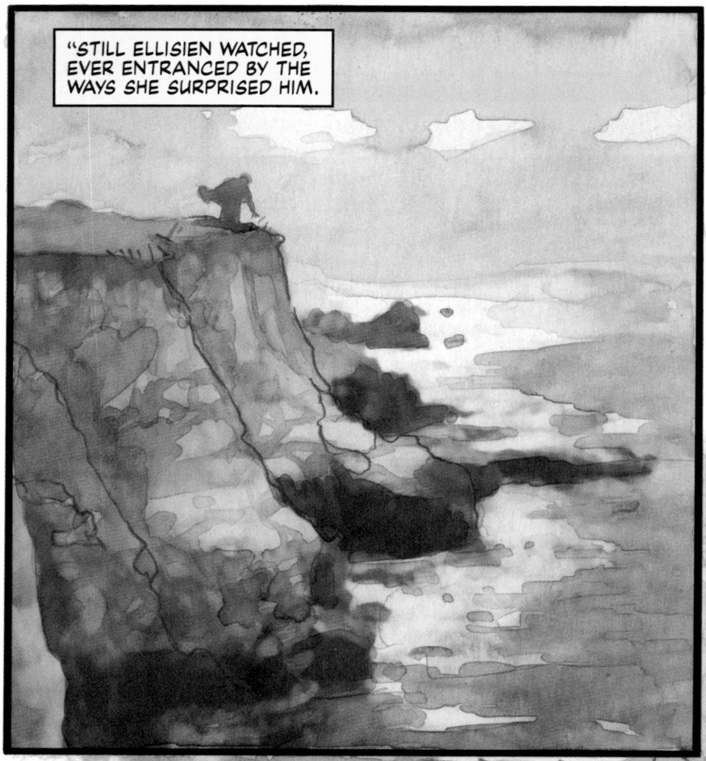
"STILL ELLISIEN WATCHED, EVER ENTRANCED BY THE WAYS SHE SURPRISED HIM.

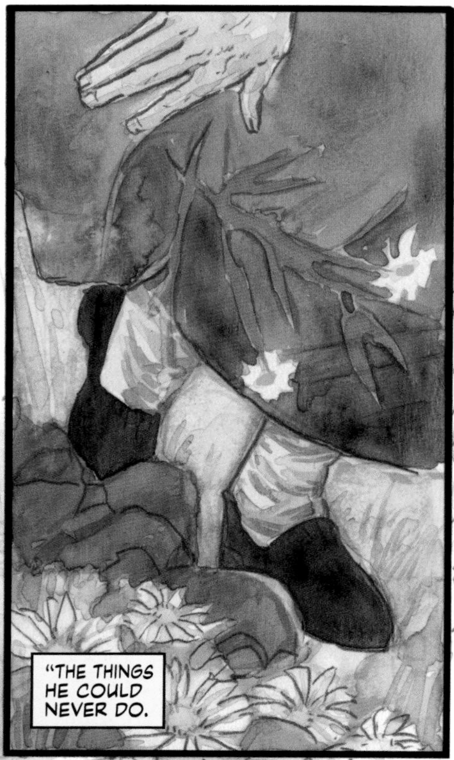
"THE THINGS HE COULD NEVER DO.

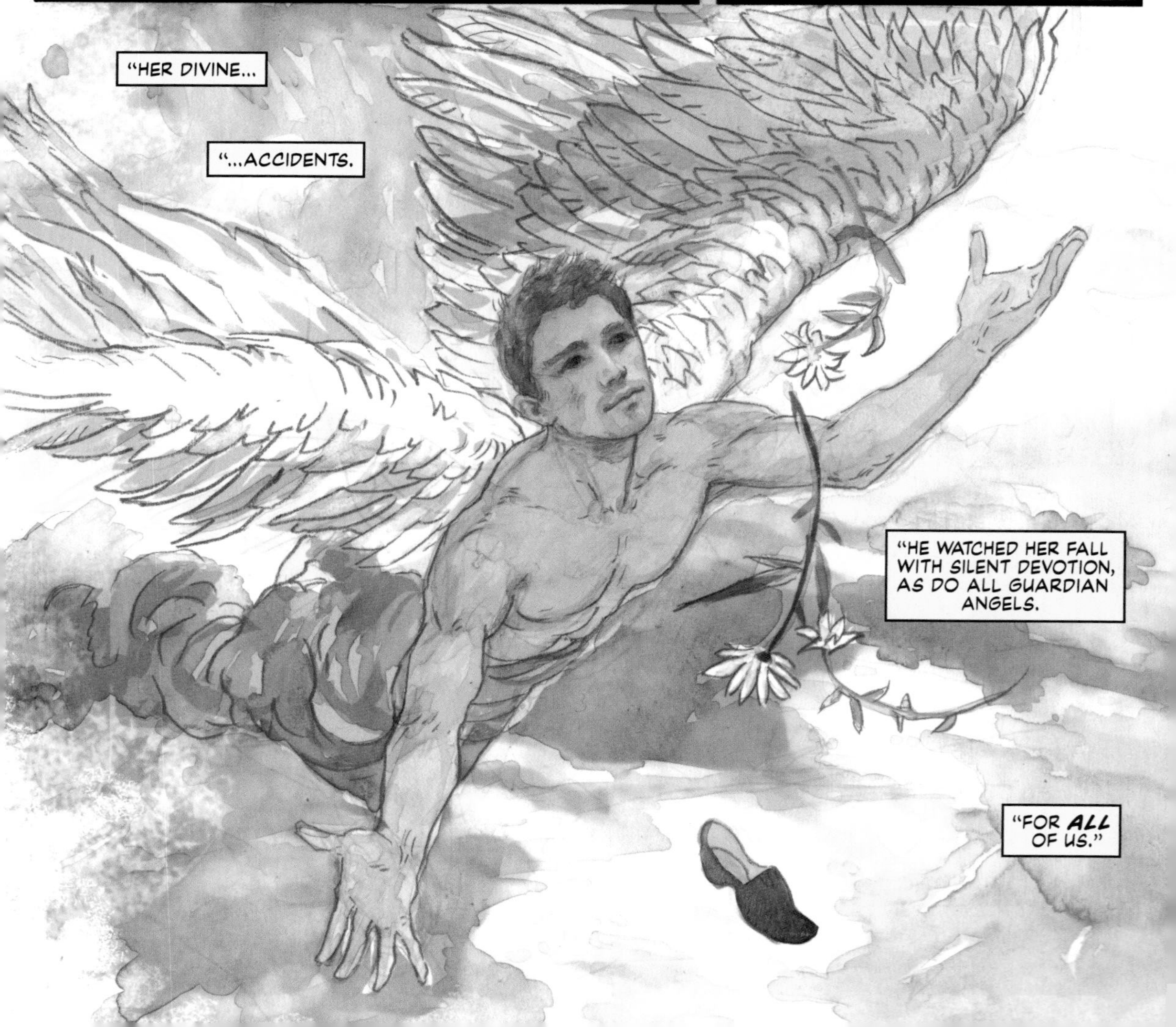
"HER DIVINE...
"...ACCIDENTS.
"HE WATCHED HER FALL WITH SILENT DEVOTION, AS DO ALL GUARDIAN ANGELS.
"FOR ***ALL*** OF US."

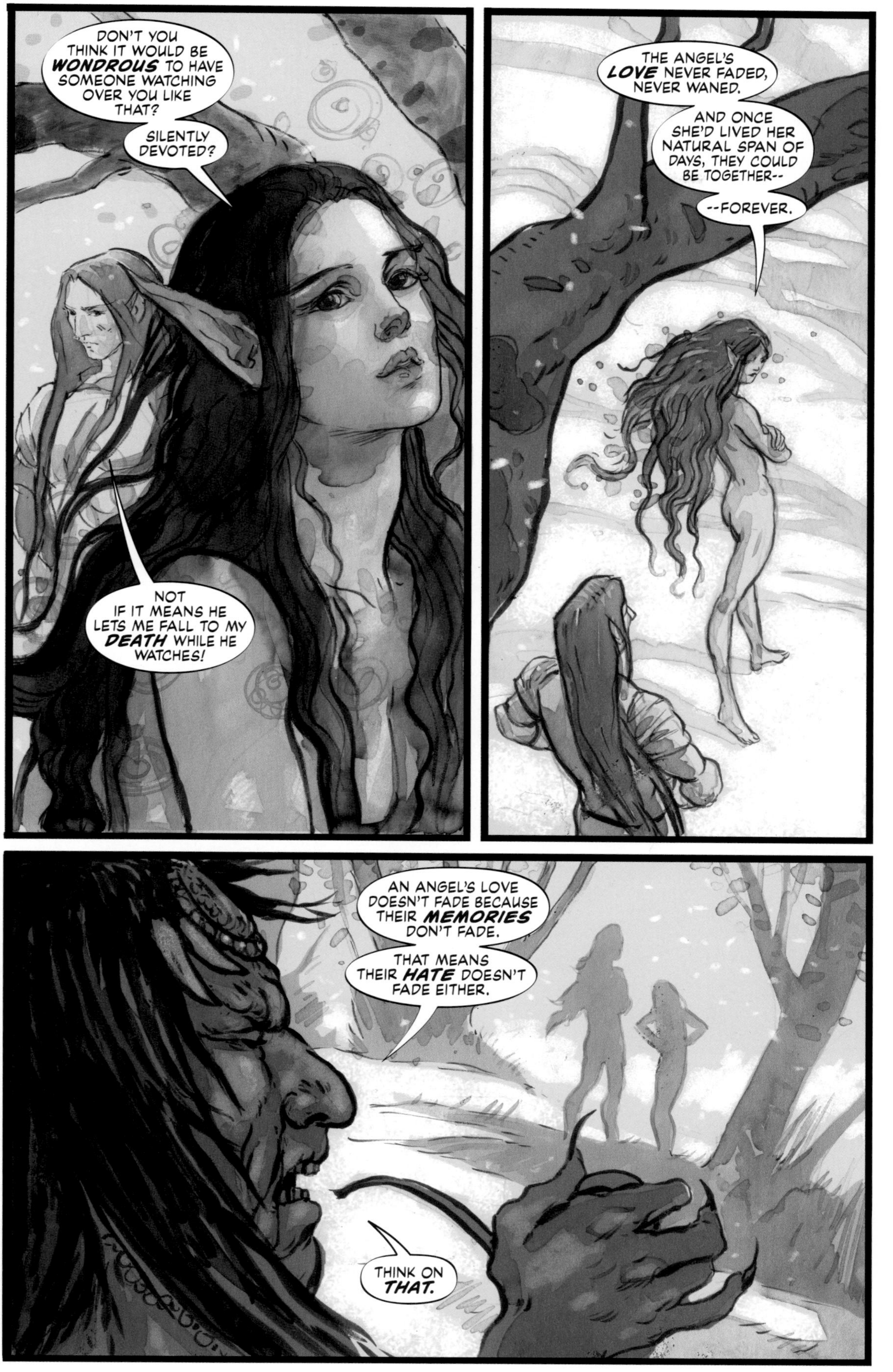
DON'T YOU THINK IT WOULD BE *WONDROUS* TO HAVE SOMEONE WATCHING OVER YOU LIKE THAT?
SILENTLY DEVOTED?
NOT IF IT MEANS HE LETS ME FALL TO MY *DEATH* WHILE HE WATCHES!
THE ANGEL'S *LOVE* NEVER FADED, NEVER WANED.
AND ONCE SHE'D LIVED HER NATURAL SPAN OF DAYS, THEY COULD BE TOGETHER--
--FOREVER.
AN ANGEL'S LOVE DOESN'T FADE BECAUSE THEIR *MEMORIES* DON'T FADE.
THAT MEANS THEIR *HATE* DOESN'T FADE EITHER.
THINK ON *THAT.*

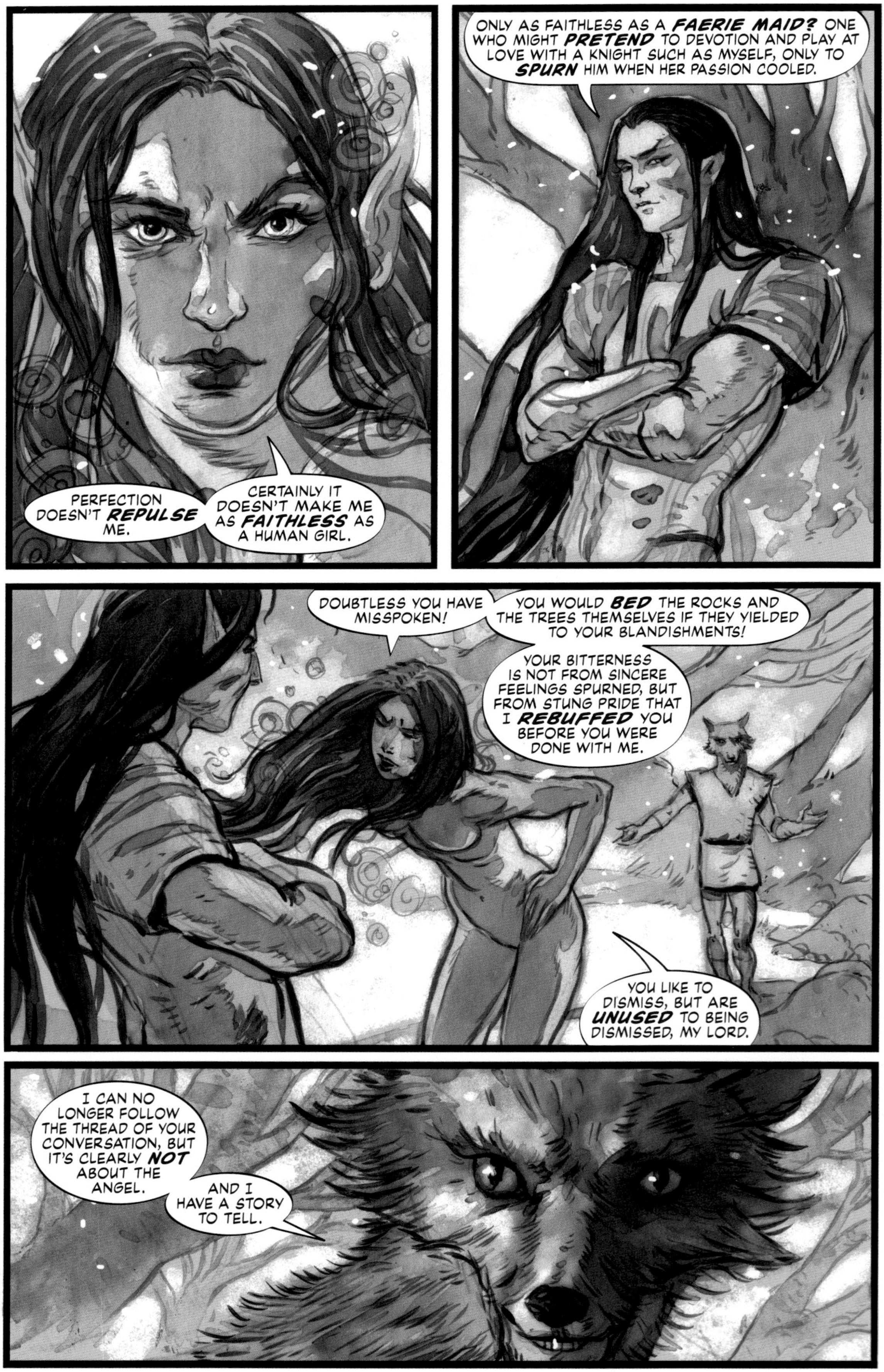
PERFECTION DOESN'T REPULSE ME.
CERTAINLY IT DOESN'T MAKE ME AS FAITHLESS AS A HUMAN GIRL.
ONLY AS FAITHLESS AS A FAERIE MAID? ONE WHO MIGHT PRETEND TO DEVOTION AND PLAY AT LOVE WITH A KNIGHT SUCH AS MYSELF, ONLY TO SPURN HIM WHEN HER PASSION COOLED.
DOUBTLESS YOU HAVE MISSPOKEN!
YOU WOULD BED THE ROCKS AND THE TREES THEMSELVES IF THEY YIELDED TO YOUR BLANDISHMENTS!
YOUR BITTERNESS IS NOT FROM SINCERE FEELINGS SPURNED, BUT FROM STUNG PRIDE THAT I REBUFFED YOU BEFORE YOU WERE DONE WITH ME.
YOU LIKE TO DISMISS, BUT ARE UNUSED TO BEING DISMISSED, MY LORD.
I CAN NO LONGER FOLLOW THE THREAD OF YOUR CONVERSATION, BUT IT'S CLEARLY NOT ABOUT THE ANGEL.
AND I HAVE A STORY TO TELL.

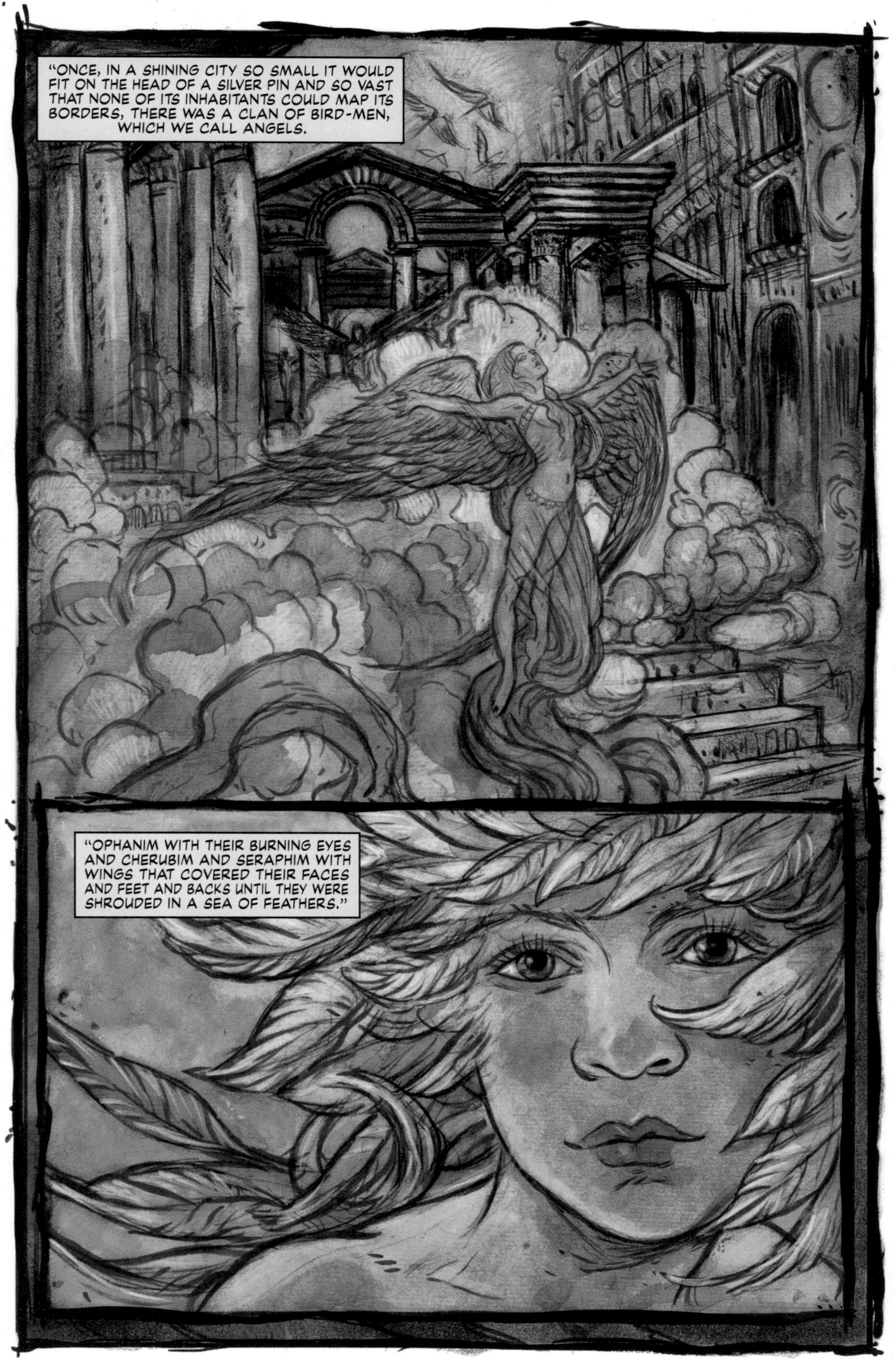
"ONCE, IN A SHINING CITY SO SMALL IT WOULD FIT ON THE HEAD OF A SILVER PIN AND SO VAST THAT NONE OF ITS INHABITANTS COULD MAP ITS BORDERS, THERE WAS A CLAN OF BIRD-MEN, WHICH WE CALL ANGELS.
"OPHANIM WITH THEIR BURNING EYES AND CHERUBIM AND SERAPHIM WITH WINGS THAT COVERED THEIR FACES AND FEET AND BACKS UNTIL THEY WERE SHROUDED IN A SEA OF FEATHERS."

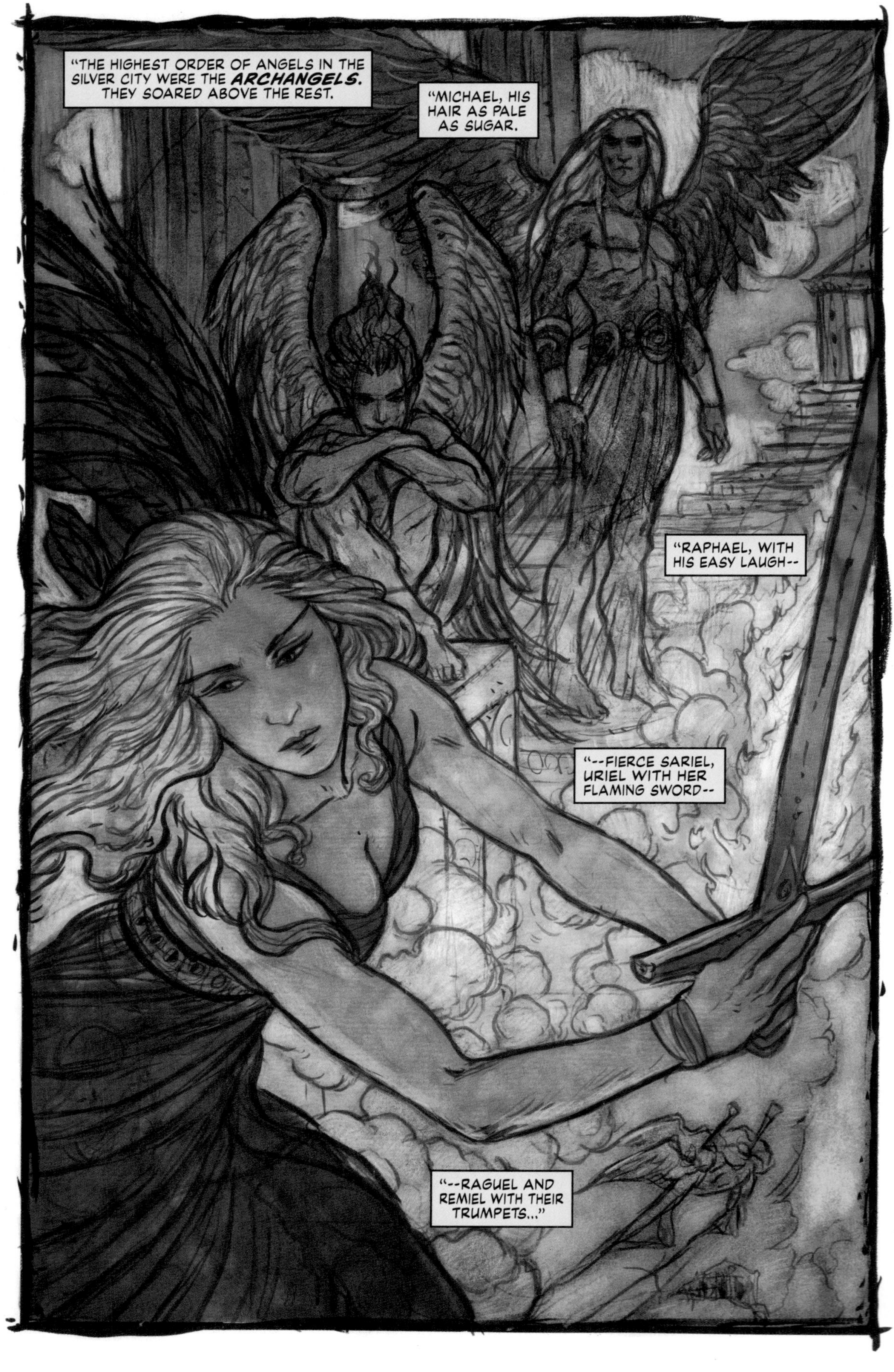
"THE HIGHEST ORDER OF ANGELS IN THE SILVER CITY WERE THE ARCHANGELS. THEY SOARED ABOVE THE REST.
"MICHAEL, HIS HAIR AS PALE AS SUGAR.
"RAPHAEL, WITH HIS EASY LAUGH--
"--FIERCE SARIEL, URIEL WITH HER FLAMING SWORD--
"--RAGUEL AND REMIEL WITH THEIR TRUMPETS..."

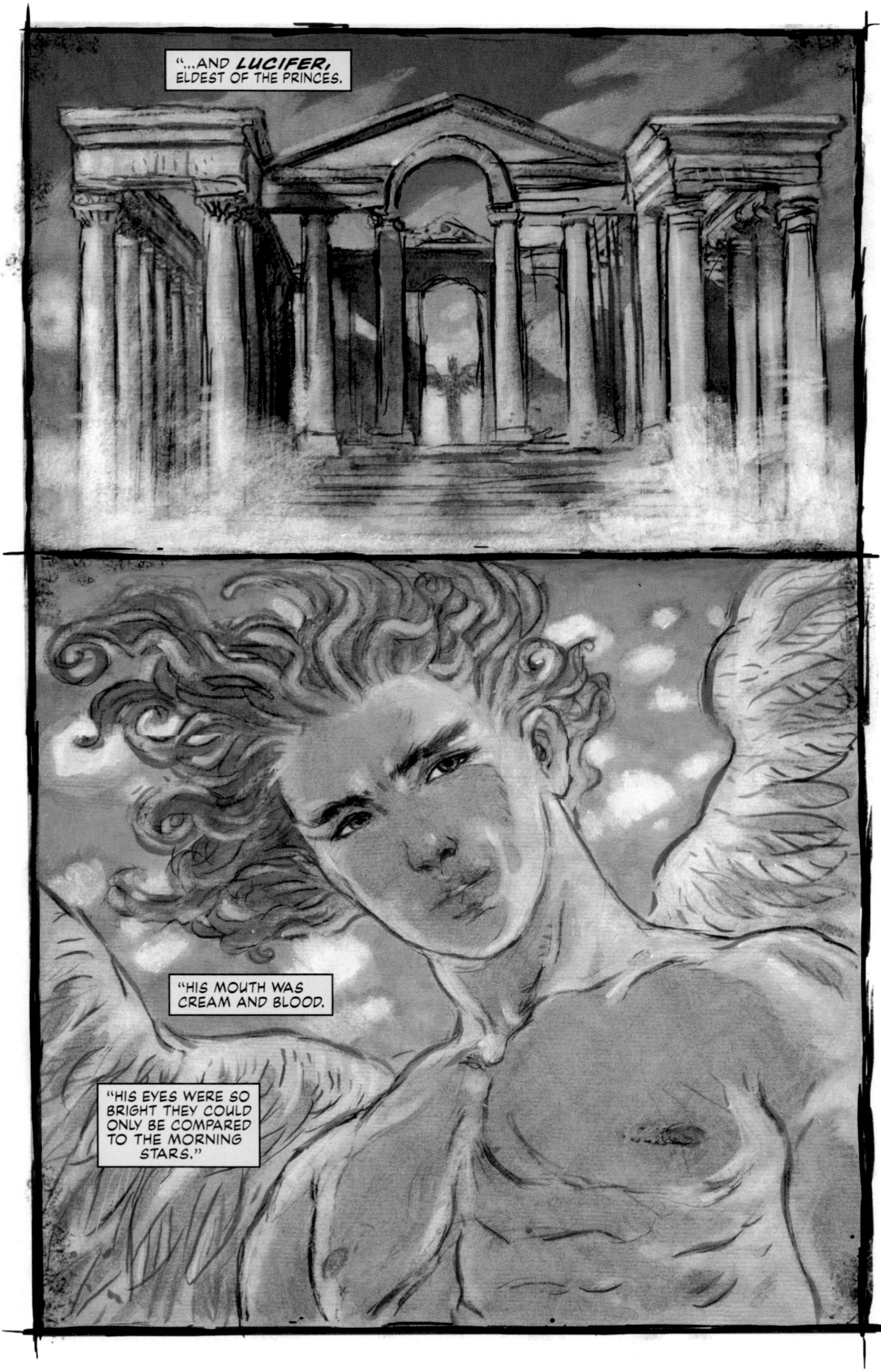
"...AND LUCIFER, ELDEST OF THE PRINCES.
"HIS MOUTH WAS CREAM AND BLOOD.
"HIS EYES WERE SO BRIGHT THEY COULD ONLY BE COMPARED TO THE MORNING STARS."

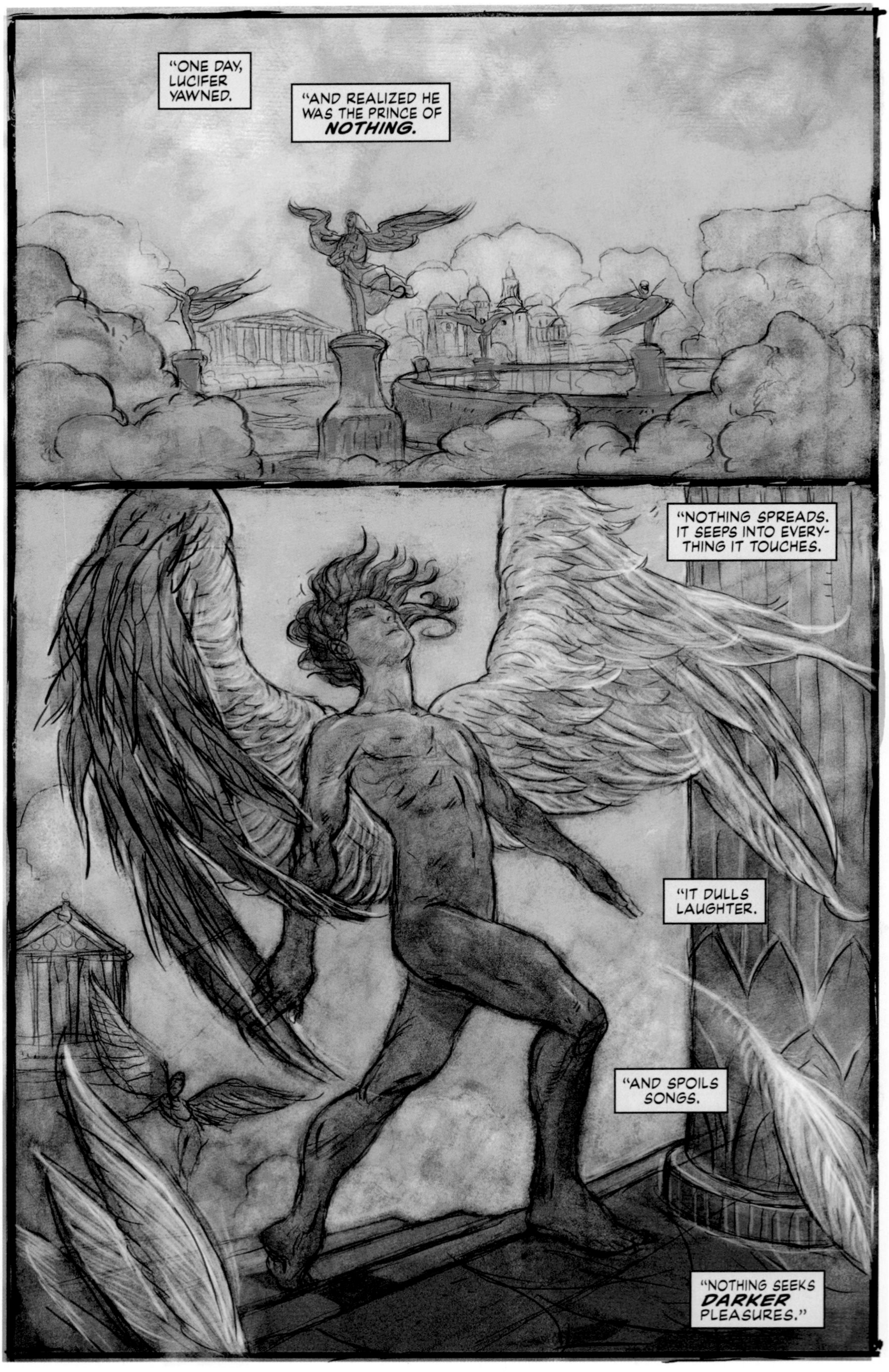
"ONE DAY, LUCIFER YAWNED.
"AND REALIZED HE WAS THE PRINCE OF NOTHING.
"NOTHING SPREADS. IT SEEPS INTO EVERY-THING IT TOUCHES.
"IT DULLS LAUGHTER.
"AND SPOILS SONGS.
"NOTHING SEEKS DARKER PLEASURES."

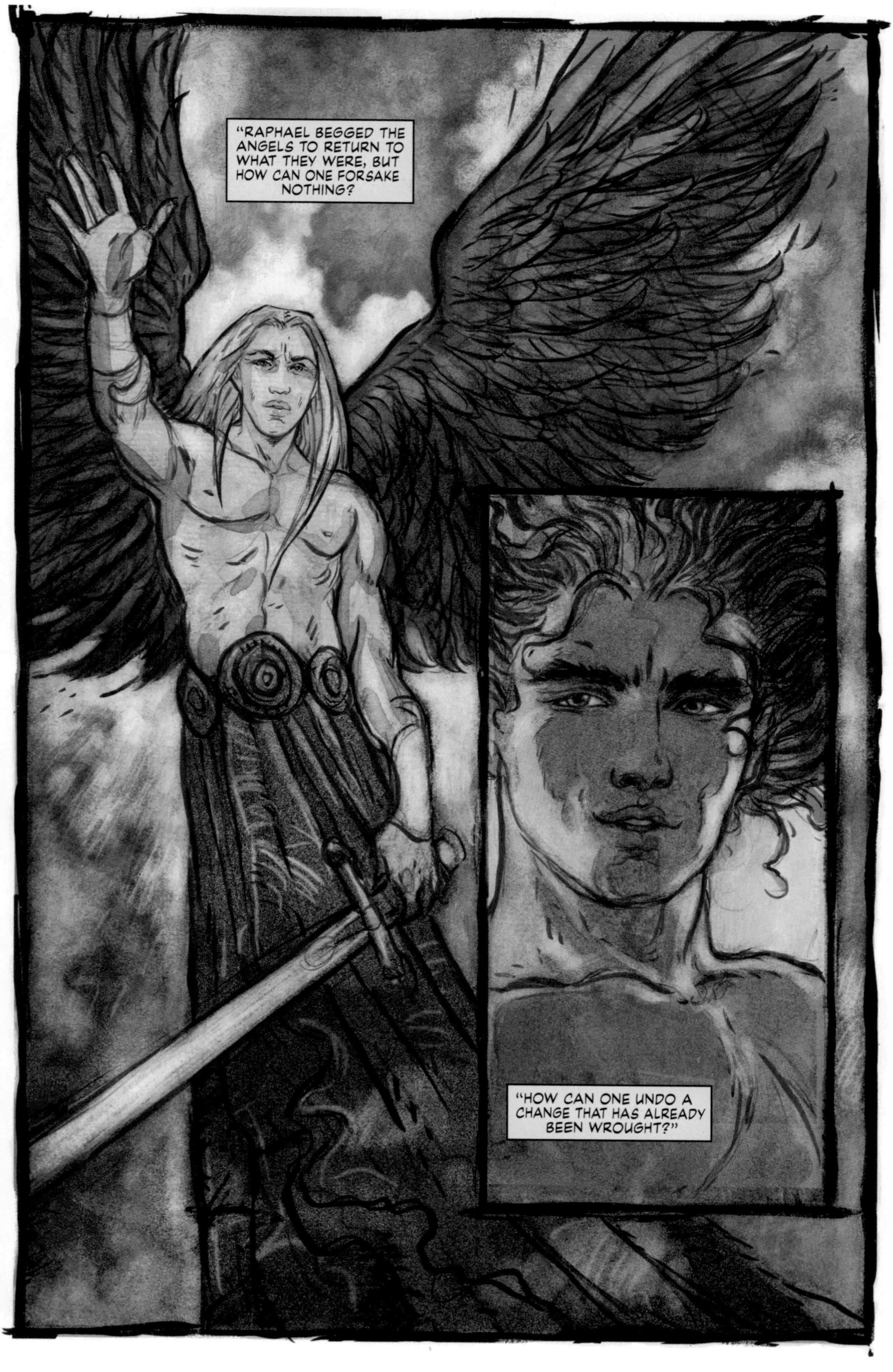
"RAPHAEL BEGGED THE ANGELS TO RETURN TO WHAT THEY WERE, BUT HOW CAN ONE FORSAKE NOTHING?
"HOW CAN ONE UNDO A CHANGE THAT HAS ALREADY BEEN WROUGHT?"

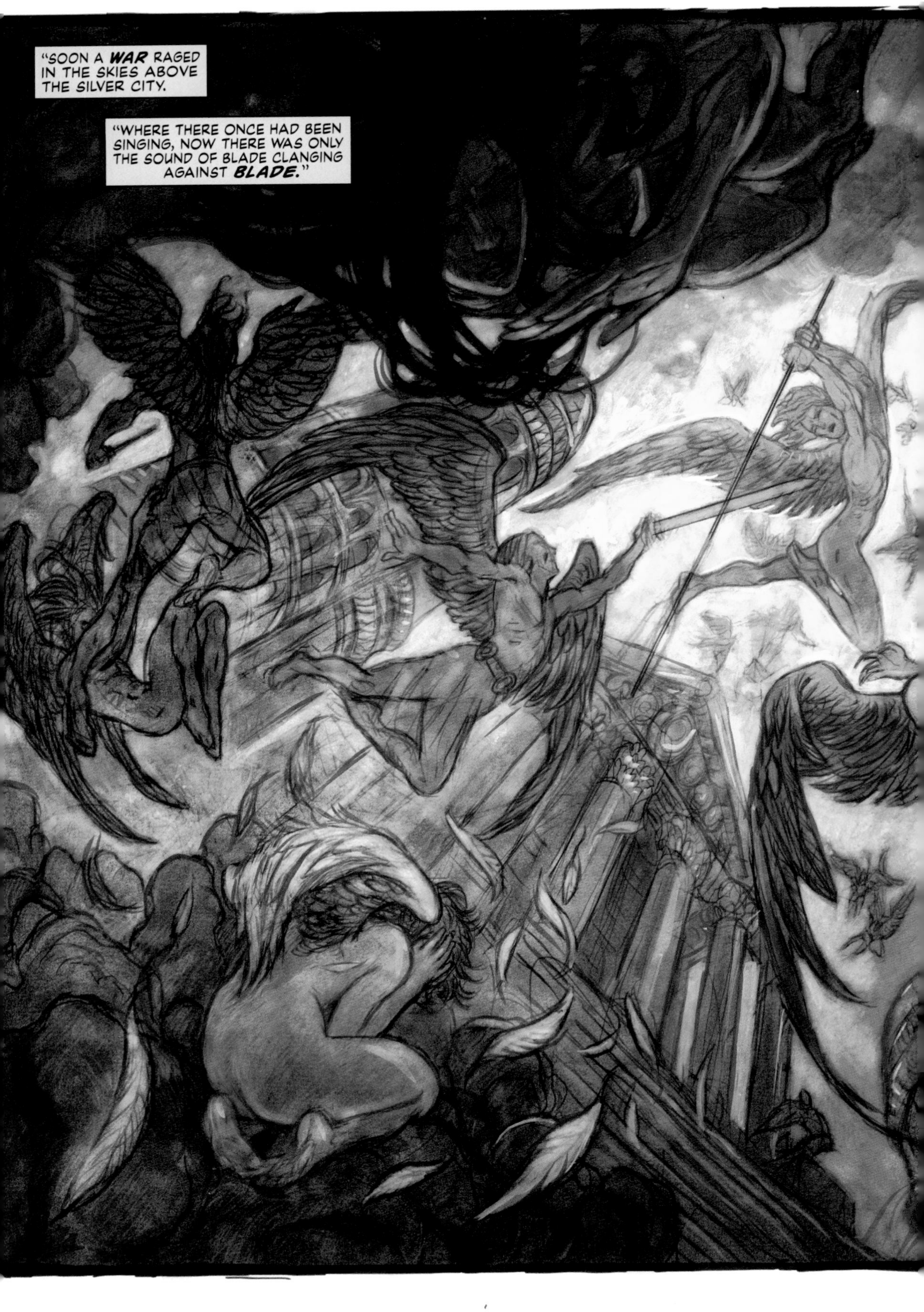
"SOON A WAR RAGED IN THE SKIES ABOVE THE SILVER CITY.
"WHERE THERE ONCE HAD BEEN SINGING, NOW THERE WAS ONLY THE SOUND OF BLADE CLANGING AGAINST BLADE."

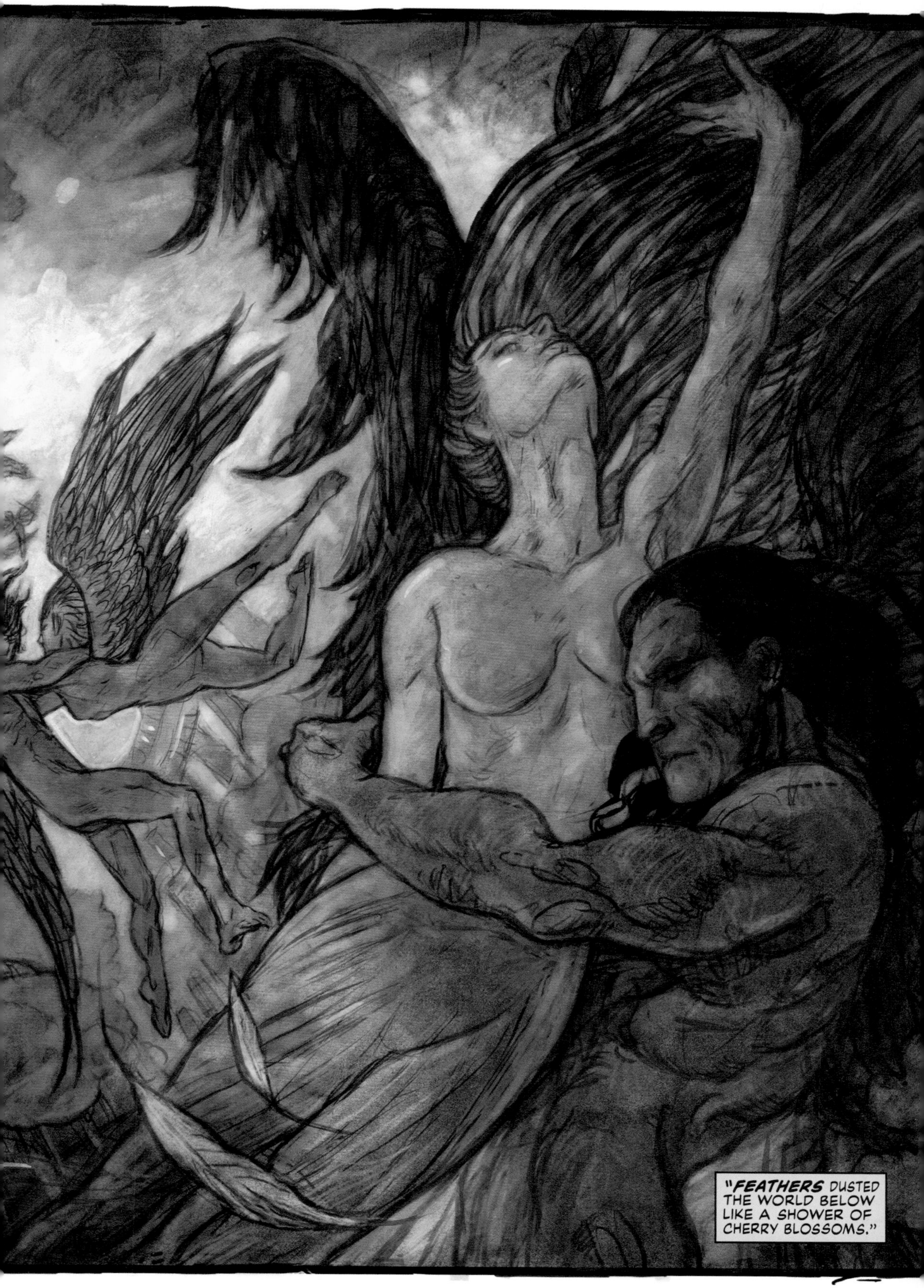
"FEATHERS DUSTED THE WORLD BELOW LIKE A SHOWER OF CHERRY BLOSSOMS."

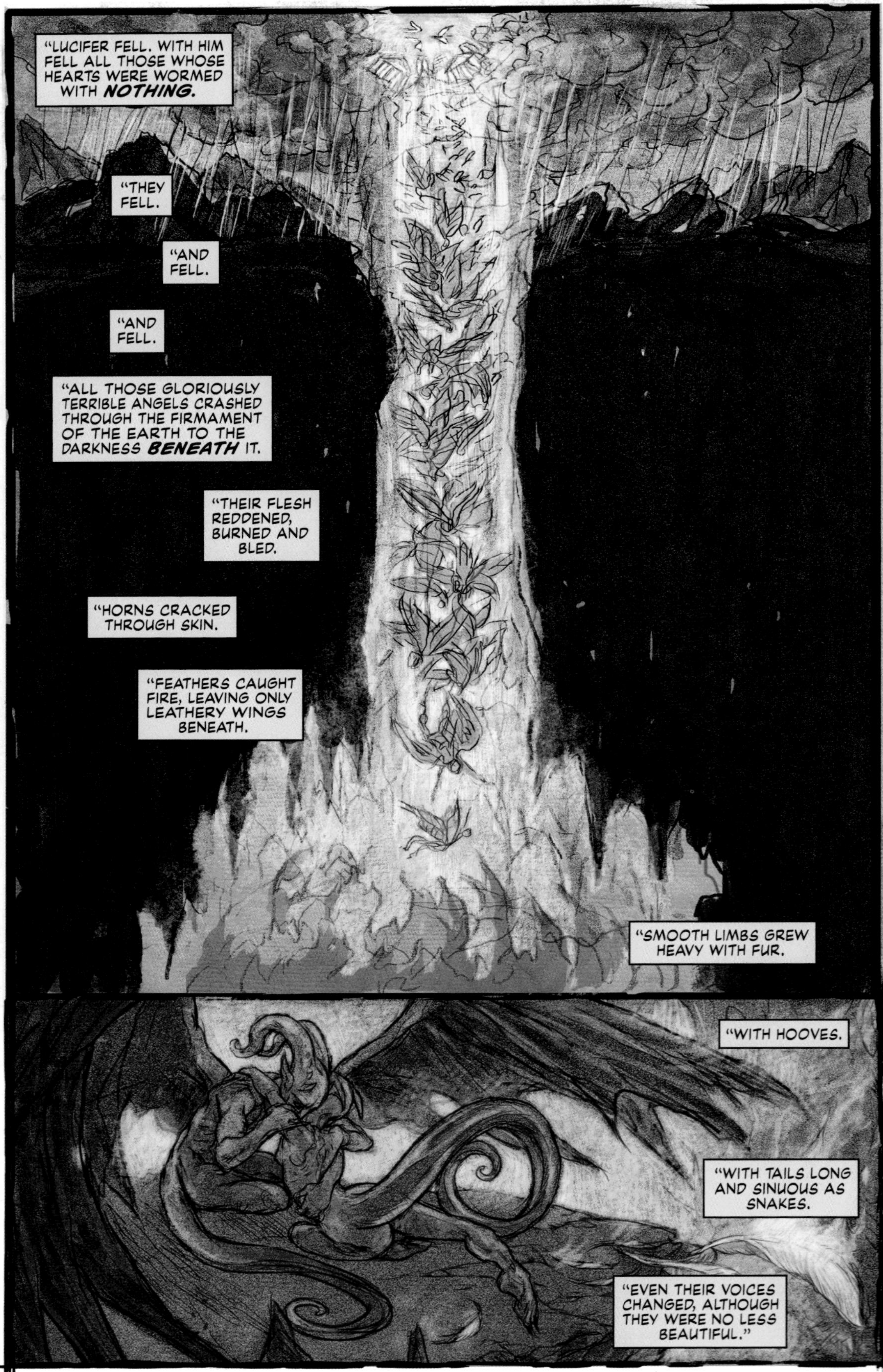
"LUCIFER FELL. WITH HIM FELL ALL THOSE WHOSE HEARTS WERE WORMED WITH ***NOTHING.***
"THEY FELL.
"AND FELL.
"AND FELL.
"ALL THOSE GLORIOUSLY TERRIBLE ANGELS CRASHED THROUGH THE FIRMAMENT OF THE EARTH TO THE DARKNESS ***BENEATH*** IT.
"THEIR FLESH REDDENED, BURNED AND BLED.
"HORNS CRACKED THROUGH SKIN.
"FEATHERS CAUGHT FIRE, LEAVING ONLY LEATHERY WINGS BENEATH.
"SMOOTH LIMBS GREW HEAVY WITH FUR.
"WITH HOOVES.
"WITH TAILS LONG AND SINUOUS AS SNAKES.
"EVEN THEIR VOICES CHANGED, ALTHOUGH THEY WERE NO LESS BEAUTIFUL."

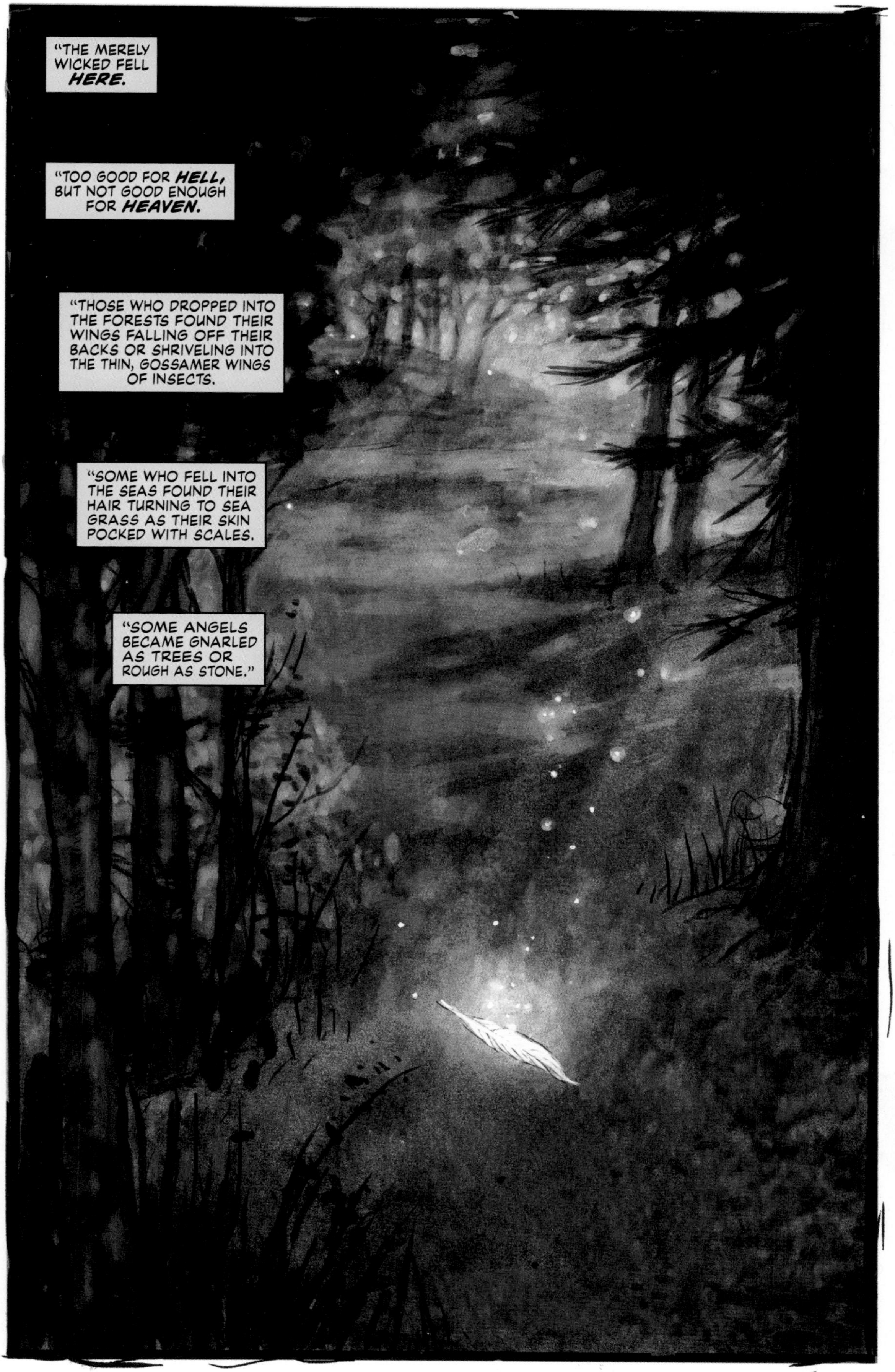
"THE MERELY WICKED FELL *HERE*.
"TOO GOOD FOR *HELL*, BUT NOT GOOD ENOUGH FOR *HEAVEN*.
"THOSE WHO DROPPED INTO THE FORESTS FOUND THEIR WINGS FALLING OFF THEIR BACKS OR SHRIVELING INTO THE THIN, GOSSAMER WINGS OF INSECTS.
"SOME WHO FELL INTO THE SEAS FOUND THEIR HAIR TURNING TO SEA GRASS AS THEIR SKIN POCKED WITH SCALES.
"SOME ANGELS BECAME GNARLED AS TREES OR ROUGH AS STONE."

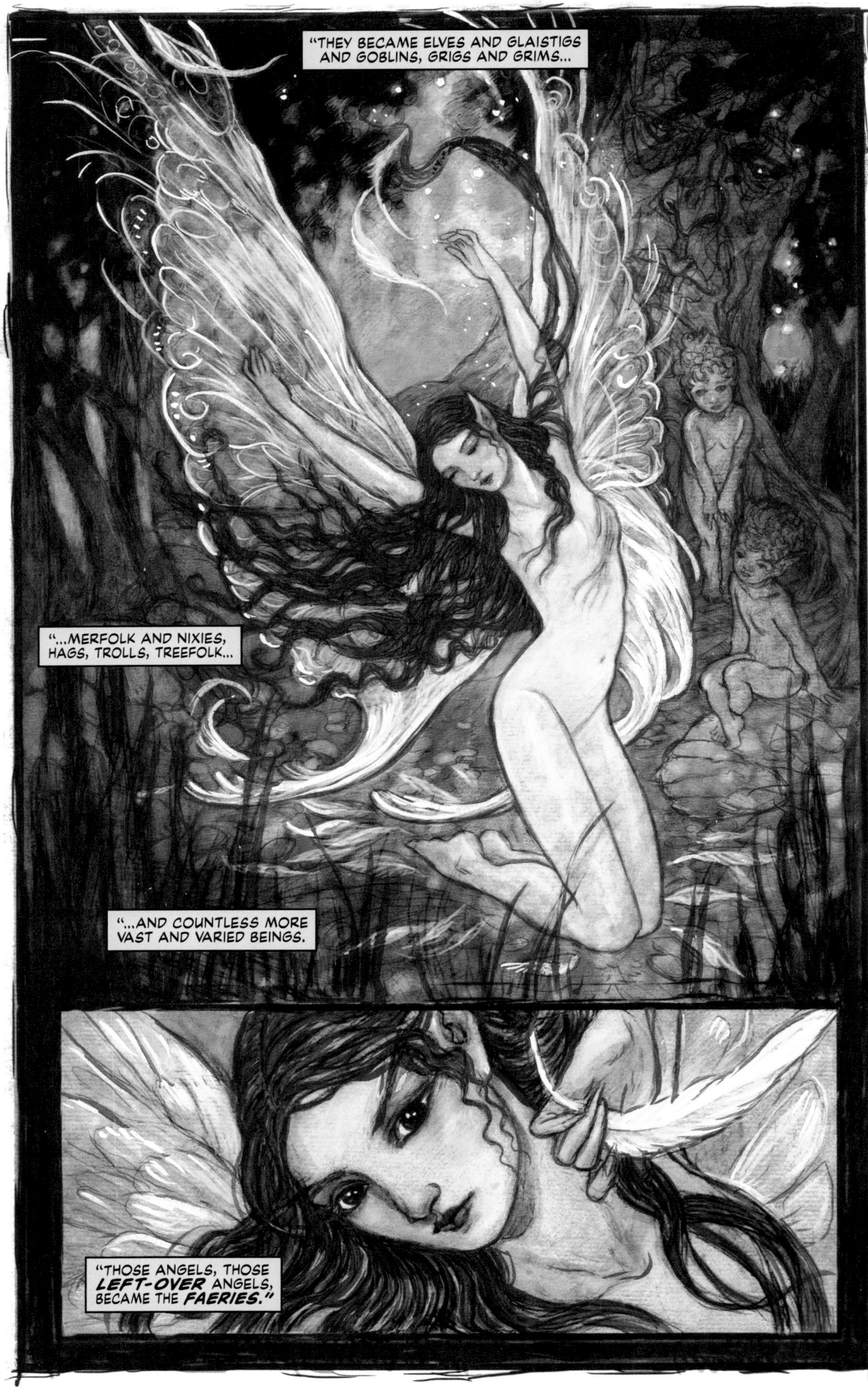
"THEY BECAME ELVES AND GLAISTIGS AND GOBLINS, GRIGS AND GRIMS...
"...MERFOLK AND NIXIES, HAGS, TROLLS, TREEFOLK...
"...AND COUNTLESS MORE VAST AND VARIED BEINGS.
"THOSE ANGELS, THOSE LEFT-OVER ANGELS, BECAME THE FAERIES."

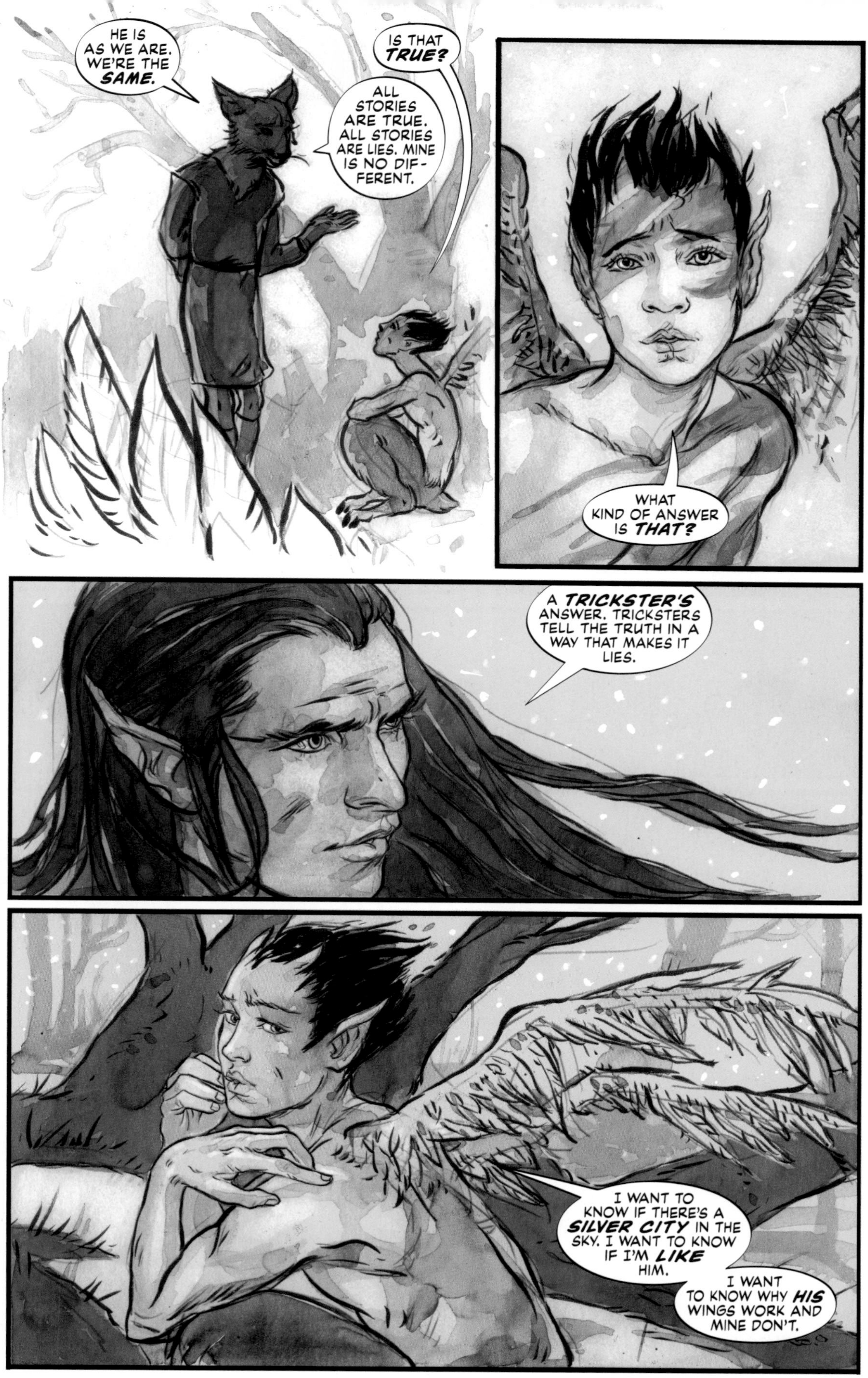
HE IS AS WE ARE. WE'RE THE *SAME.*
IS THAT *TRUE?*
ALL STORIES ARE TRUE. ALL STORIES ARE LIES. MINE IS NO DIF-FERENT.
WHAT KIND OF ANSWER IS *THAT?*
A *TRICKSTER'S* ANSWER. TRICKSTERS TELL THE TRUTH IN A WAY THAT MAKES IT LIES.
I WANT TO KNOW IF THERE'S A *SILVER CITY* IN THE SKY. I WANT TO KNOW IF I'M *LIKE* HIM.
I WANT TO KNOW WHY *HIS* WINGS WORK AND MINE DON'T.

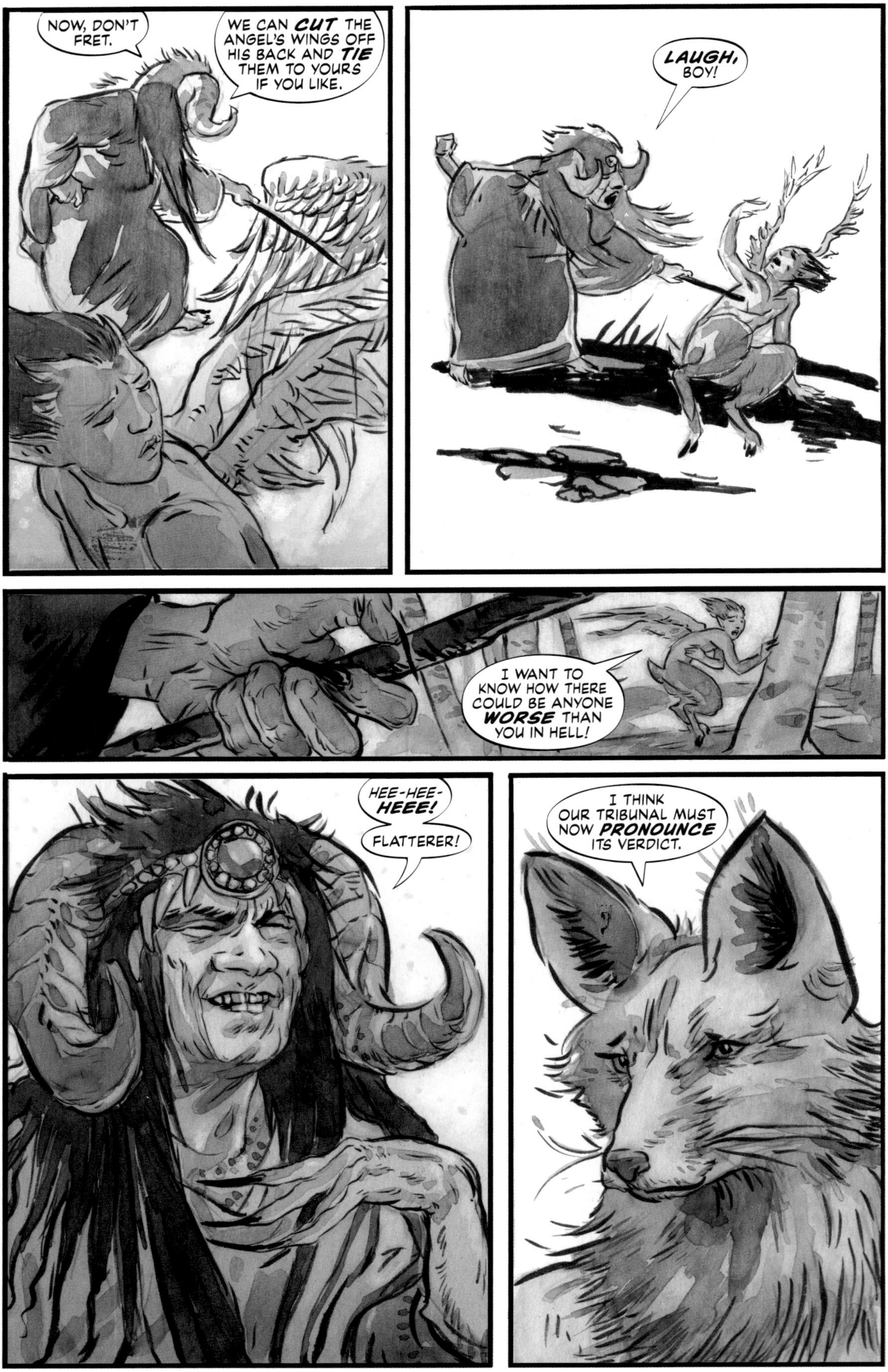
NOW, DON'T FRET.
WE CAN CUT THE ANGEL'S WINGS OFF HIS BACK AND TIE THEM TO YOURS IF YOU LIKE.
LAUGH, BOY!
I WANT TO KNOW HOW THERE COULD BE ANYONE WORSE THAN YOU IN HELL!
HEE-HEE-HEEE!
FLATTERER!
I THINK OUR TRIBUNAL MUST NOW PRONOUNCE ITS VERDICT.

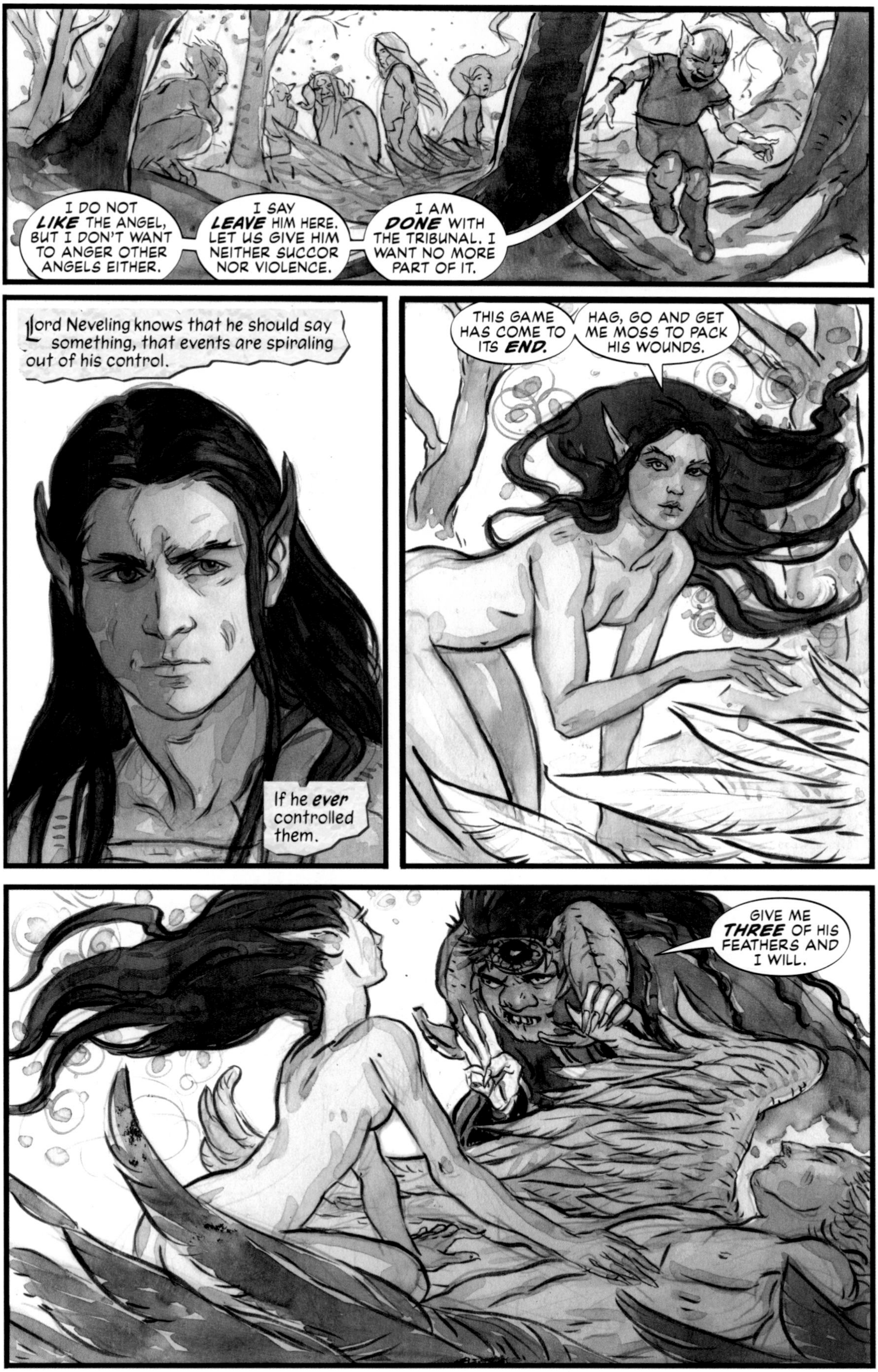
I DO NOT *LIKE* THE ANGEL, BUT I DON'T WANT TO ANGER OTHER ANGELS EITHER.
I SAY *LEAVE* HIM HERE. LET US GIVE HIM NEITHER SUCCOR NOR VIOLENCE.
I AM *DONE* WITH THE TRIBUNAL. I WANT NO MORE PART OF IT.
Lord Neveling knows that he should say something, that events are spiraling out of his control.
If he *ever* controlled them.
THIS GAME HAS COME TO ITS *END.*
HAG, GO AND GET ME MOSS TO PACK HIS WOUNDS.
GIVE ME *THREE* OF HIS FEATHERS AND I WILL.

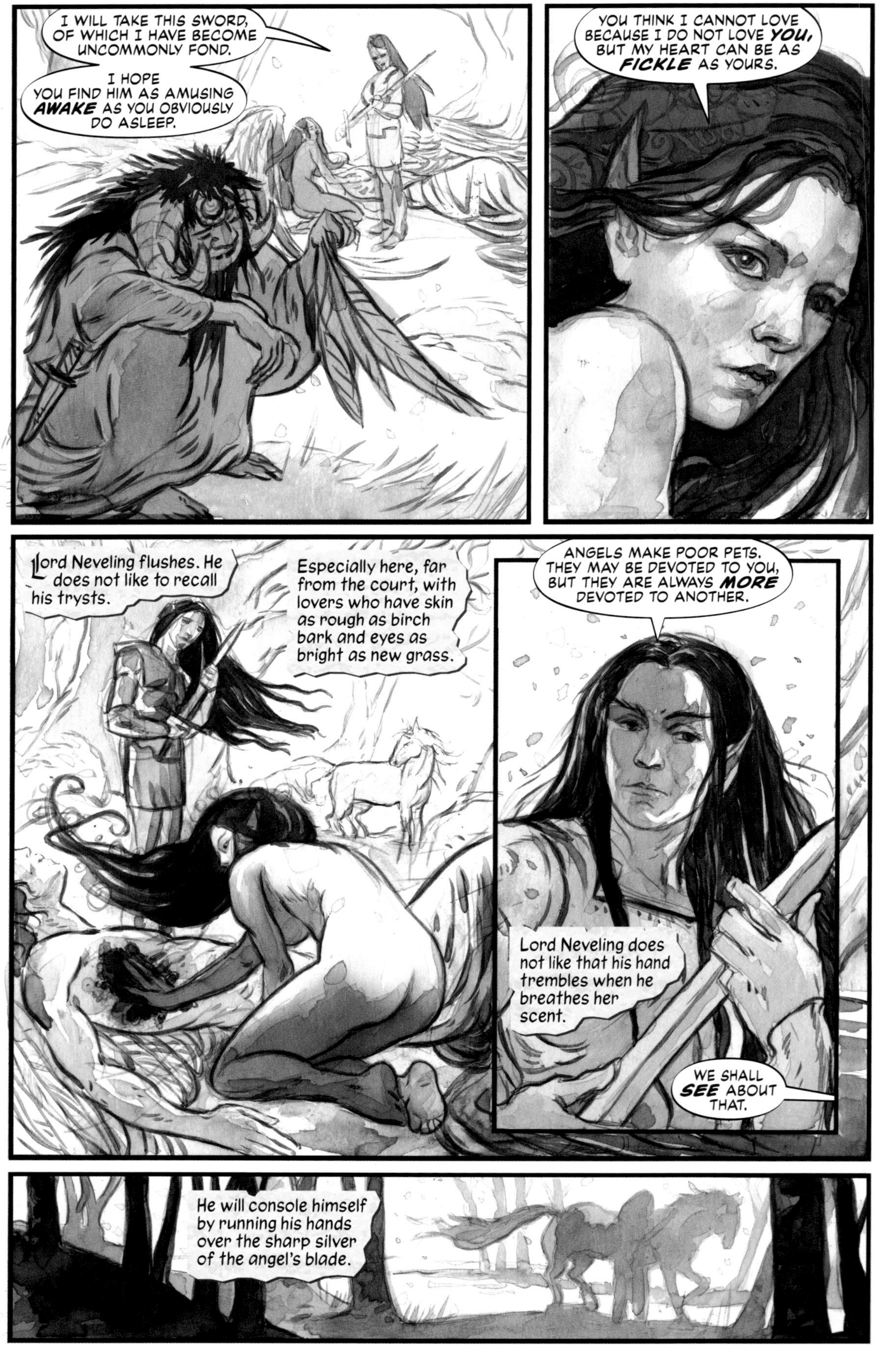
I WILL TAKE THIS SWORD, OF WHICH I HAVE BECOME UNCOMMONLY FOND.
I HOPE YOU FIND HIM AS AMUSING **AWAKE** AS YOU OBVIOUSLY DO ASLEEP.
YOU THINK I CANNOT LOVE BECAUSE I DO NOT LOVE **YOU,** BUT MY HEART CAN BE AS **FICKLE** AS YOURS.
Lord Neveling flushes. He does not like to recall his trysts.
Especially here, far from the court, with lovers who have skin as rough as birch bark and eyes as bright as new grass.
ANGELS MAKE POOR PETS. THEY MAY BE DEVOTED TO YOU, BUT THEY ARE ALWAYS **MORE** DEVOTED TO ANOTHER.
Lord Neveling does not like that his hand trembles when he breathes her scent.
WE SHALL **SEE** ABOUT THAT.
He will console himself by running his hands over the sharp silver of the angel's blade.

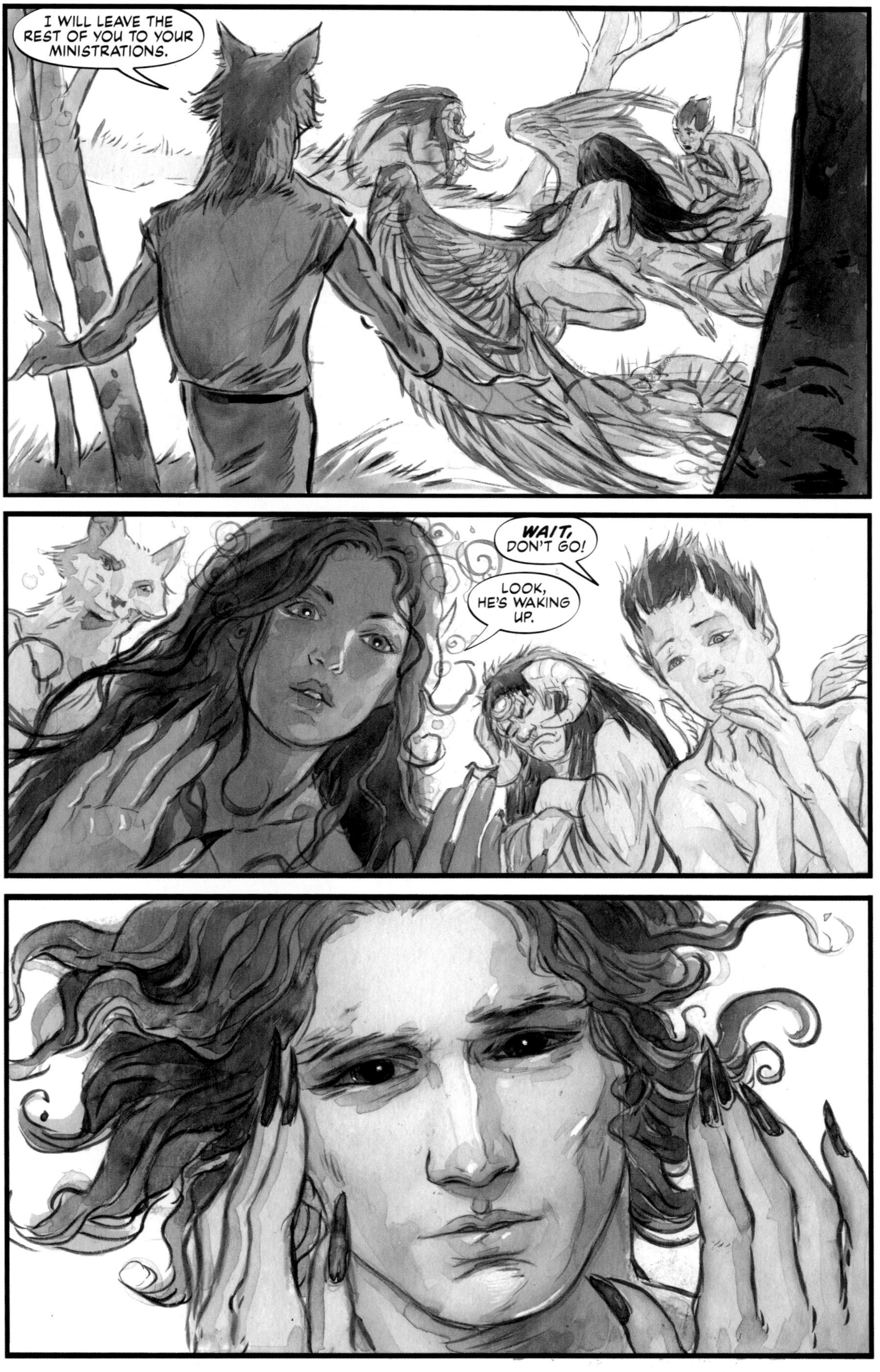
I WILL LEAVE THE REST OF YOU TO YOUR MINISTRATIONS.
WAIT, DON'T GO!
LOOK, HE'S WAKING UP.

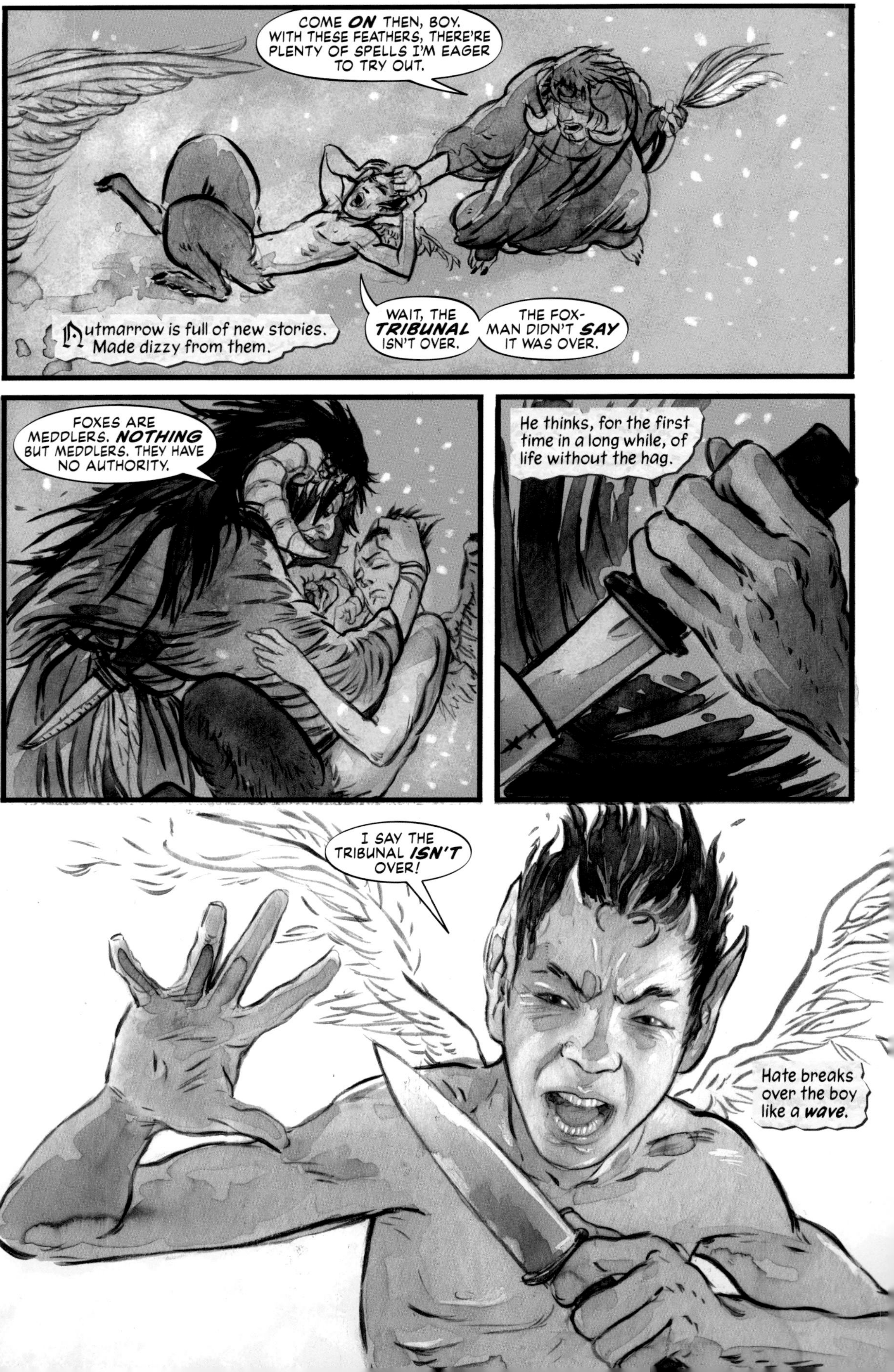
COME ON THEN, BOY. WITH THESE FEATHERS, THERE'RE PLENTY OF SPELLS I'M EAGER TO TRY OUT.
Outmarrow is full of new stories. Made dizzy from them.
WAIT, THE TRIBUNAL ISN'T OVER.
THE FOX-MAN DIDN'T SAY IT WAS OVER.
FOXES ARE MEDDLERS. NOTHING BUT MEDDLERS. THEY HAVE NO AUTHORITY.
He thinks, for the first time in a long while, of life without the hag.
I SAY THE TRIBUNAL ISN'T OVER!
Hate breaks over the boy like a wave.

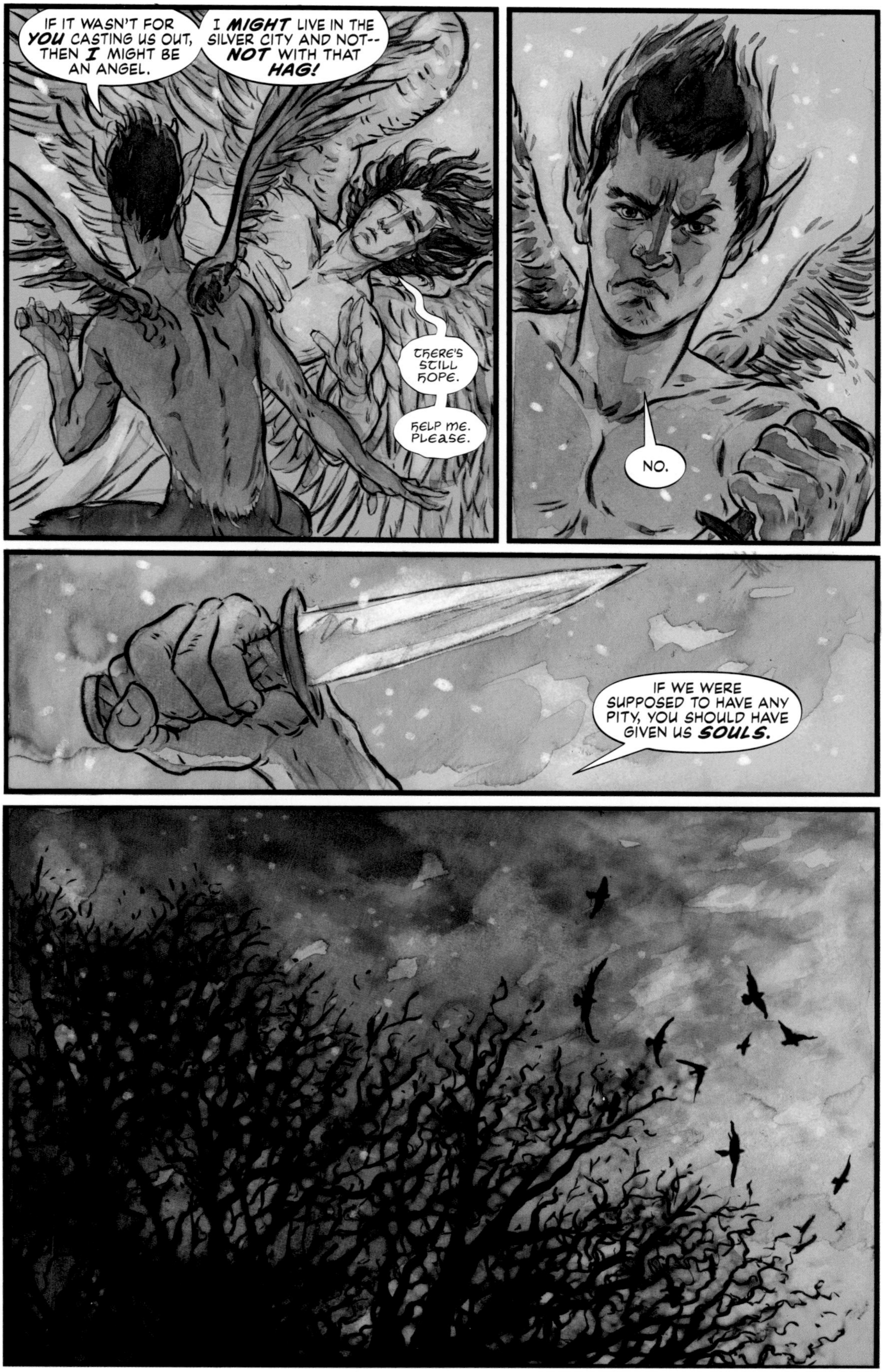
IF IT WASN'T FOR YOU CASTING US OUT, THEN I MIGHT BE AN ANGEL.
I MIGHT LIVE IN THE SILVER CITY AND NOT-- NOT WITH THAT HAG!
THERE'S STILL HOPE.
HELP ME. PLEASE.
NO.
IF WE WERE SUPPOSED TO HAVE ANY PITY, YOU SHOULD HAVE GIVEN US SOULS.

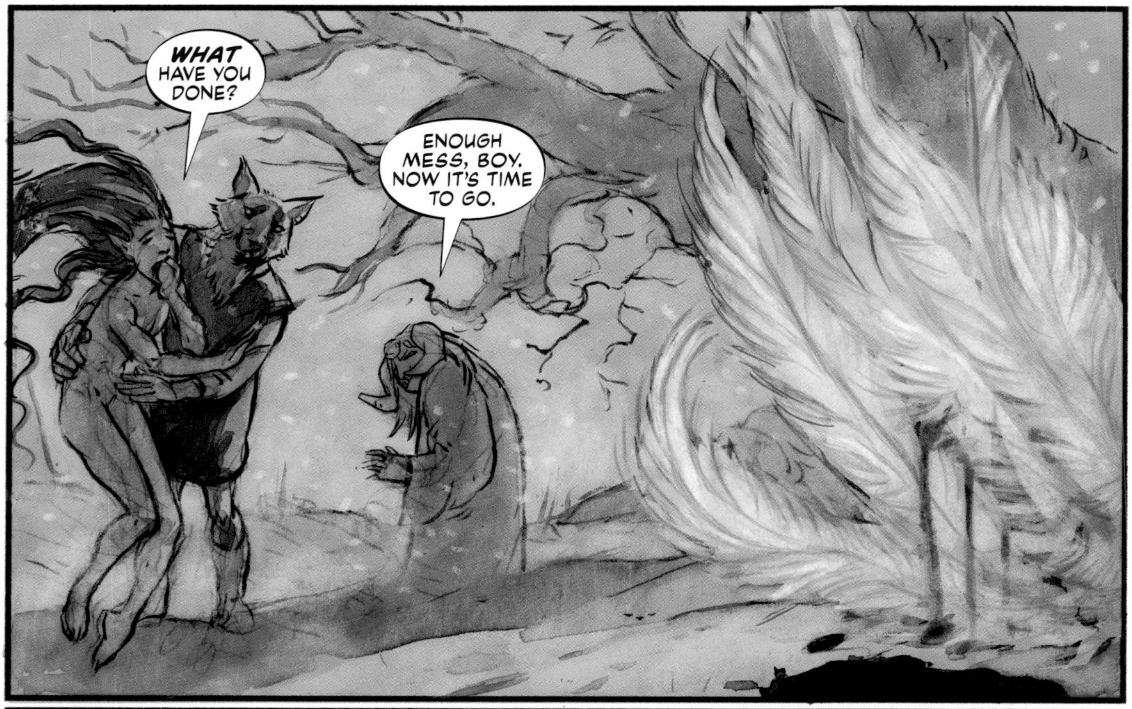
WHAT HAVE YOU DONE?
ENOUGH MESS, BOY. NOW IT'S TIME TO GO.

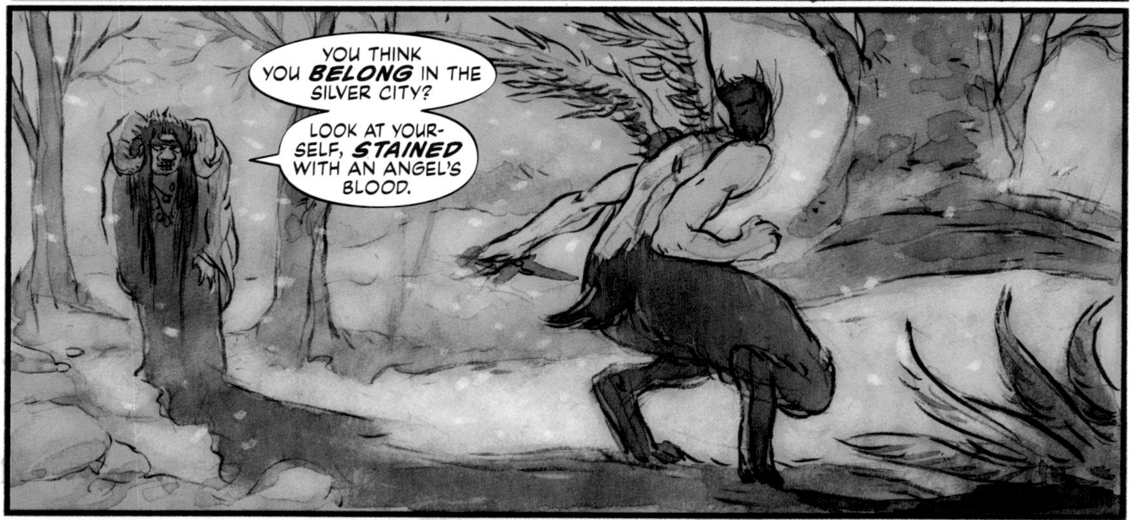
YOU THINK YOU BELONG IN THE SILVER CITY?
LOOK AT YOURSELF, STAINED WITH AN ANGEL'S BLOOD.

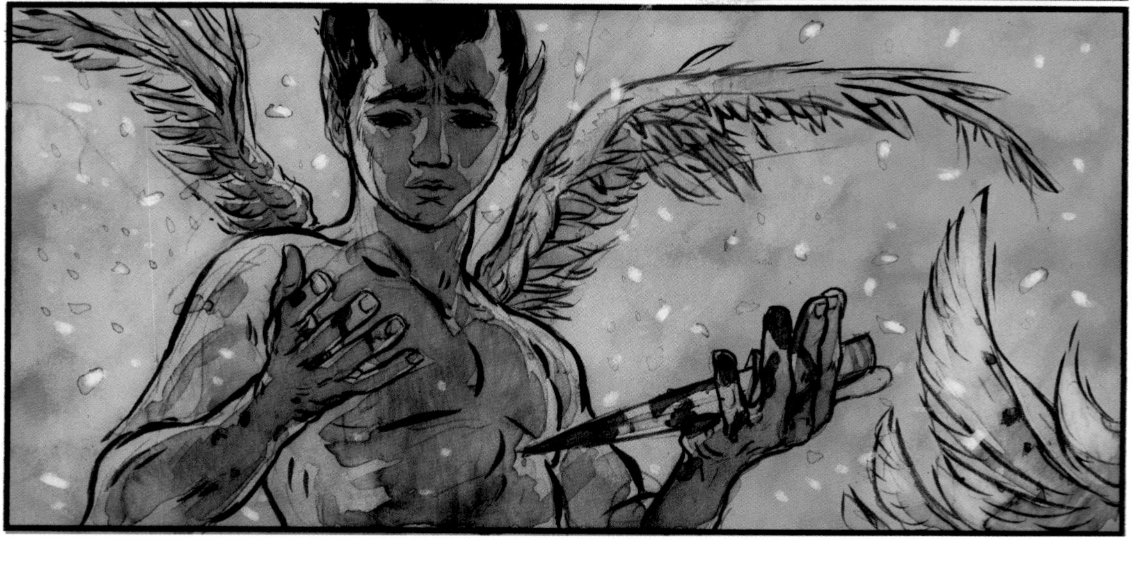

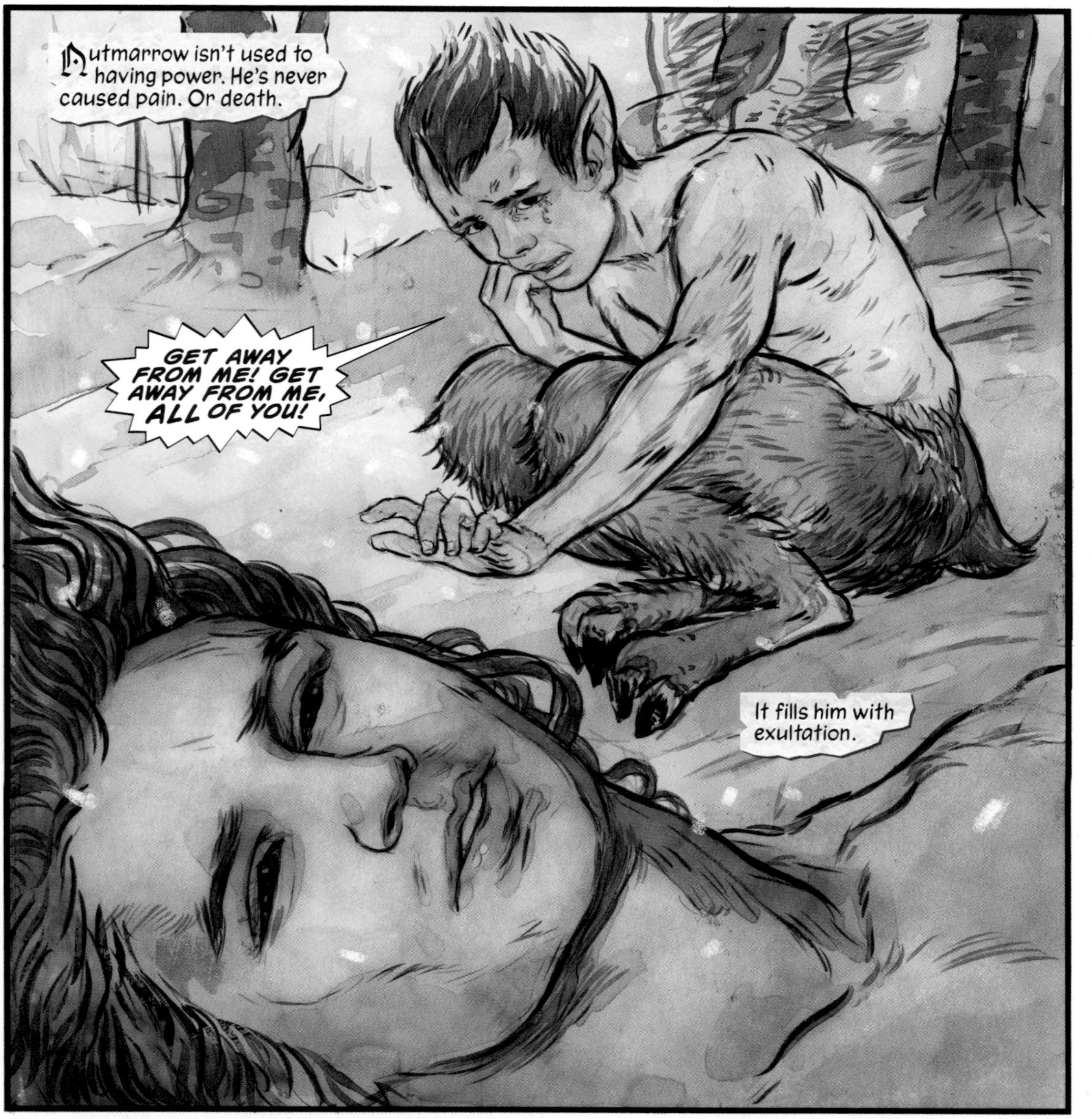
Nutmarrow isn't used to having power. He's never caused pain. Or death.
GET AWAY FROM ME! GET AWAY FROM ME, ALL OF YOU!
It fills him with exultation.

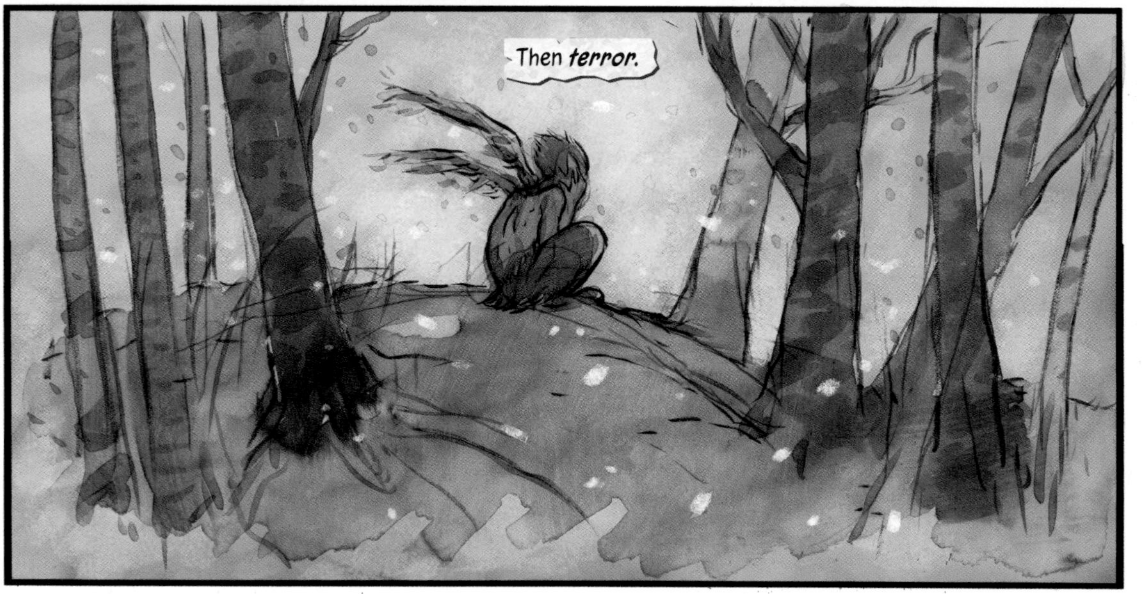
Then terror.

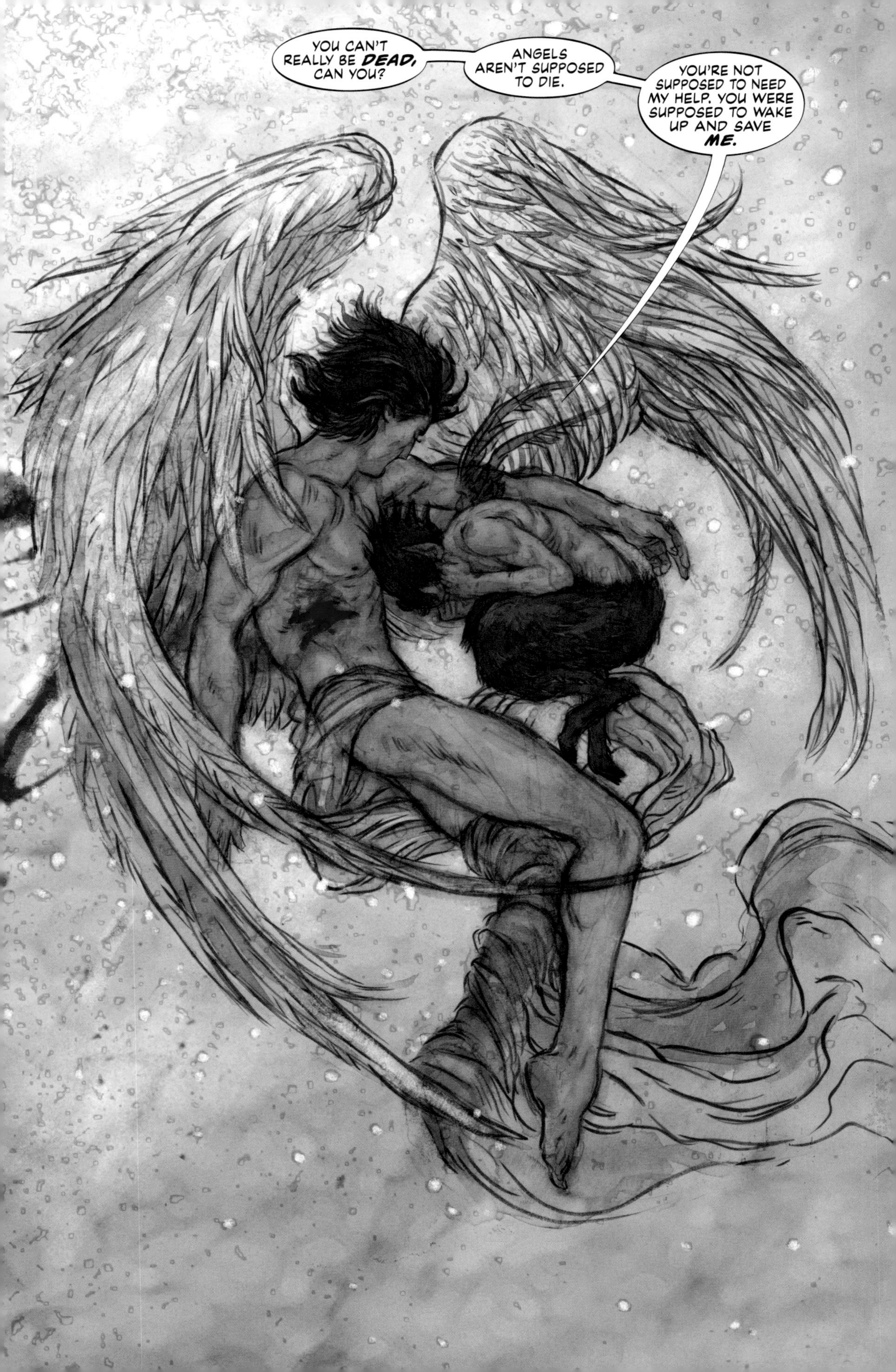
YOU CAN'T REALLY BE DEAD, CAN YOU?
ANGELS AREN'T SUPPOSED TO DIE.
YOU'RE NOT SUPPOSED TO NEED MY HELP. YOU WERE SUPPOSED TO WAKE UP AND SAVE ME.

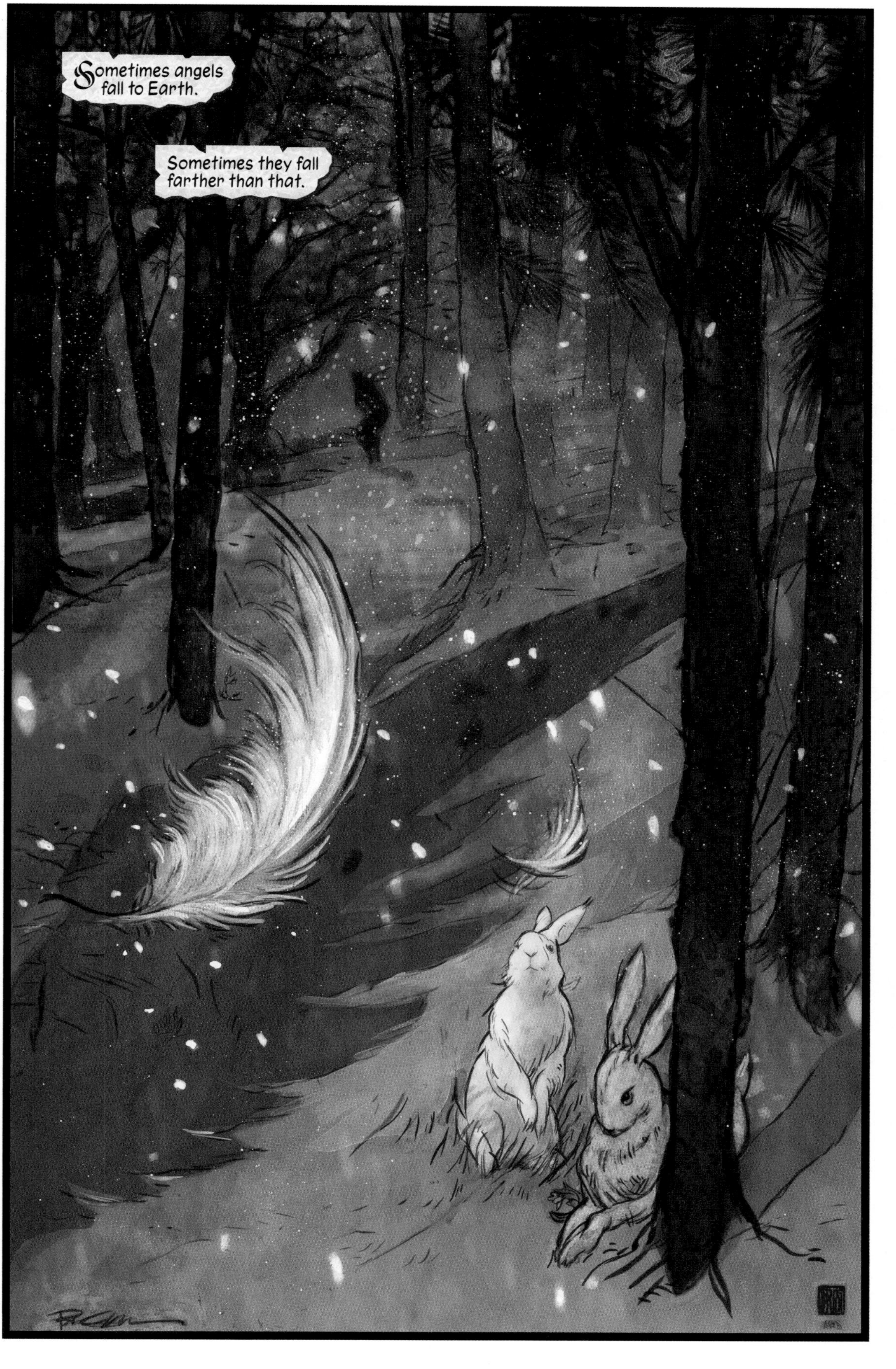
Sometimes angels fall to Earth.
Sometimes they fall farther than that.

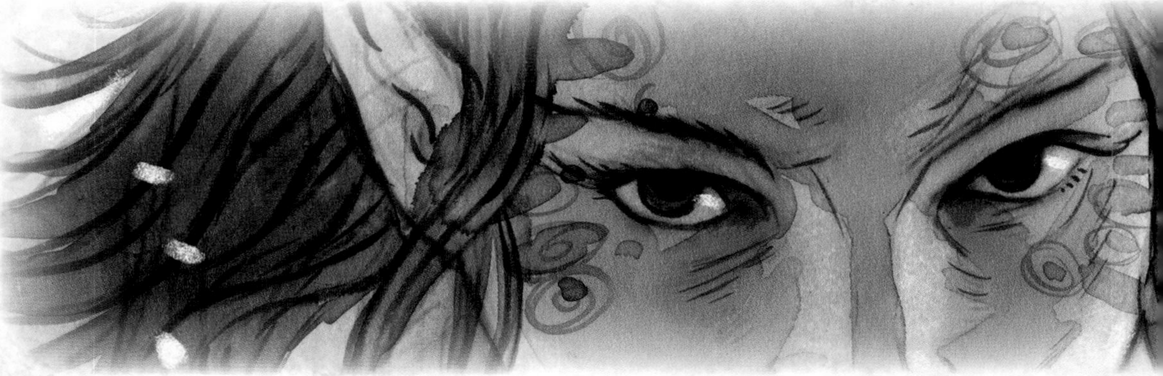

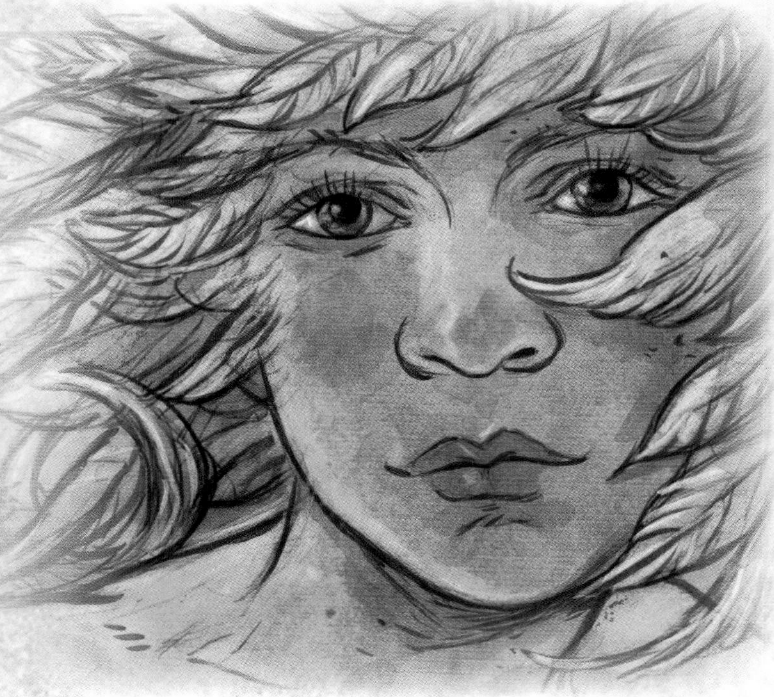

HOLLY BLACK is the best-selling author of contemporary fantasy novels for teens and children. She collaborated with a longtime friend, Caldecott award-winning artist Tony DiTerlizzi, to create the best-selling *Spiderwick Chronicles*, which has been translated into 32 languages and was adapted into a film in 2008. Holly has also been a frequent contributor to anthologies, and her first collection of short fiction, *Poison Eaters and Other Stories*, was published in 2010. She has just finished the third book in her Eisner-nominated graphic novel series *The Good Neighbors* and is working on *Red Glove*, the second novel in *The Curse Workers* series. Holly lives in Massachusetts with her husband, Theo, in a house with a secret library.

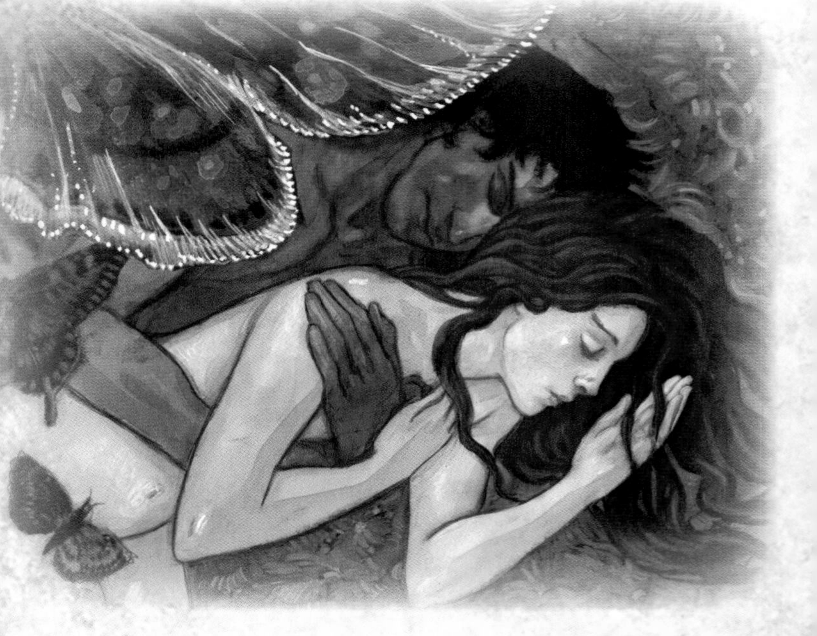

LOUISE HAWES has written over fifteen books for children, teenagers, and adults. She has received two New Jersey Writing Fellowships and the New Jersey Authors' Award, and her work has earned Children's Book Council/IRA Choices, New York Public Library Best Books, Bank Street College Best Books, and Independent Booksellers Picks. She has served as a John Grisham Visiting Author at the University of Mississippi, a Writer in Residence at the University of New Mexico, and Reading Initiative Author at the Mississippi University for Women. She is currently on faculty at the Vermont College of Fine Arts.

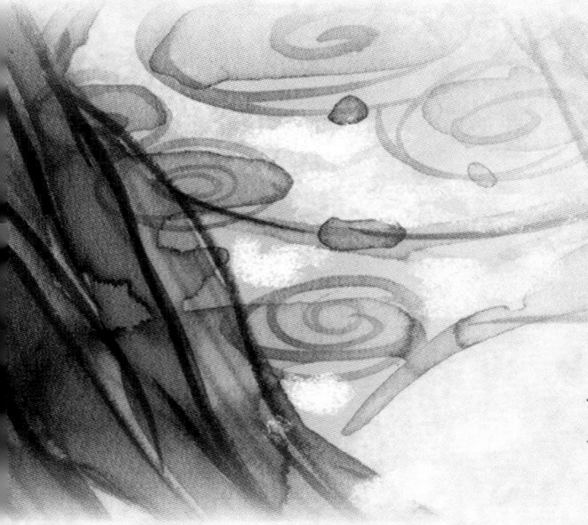

REBECCA GUAY is known for her lyrical figures and emotional, poignant content evoking an earlier age of art. A graduate of Pratt Institute, she has achieved success in the fields of fine art, commercial illustration and has been widely published throughout fantasy, children's books and comics, illustrating the stories of Ursula K. Le Guin, Bruce Coville, Jane Yolen and many others. A 2011 recipient of two Spectrum Gold medal awards, Rebecca has had her work displayed at the Society of Illustrators Spectrum exhibit in 2005, 2009, The Earth show 2010, and in the Annual 2011 show. In 2010, one of her large oils was acquired for the permanent collection at The American Museum of Illustration at the Society of Illustrators in New York City. Rebecca lives with her husband Matthew Mitchell (also a painter) and daughter Vivian in western Massachusetts.

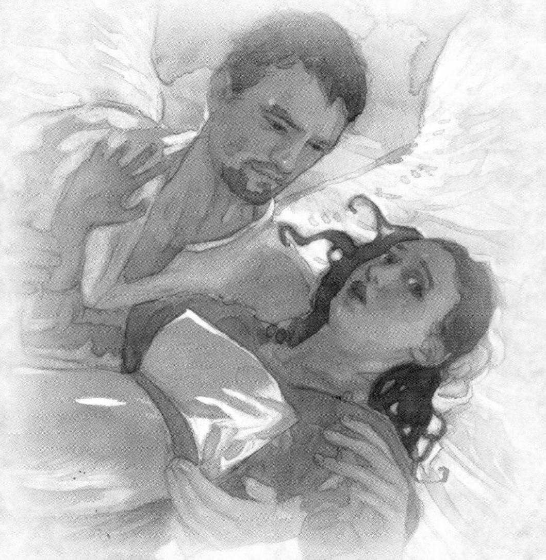

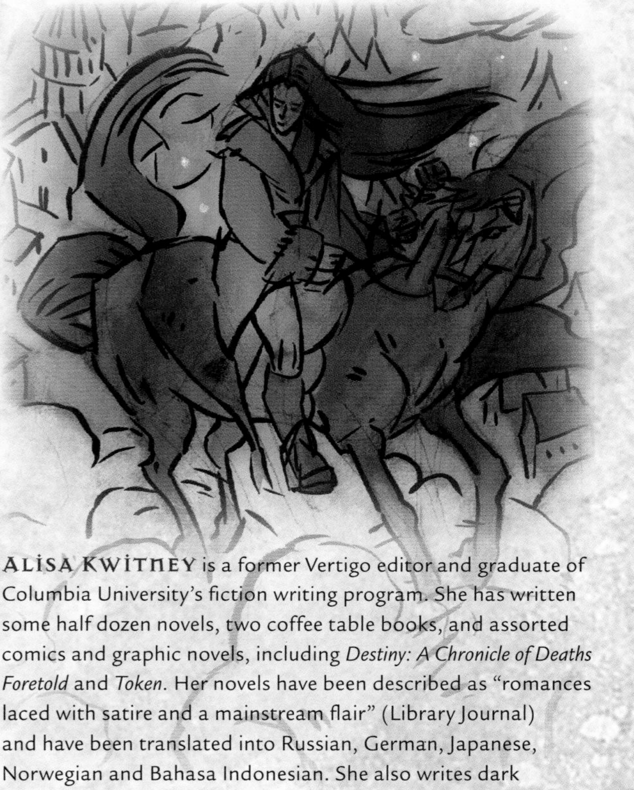

TODD MITCHELL is the author of the young adult novels *The Secret to Lying* and *The Traitor King*. He has also published several short stories, essays, and poems in national and international journals. Currently, he teaches creative writing at Colorado State University in Fort Collins, Colorado, where he lives with his wife, dog, and two occasionally angelic daughters.

ALISA KWITNEY is a former Vertigo editor and graduate of Columbia University's fiction writing program. She has written some half dozen novels, two coffee table books, and assorted comics and graphic novels, including *Destiny: A Chronicle of Deaths Foretold* and *Token*. Her novels have been described as "romances laced with satire and a mainstream flair" (Library Journal) and have been translated into Russian, German, Japanese, Norwegian and Bahasa Indonesian. She also writes dark fantasy/paranormal romance under the name Alisa Sheckley.

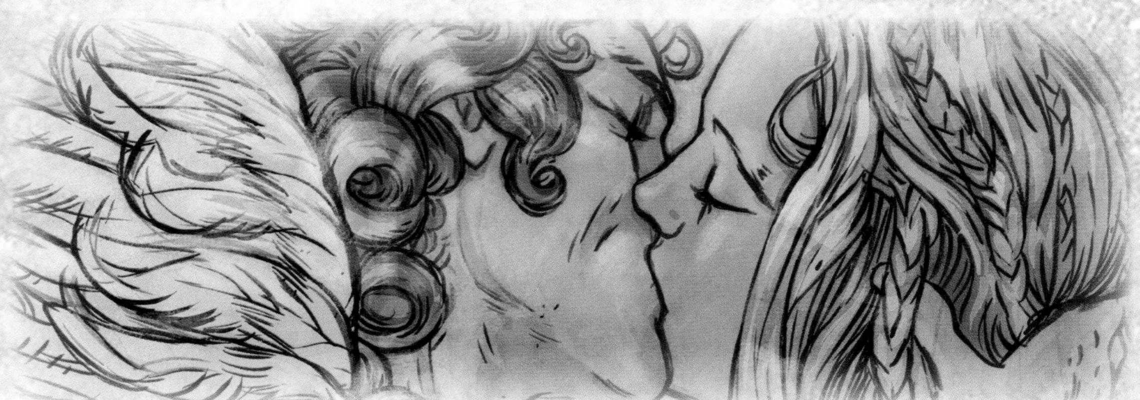

BILL WILLINGHAM is the writer and creator of *Fables*. He has been writing, and sometimes drawing, comics for more than twenty years on titles including *Elementals*, *Coventry*, *Proposition Player* and *Fables*. His prose novels include *Peter & Max: A Fables Novel*, and the children's book *Down the Mysterly River*. His work has been nominated for many awards, including the Eisner, Harvey and Ignatz comic industry awards, plus the Hugo and the International Horror Guild award. Bill lives in the woods in Minnesota, a brother of dragons and companion to owls.

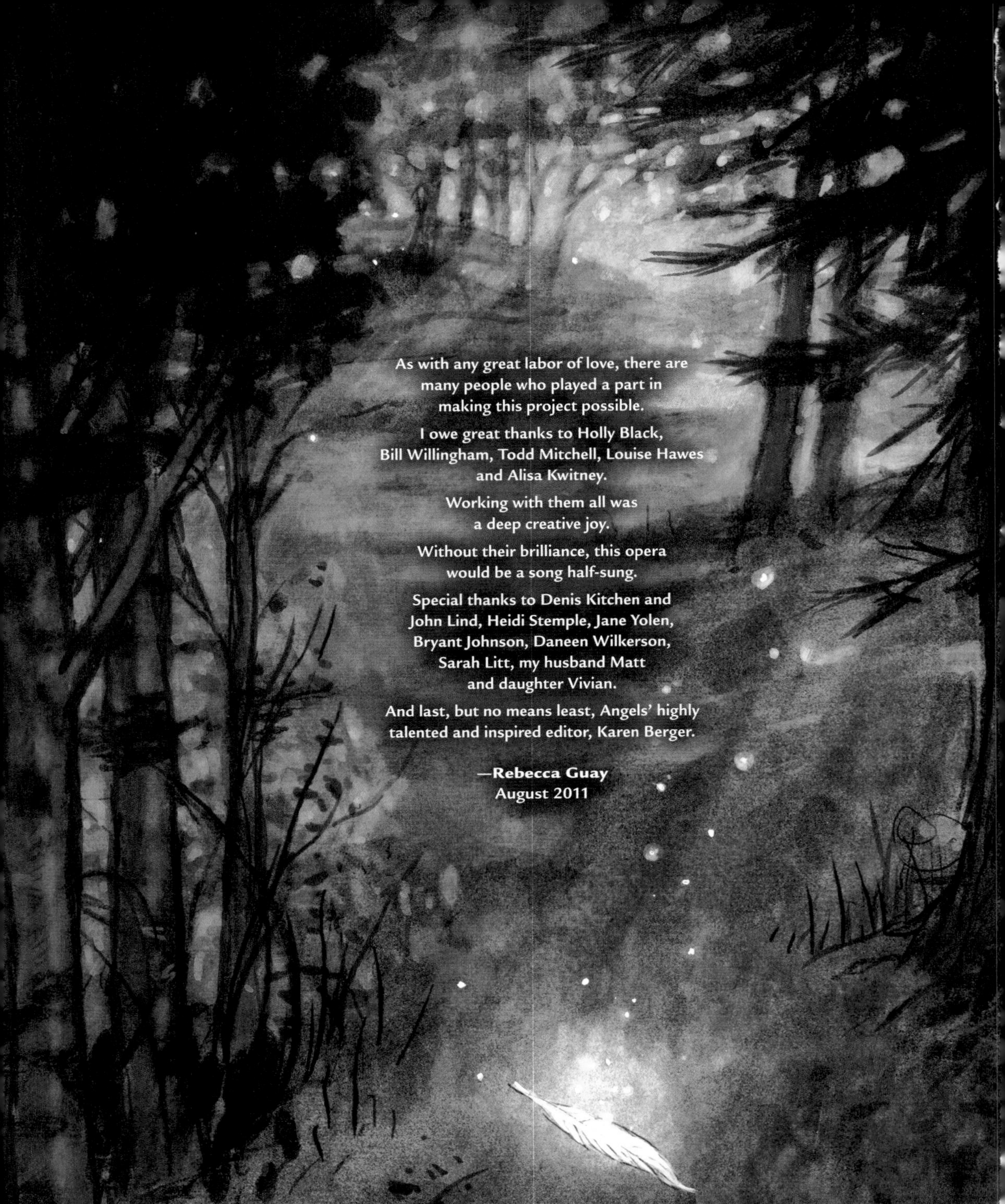

As with any great labor of love, there are many people who played a part in making this project possible.

I owe great thanks to Holly Black, Bill Willingham, Todd Mitchell, Louise Hawes and Alisa Kwitney.

Working with them all was a deep creative joy.

Without their brilliance, this opera would be a song half-sung.

Special thanks to Denis Kitchen and John Lind, Heidi Stemple, Jane Yolen, Bryant Johnson, Daneen Wilkerson, Sarah Litt, my husband Matt and daughter Vivian.

And last, but no means least, Angels' highly talented and inspired editor, Karen Berger.

—**Rebecca Guay**
August 2011

Karen Berger Senior VP – Executive Editor, Vertigo **Sarah Litt** Assistant Editor
Robbin Brosterman Design Director – Books **Bob Harras** VP – Editor in Chief **Curtis King Jr.** Publication Design

Diane Nelson President **Dan DiDio** and **Jim Lee** Co-Publishers **Geoff Johns** Chief Creative Officer **John Rood** Executive VP – Sales, Marketing and Business Development **Amy Genkins** Senior VP – Business and Legal Affairs **Naìri Gardiner** Senior VP – Finance **Jeff Boison** VP – Publishing Operations **Mark Chiarello** VP – Art Direction and Design **John Cunningham** VP – Marketing **Terri Cunningham** VP – Talent Relations and Services **Alison Gill** Senior VP – Manufacturing and Operations **David Hyde** VP – Publicity **Hank Kanalz** Senior VP – Digital **Jay Kogan** VP – Business and Legal Affairs, Publishing **Jack Mahan** VP – Business Affairs, Talent **Nick Napolitano** VP – Manufacturing Administration **Sue Pohja** VP – Book Sales **Courtney Simmons** Senior VP – Publicity **Bob Wayne** Senior VP – Sales

Logo design by **Nancy Ogami**

A FLIGHT OF ANGELS
Published by DC Comics, 1700 Broadway, New York, NY 10019.

Printed in the USA. First Printing. DC Comics, a Warner Bros. Entertainment Company.
HC ISBN: 978-1-4012-3200-9 SC ISBN: 978-1-4012-2147-8

SUSTAINABLE FORESTRY INITIATIVE
Certified Chain of Custody
Promoting Sustainable Forest Management
www.sfiprogram.org

Fiber used in this product line meets the sourcing requirements of the SFI program.
www.sfiprogram.org SGS-SFI/COC-US10/81072

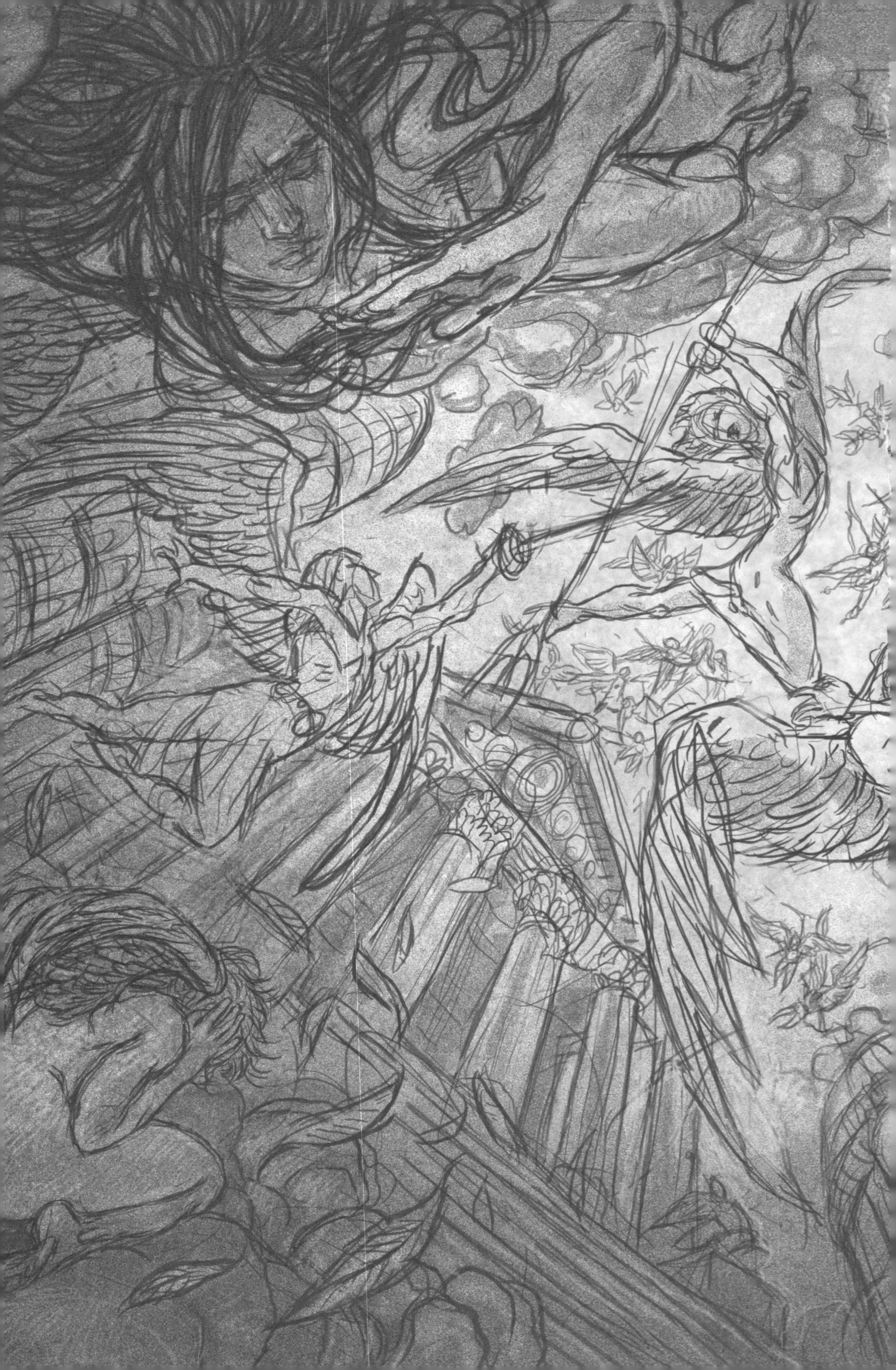